FISH OHIO
100 Ohio Lakes

by Bill Bailey

Copyright 1997 by Glovebox Guidebooks of America

Cover design and layout by Dan Jacalone
Cover photo by Mari Romanack
Cover photo: Mark Romanack, outdoor writer and
professional walleye fisherman
Research assistance by Steve DeKett
Managing editor: Penny Weber-Bailey
Editor: Bill Cornish

Published by
Glovebox Guidebooks of America
1112 Washburn Place East
Saginaw, Michigan 48602
(517) 792-8363

Library of Congress - C.I.P.

Bailey, William L., 1952-

Fish Ohio: 100 Lakes
(A Glovebox Guidebook of America)
ISBN 1-881139-19-0

Printed in the United States of America

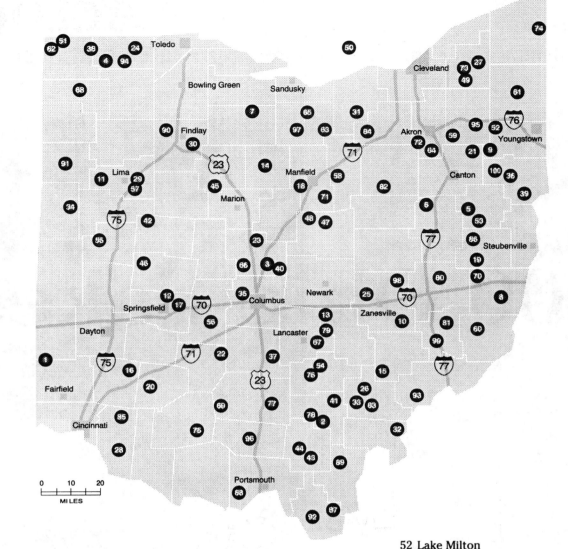

Introduction

Time. There will never be enough time. It is the enemy. It slips away too quickly. Without planning, the weekends flash by, the kids grow up and memories fade. Too often a lack of planning and information is the reason why we don't do more fishing.

Fishing is a place where family memories are stored, where friends relish a Saturday afternoon together—remembering the adventure over and over for years to come. It may sound corny, but fishing can be an anchor in our lives that we only fully appreciate years later.

That's why I wrote this book—to help families, husbands and wives, single moms and old pals, build memories and to get outdoors to reconnect with nature or family. This book is not for expert anglers (although they will learn lots too), it's for everybody. An easy-to-use guide to 100 top lakes evenly scattered around Ohio. The mission of the book is to motivate you—and help you plan a weekend on a top nearby fishing lake.

With the expert help of Steve DeKett, we have talked with 20 wildlife division fish biologists, more than 50 bait and tackle shop owners and nearly 100 anglers that know these waters. We have carefully distilled the information so that you can quickly learn the lake, catch fish and build memories. We have also fished most of the lakes—well, somebody has to do it!

I hate to make a list (because you always leave somebody off), but here are some key wildlife division biologists and staff that were super helpful: Jerry Gallant, Marty Webb, Vince LaConte, Doug Maloney, Dave Bright, John Wisse, Richard Day, Mike Burr, Debbie Walters, Steve Graham, Mike Greenlee and many other dedicated state staff members.

Fish Ohio is a book for all seasons. It will guide you to top sustainable lakes, suggest tackle and point you to the hotspots. It will help you enjoy Ohio's incredible and diverse lakes—and help you to fish more!

Good luck and best fishes.

Acton Lake

■ 625 acres of fishing water ■ 8 miles of shoreline PREBLE & BUTLER COUNTIES

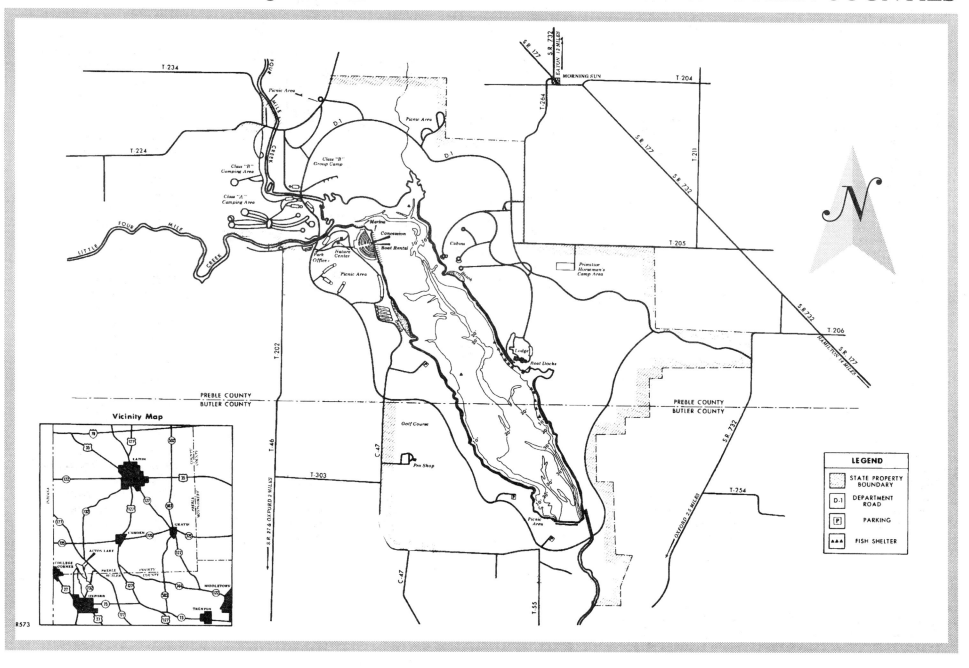

Location: At Hueston Woods State Park, SR 732 and SR 177, five miles northwest of Oxford. 40 miles west and slightly south of Dayton, four miles from the Indiana/Ohio state line. It's in Preble and Butler counties.

Wildlife district office: (513) 372-9261.

Fishing opportunities: Bass, crappies, bluegill, a few tiger muskie and bullheads.

Boat rental and marina, 10 hp limit on the lake. Marina, (513) 523-8859.

Up to 2 million visitors to the park and lake annually.

State park is 3,596 acres and surrounds the lake.

Water conditions: Muddy, especially after heavy rains; 98 square miles of farmland drain to the lake.

Bottom structure: stilted (regular dredging is conducted).

No weedbeds or significant aquatic growth.

Lodge: Dining room, 94 rooms, 59 cabins. Call (800) 282-7275.

Camping: Up to 3,000 people can be accommodated in the state park's 490-site campground. Call (513) 523-8081.

Several bait and tackle shops are in the area.

Special regulations: Bass must be 15 inches.

Overview: Lake turbidity and productivity are high, so high that a huge overpopulation of bite-size shad offer a constant forage base. The conditions (mostly turbidity) at Acton Lake keep the shad small enough that they are a continual source of food for predator fish. In fact, biologists report that each year, shocked fish roll to the surface stuffed with natural food.

Therefore fishing can be very good—or very bad—for long periods of time. Local anglers and area bait and tackle shops know when the shad population is off, which can be early spring and late fall. Even with plenty of natural food, predatory fish will bite, if you can make them mad enough. Bass and crappie fishing can be very good if you visit when they are biting.

Underwater structure: Due to muddy water, little aquatic plant growth is found. Christmas trees are annually sunk (a map is available that details the locations of installed structure). Fallen timber is found in coves. Submerged barn foundations and stumps provide holding, feeding and hiding places for many species.

Hot spots: Christmas trees have been sunk near the blue pipe north of the lodge on the east side of the lake; south of the lodge at two small coves, in front of the dam and just north of the dam on the east side of the lake at the end of a point.

How to catch 'em: Crappie go for live bait (waxworms, minnows, redworms and nightcrawlers) along the northeastern and west shore; bass are best angered by flashy buzzing spinner baits, topwater and noisy crankbaits. Populations of bass also hold around fallen trees on the southeast shore. Catfish are most easily taken after summer rains when they migrate to the inlets. You can catch jumbo catfish one right after the other following a warm rain. Use cut or live bait.

The deepwater, handicapped accessible fishing pier is an excellent site near the Sugar Camp for youth and anglers with disabilities. Many of the sea walls, near docks, are also excellent places to shoreline fish (bring your lawn chair!). Young shoreline anglers have their best luck with bluegills, using bobbers and live bait.

Although lake depth reaches 30 feet near the dam, most anglers fish the other end of the lake or along the shoreline near the lodge or near the dam.

Public access: Shoreline fishing is available around the entire lake. The lake has eight miles of shoreline.

Ice fishing: This is excellent for big crappies, one of the best kept secrets in the state. One of the most popular ice fishing areas is near the Sugar Camp fishing pier. Many wintertime crappies are 10-12 inches.

Insider tips: The state park has a small free zoo (mountain lion, bobcats, bald eagles), beautiful lodge, pioneer farm, cabins and a modern 490-site campground. Pick up a map that details the underwater structure and park amenities from the park office.

Lake Alma

VINTON COUNTY ■ 64 acres of fishing water

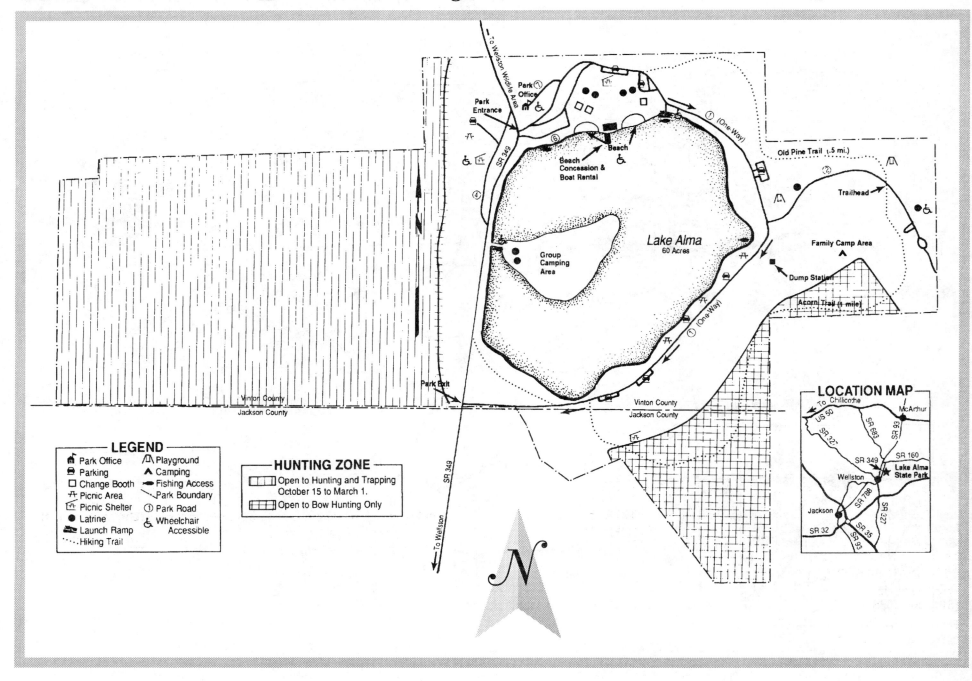

LEGEND
- 🏚 Park Office
- 🅿 Parking
- ☐ Change Booth
- ⛱ Picnic Area
- 🏕 Picnic Shelter
- ● Latrine
- 🚤 Launch Ramp
- ⋯ Hiking Trail
- ⛸ Playground
- ⛺ Camping
- ⬥ Fishing Access
- ⋰ Park Boundary
- ① Park Road
- ♿ Wheelchair Accessible

HUNTING ZONE
- ▦ Open to Hunting and Trapping October 15 to March 1.
- ▦ Open to Bow Hunting Only

LOCATION MAP

Location: Follow U.S. 93 to Wellston, then two miles north on SR 349 to the state park and lake.

Wildlife district office: (614) 594-2211.

Fishing opportunities: Largemouth bass, crappie, bluegill and channel catfish.

Water conditions: Light tea-colored to clear.

Bottom composition: Mud, silt.

Horsepower restriction: Electric motors only.

Stocking: Channel catfish, bi-annually.

Camping: 64 shady sites in the state park; call (614) 384-4474.

Boat rental: at marina and concession.

Outlook:
Bluegill, redear - good
Channel catfish - good
Largemouth bass - excellent
Crappie - good

Ohio lakes are often created for flood control, drinking water, old canals or simply for water-based recreation. Lake Alma is a breed apart. The 64-acre lake was created in 1903 when C. K. Davis, a wealthy local resident, dammed up Little Raccoon Creek, named the resulting lake in honor of his wife, and opened the area as an amusement park. The merriment didn't last long. By 1910 the amusement park filled with merry-go-rounds and other period rides had faded. The park and lake are very pleasant, used lightly and a good secret to keep.

How to catch 'em: Several year classes of largemouth bass are represented in the small lake. Biologists say there are a lot of fish in the 15-19 inch range, and at least one 23-inch largemouth was surveyed recently. There are also reports of a good number of eight-pound fish caught annually. Bring your best weedless lures when you visit Lake Alma for some terrific bass angling. Due to weedbed growth, plan a spring visit, or bring your vertical jigs and plastic worms to work in and around the lily pads. Locals use chartreuse and black spinnerbaits, cast past the weedy edges and work slowly and steadily. Texas-style worm rigs also do a good job here.

The best crappie fishing is from the pedestrian bridge to the island, which was once an amusement park. Spring and fall crappie fishing is good, with plenty of eight- to 10-inch fish. Channel cats, usually eight inch yearlings, are planted on even numbered years. There are several year classes represented and the fishing is good. Catfish love chicken livers and bait shrimp. Crappie anglers should try chartreuse jigs and live minnows. Bluegill are known to devour waxworms and nightcrawlers.

Hot spots: Concentrate your fishing efforts around the island and along the state highway. Although efforts to clear excessive aquatic vegetation are underway, mid-summer fishing and boating can be tough in the dense weeds. Grass carp have been introduced and selective herbicide treatments will help. Local anglers have learned to fish the pockets and edges around thick weedbeds. Bass sometimes hide where two weedbeds meet. Fish the shady and windless side of weedbeds in the summer. Both of the boat docks and from the pedestrian bridge can be good fishing sites.

Underwater structure: Little, if any manmade structure has ever been placed in the lake. The shallow lake does, however, have abundant lily pads and coontail growth. The weeds can be hard on electric trolling motors. A few clumps of Christmas trees have been placed near the east beach. A few rock outcrops are scattered around the lake.

Boat launching: The recently improved twin-lane ramp near the beach is a great improvement over the old, steep gravel launching ramp.

Ice fishing: Panfish ice fishing is fair to good.

Insider tips: The pleasant 323-acre state park has family-oriented camping (many sites with electricity), two hiking trails, a small boat ramp, naturalist programs, island, twin swimming beaches and well-spaced day-use areas around the shoreline. If caught, grass carp (white amur) must be released unharmed. A bike path circles the lake. Bikes are rented at the state park.

Alum Creek Lake

■ 3,387 acres of fishing water ■ 46 miles of shoreline DELAWARE COUNTY

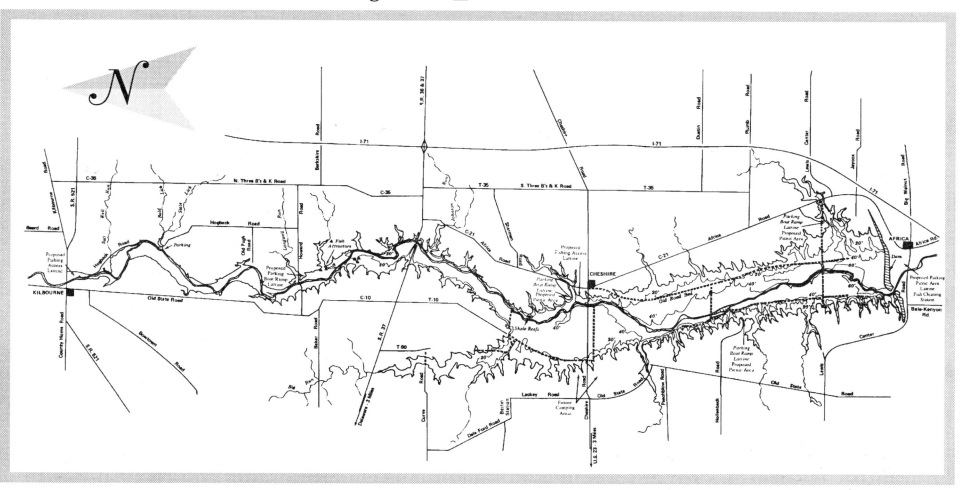

Location: In Delaware County, only minutes north of Columbus, between I-71 and U.S. 23, at the Alum Creek State Park.

Wildlife district office: (614) 265-7038.

Fishing opportunities: Muskie, crappie, large- and smallmouth bass, catfish and bluegill.

Water conditions: One of the clearest and cleanest lakes in Ohio.

Bottom composition: Rock sandbars on a mud base, manmade shale reefs (for walleye spawning).

Stocking: The state started planting muskies annually in 1990. Several Huskie Muskies have come from the lake. Annual put-and-take stocking program for saugeye, about 30,000 are placed yearly.

Camping: Alum Creek State Park, (614) 548-4631. 297 Class A sites.

Shoreline: The entire lake is surrounded by state property. The southwest side of the lake has shoreline access. Weedbeds are common.

Marina: Fishing boats, pontoon and personal watercraft are rented.

Bait and tackle: Cheshire Market, Creek Bait and Tackle (off Rt. 36/37) and Tackle Express

Outlook:

Largemouth bass - excellent
Channel catfish - good
Bluegill, redear - good
Saugeye - very good
Muskie - very good

Alum Creek Lake is one of the cleanest and clearest lakes in the state. Most of the runoff is off of shale and feeder creeks which are carved through rock. There is little farm runoff into the lake that is surrounded by beech-maple woodlots and shale deposits. The fish from this lake are firm and have excellent taste—white bass even taste good!

One of the great advantages of Alum Creek Lake is the no-wake zone that benefits fishermen—especially muskie anglers. The lake is becoming an increasingly well known muskie fishery. The quiet zones of the lake are wide expanses of water where anglers can troll plugs, waiting for the king of predatory fish to go on the bite. Anglers also use planer boards and troll large crankbaits under the bank, fish the weedbeds with crankbaits, troll a big crankbait in the prop-wash of their motor (even in 30 feet of water, curious muskie will come to the surface and hit baits in the agitated water) and cast and retrieve across weeds, points and holding areas. The best period to fish muskie is from mid-March to early May. In the summer, look for a weedbed near a bay (try near the dam for this habitat) and cast crankbaits along the edge and through the weeds.

Saugeye, which never get as big as walleye and don't mind turbid waters, are common in the lake both during warm weather and winter. Eight- to 10 pound saugeye are common. Walleye have been planted in the lake, but due to the fluctuation in lake levels, natural reproduction has been low.

Because of the maturing muskie, larger crappies are being taken. Twelve- to 15-inch crappies are common. Nine- to 12-inch fish can be consistently caught in the spring. Most of the crappies are the white variety.

How to catch 'em: You can put a lot of food on your plate at Alum Creek Lake. Crappie and bluegills can be taken from most parts of the lake (best areas is the upper lake, above SR 36 and 37). Many saugeye anglers can limit out in a hurry. The average size of the saugeye is 15-20 inches, with 26-28-inchers commonly taken. Many saugeye can be taken on crankbaits—especially a Rattling Road-type that can be worked and jerked to different depths. Some saugeye anglers report good success on nightcrawler harnesses trolled slowly (use your trolling motor) or spinners with a small piece of worm.

Local experts says Texas Rigs, worms and plastic worms work well on bass.

Crappie fishing is excellent in April and in any cove with brush on the lake. Local experts say not to overlook shallow water during this time of the year. Many crappies are on nests and easy to take with tiny artificial lures, weighted hooks on jigs, and bobber and minnows. Fish near any brush for crappies. Some anglers also suspend a tube jig about two feet below a bobber to tease the crappies onto the hook.

The original creek (Alum Creek, from SR 521, east of Kilbourne to the upper reaches) holds smallmouth bass. Rangers say they see seven-pound smallmouth taken even in spring and summer. 12-14 pound channel catfish are taken regularly on cut gizzard shad (scale the shad, cut off a piece of meal and take the gut out of the fish and hang it on the hook, holding the meal). The cats taste great, especially if they are taken in the spring and early summer.

Underwater structure: The north end of the lake, where it is a little shallower, has many coves with fallen trees and brush that can be filled with crappies. The shale reefs are in three areas near flats. In places the top of the reef is just two feet underwater, then drops off to 30 feet deep. The shale pile offers excellent ledge effects where the fish can suspend near flats that run out to the main creek channels. Most of the largest fish are at the end of the longest, narrowest sandbar that runs out to a creekbed. The big fish move into this habitat daily, maybe for just a half-hour, to feed.

Also in the lake are old roadbeds and a bridge. Local anglers say that if you follow the old Africa Roadbed to a weedbed, you'll find muskie. South of Cheshire, you'll find a deep weedbed that is an excellent habitat for many species. Try jigging there.

The lake hosts many small bass tournaments. Many anglers stay in the state park campground.

Boat launching: There are four launching ramps on the lake. Three of the launches have two lanes. The lake allows unlimited horsepower.

Insider tips: Try below the dam in late March for muskie and saugeye. If there is a water release at the dam, an influx of bait fish are swept along and the fishing can be very good at these times. Grass carp were introduced to the lake in 1992 to help reduce nuisance vegetation. High-density vegetation limits access to this excellent bass fishery from mid- to late summer.

Archibold Reservoirs

FULTON COUNTY ■ 20 acres and 45 acres of fishing water

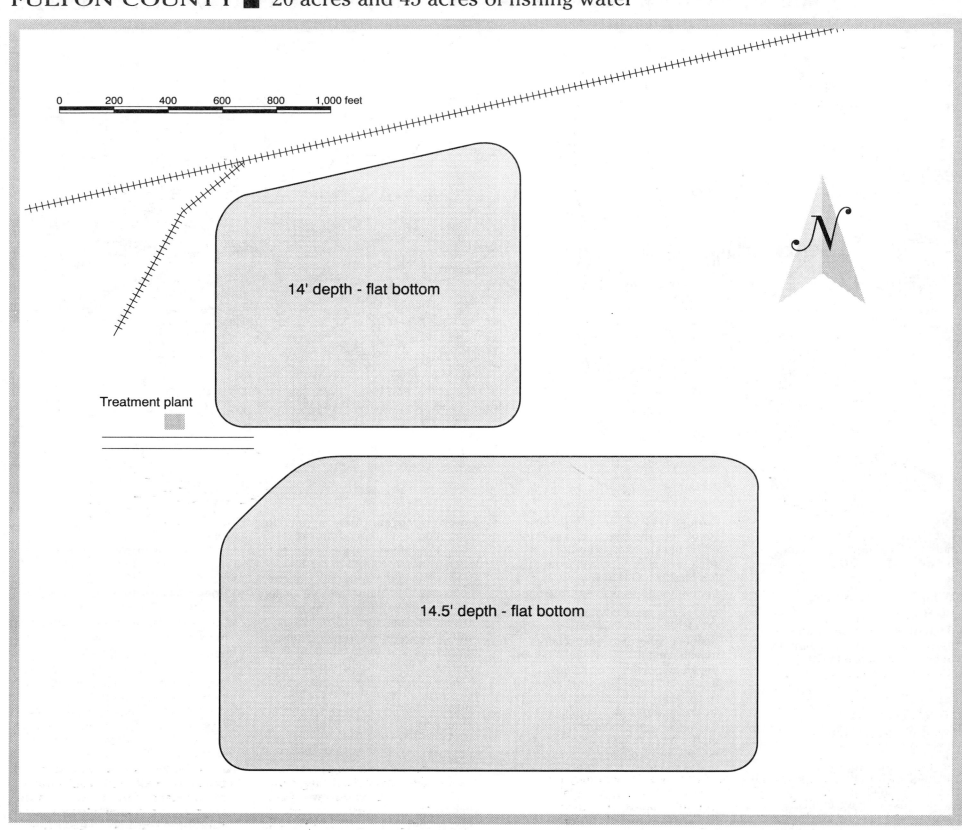

0   200   400   600   800   1,000 feet

14' depth - flat bottom

Treatment plant

14.5' depth - flat bottom

N

Location: In northwestern Ohio. One mile east of Archbold, off 22nd Road.

Wildlife district office: (419) 424-5000.

Fishing opportunities: Saugeye, walleye, largemouth bass, bluegill, crappie, yellow perch, channel catfish, bluegill and bullhead.

Water conditions: Medium clear.

Bottom composition: Mud.

Horsepower restriction: Electric motors only.

Stocking: Saugeye and walleye.

Maximum depth: 20 feet.

Outlook:
Saugeye - very good
Walleye - very good

Channel catfish - good
Bluegill - fair
Bullhead - fair to good

Both Archbold reservoirs are upground sites with riprap shoreline improvements. They have flat bottoms, with little structure. The bodies of water, adjacent to each other, are in a rural area, near the village of Archbold.

How to catch 'em: Saugeye can run 12-21 inches in the water supply reservoirs. Saugeye and walleye can often be taken along the riprap shoreline or drift fishing from a small boat. Fair to good populations of bluegill that average 6-8 inches can be taken throughout the season on tiny jigs with worms attached.

Bring the kids, small hooks and lots of sinkers, worms and bobbers for some very good bullhead fishing on

both reservoirs. Some report taking 12-inch bullheads, while most are 8-10 inches.

The reservoirs have fair to good populations of channel catfish. Most are 16-22 inches, but there can be some much bigger individuals taken. Most catfish anglers drop cutbait on the bottom and take a nap. The lazy reservoirs are not heavily fished and the catfish are slow to bite. Evenings and nights fishing livers, gobs of crawlers or commercially prepared doughballs are good choice.

Hot spots: Along the stony shoreline, casting long is the best advice on these small reservoirs.

Underwater structure: Both of the reservoirs have some small humps, shelves and improved shoreline that hold fish. Inlets and places where water moves are locations to key

your efforts on.

Boat launching: Carry on and hand loading small boats only.

Insider tip: These lightly fished reservoirs can be good close to home places to bring the family for an afternoon of safe shoreline fishing.

OHIO

Atwood Lake

■ 1,540 acres of fishing water ■ 28 miles of shoreline CARROLL COUNTY

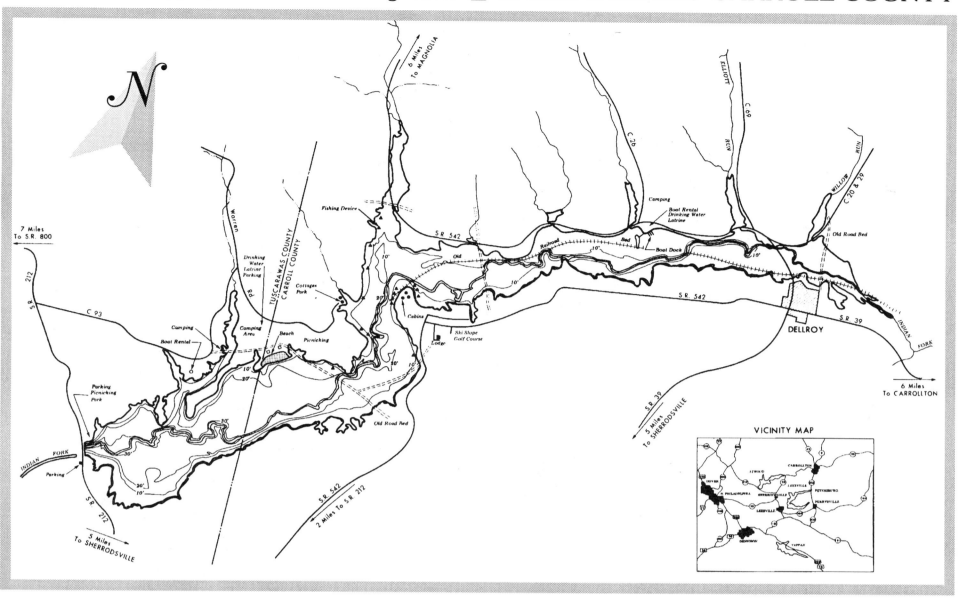

Location: Between Canton and New Philadelphia, I-77 exit 93, 11 miles to State Route 212 to County Road 93. Most of the lake is in Carroll County with some along the western edge of Tuscarawas County.

Wildlife district office: (330) 644-2293.

Fishing opportunities: Largemouth bass, bluegill, northern pike, crappies, channel catfish, yellow perch and saugeye.

Average depth: 34 feet, deepest 40 feet.

Stocking: Saugeye stocking started in 1985; about 300,000 saugeye are stocked by the ODNR every two or three years (155,000 fingerlings in 1995). Other species are stocked.

Water conditions: overall water quality is good; muddy after rains; clear in late season.

Horsepower limit: 25 hp.

Marina and boat rental: Call (800) 882-6339 (west end) or (216) 735-2323 (east end).

No wake zones: In residential areas, park areas, dam and certain inlets.

Bottom structure: A manmade lake, mostly firm composition with mud flats. Some aquatic plants.

Shoreline: Some rocky shoals, flats and weedbeds.

Camping: 532 sites; lodge.

Fishing forecast number: (216) 735-2559.

Outlook:
Saugeye - excellent
Bass - good
Black and white crappies - good

Atwood Dam was constructed in 1937 on the Indian Fork Creek for flood control. The Muskingum Watershed Conservancy District owns and manages the lake and surrounding lands. The district cooperates with the ODNR for fisheries management and stocking. There are about 3,000 acres of public lands adjacent to the lake. The conservancy district was organized under state law in 1933 for the primary purposes of flood control, conservation and recreation. In 1939 the flood control aspect became the responsibility of the U.S. Army Corps of Engineers. The are 16,000 acres of lake and 365 miles of shoreline in the watershed district for anglers to enjoy.

Anglers are advised that the lake is busy with recreational boaters on summer weekends from Memorial Day to Labor Day. Some of the best fishing is done on weekdays in both the spring and fall.

How to catch 'em: Bass and panfishing in the coves during the spring are considered excellent. As the water warms the bass move into deeper water, and the best method is casting the shoreline with rubber worms and spinners.

Atwood Lake is an excellent crappie and saugeye fishery. Average saugeyes are 14 to 28 inches. Cat fishing is very good. Standard live bait presentations are recommended by area bait and tackle shops. Most bluegills are taken out of the lake using redworms, maggots or tiny popper flies. Local experts advise mid-summer anglers to move to the deep channels, fishing slow and during the evening. Try night fishing for catfish using shrimp, cut bait or nightcrawlers over the sand and gravel bars. Use spoons or live bait in the shallows in the early spring for northern pike. Bass are under fished, despite good numbers and sizes.

Public access: Significant sections of the shoreline are accessible for fishing.

Boat launching: Three ramps are available at the lake; one at each marina, and a new ramp with a courtesy dock near the dam (parking for 75 vehicles and trailers) off SR 212. The lake gets heavy recreational use, including personal watercraft, pontoons and sailboat traffic. Both marinas rent a full line of boats, from bass boats to personal watercraft.

Ice fishing: Crappies through the ice are excellent and a popular take. Use meal worms, small minnows and tiny hooks. In the early spring look for brushy areas. Forty or more shanties are often on the ice in mid-winter.

Underwater structure: Certain sections of the lake have stump fields. Christmas trees are annually recycled and placed in the lake. The DNR has also dropped stumps into the lake using a helicopter to create additional fish habitat. Local bait and tackle shops have information about the location of these structures. The west marina sells topographic maps of the lake. This map also indicates current structure and other fishing and boating information. Contour maps can also be purchased by mail from the MWCD, Contour Maps, P.O. Box 349, New Philadelphia, OH 44663-0349.

Amenities: The lake and surrounding facilities are managed by the Muskingum Watershed Conservancy District. Facilities include a 532-site campground, nature center, camp store, swimming beach, 104-room resort and conference center, indoor and outdoor pool and cottages. Hunting, hiking and special events are also offered. Call (216) 343-6780 for additional information about lodging and the park.

Insider tips: Early spring is the best time for saugeye, especially in channels along the west end of the lake. The buoy line in front of the beach and off the point across from the resort are two of the more productive channels.

Beach City Lake

TUSCARAWAS COUNTY ■ 50 acres of fishing water

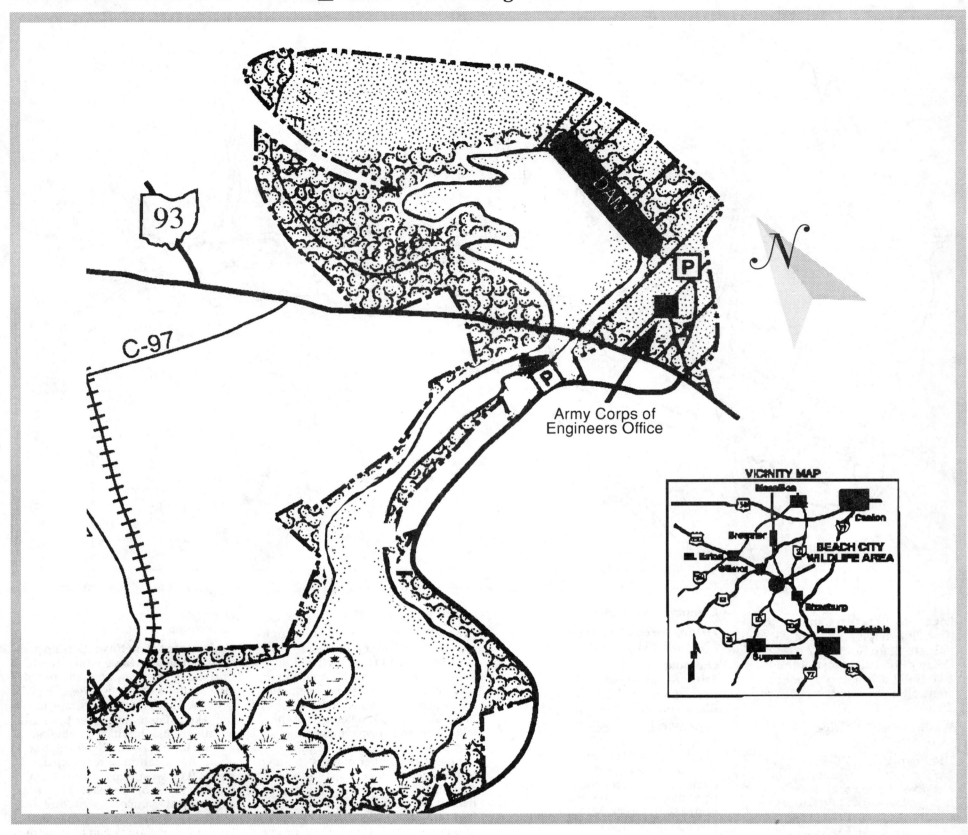

93

C-97

DAM

P

P

Army Corps of
Engineers Office

N

VICINITY MAP

BEACH CITY
WILDLIFE AREA

Location: In Tuscarawas County. State Route 93, running north-south, forms the east boundary, and U.S. 250 is at the north end of the area. The Lake is 55 miles from Cleveland and 16 miles from Canton.

Wildlife district office: (330) 644-2293.

Fishing opportunities: Saugeye, bullhead.

Water conditions: Muddy.

Bottom compositions: Mud.

Horsepower restriction: Canoe only.

Stocked: Saugeye annually.

Outlook::
Saugeye - good
Bullheads - excellent

The tiny lake is minimally managed as a fishery, largely due to the high silt load of the feeder river. The lake is only a few feet deep and filling in more each year. The body of water is now basically a wetland. The lake almost completely silted in the last 20 years.

This "wetland" is part of the 1,192-acre Beach City Wildlife Area that lies on the edge of the unglaciated Appalachian Plateau region of Ohio. Elevations vary from 948 to 1,200 feet above sea level. Much of the area is flooded, especially during the spring.

How to catch 'em: There is a tail-water fishery below the dam for saugeye, most of which are 8-22 inches. In the early spring some northern pike also frequent this area offering some springtime fun. In fact, the narrow intimate area is usu-ally underfished and could be a

great place to fly cast streamers at always spooky predatory pike. The pike are wild fish, not stocked.

Saugeye anglers stand along the bank at the tailwaters and cast jigs and minnows. Fishing is best when there is a reservoir discharge. Good saugeye angling is reported well downstream of Beach City Reservoir and the tailwater.

Not a sexy fish, bullheads can be fun to catch, especially for children. The small and shallow reservoir has an excellent population of 8-14 inch bullheads.

Hot spots: The only meaningful fish-ery, which is actually little-known, is below the dam. This area, which is close to a parking area, is only 50-75 feet wide. This tailwater is the Tuscarawas River, and some anglers fish it for smallmouth, saugeye and bullheads. Immediately below the

dam is a good fishery during the fall, winter and spring. Try below Dover Dam for saugeye.

Underwater structure: The tailwa-ters or river area has some bottom humps.

Boat launching: Only a canoe could navigate the lake or narrow tailwa-ters.

Insider tips: Bring your fly rod and streamers for a try at pike early in the season below the dam. Beach City is not a destination, but if you live nearby and time your fishing, the saugeye action can be good and the pike fun on light tackle. A few rough and stunted panfish are in the very shallow lake. Look for signs of beaver activity in the wildlife area. Hunting is allowed within the 1,912-acre managed nat-ural area.

OHIO

Beaver Creek Reservoir

■ 120 acres of fishing water WILLIAMS COUNTY

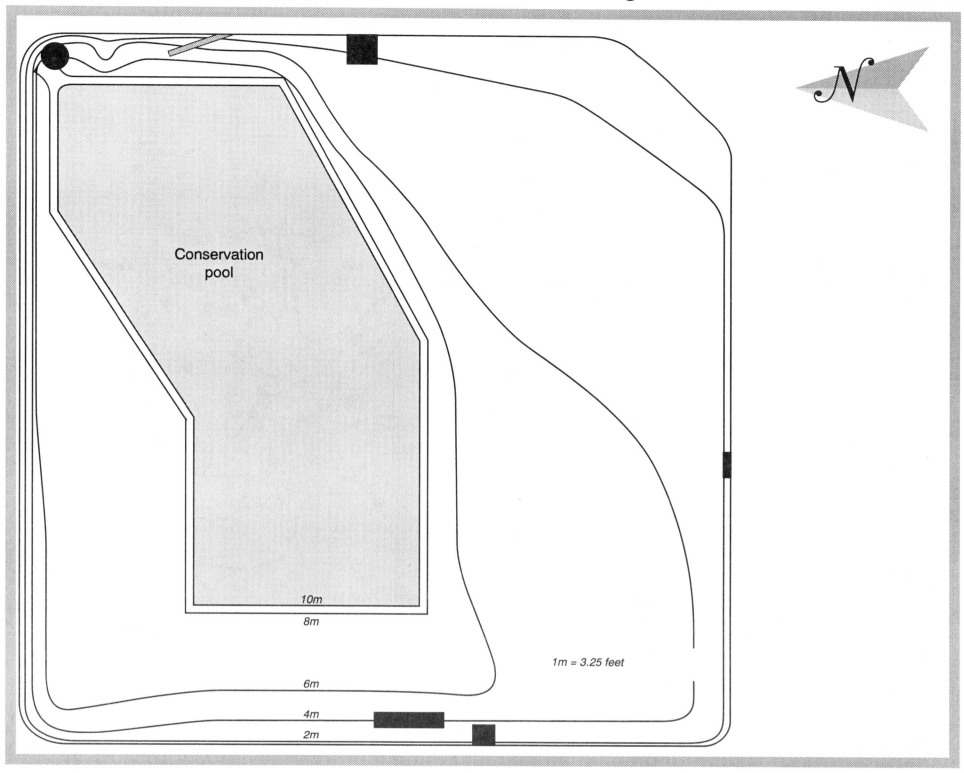

N

Conservation
pool

10m
8m

1m = 3.25 feet

6m
4m
2m

Location: In northwestern Ohio. Five miles southwest of Montpelier off I Road.

Wildlife district office: (419) 424-5000

Fishing opportunities: Walleye, white crappie, yellow perch, bluegill, channel catfish and largemouth bass.

Water conditions: Medium colored.

Bottom Composition: Muddy, soft.

Horsepower restriction: Electric motors.

Stocking: Walleye in the past.

Maximum depth: Up to 28 feet. Bring your bait.

Outlook:
Crappie - good
Walleye - good
Yellow perch - fair
Bluegill - good
Channel catfish - good
Large- and smallmouth bass - good

Beaver Creek Reservoir is an upground reservoir with heavy fishing pressure. Like most upgrounds, the underwater structure is minimal, walleye and panfish are the target species, and shoreline fishing can be good. Beaver Creek has riprap around the entire shoreline.

How to catch 'em: Live minnow and lead-head jigs are the lures and baits of choice. Most anglers who visit Beaver Creek Reservoir are there for tasty yellow perch and walleye. There is an excellent population of 10-17 inch largemouth, many of which will congregate around the weeds in the south end of the lake.

Walleye in the reservoir are in the deeper water and will chase colorful jigs tipped with a live minnow. Walleyes can range in size from 14-26 inches and they are in good numbers. Equally good-eating yellow perch are also in deeper water, typically in the northern half of the lake, and range in size from 7-13 inches.

The lake has a stable population of white crappie that average 7-12 inches. They often are along the weedbed and adjacent inlets, floating brush or underwater humps. Ice fishing for bluegills is the best way to catch them. The reservoir is small enough for anglers to move about until they find the fish. Some walleye are also taken off the bottom using a jigging spoon tipped with a minnow and stinger hook. Be sure to slowly flutter your jig 4-6 inches off the bottom.

Hot spots: The shallower area on the south of the lake is identifiable by the aquatic weed growth. Most upground reservoirs don't have much vegetation. Anglers can try working along the edges of the weedbeds. The best times to fish these expanses of weeds are July and early August. Local anglers are known to run weedless baits and plenty of jigs through the area. Flipping a plastic worm might also prove to be a successful technique.

Underwater structure: The bottom of the reservoir is flat, except for a shallow area along the south edge. The depth in the reservoir will run from about 28 feet in the north down to 12 feet on the south end of the lake.

Boat launching: A multiple-lane concrete ramp keeps the reservoir busy with small fishing boats. There is parking at the ramp.

Ice fishing: Ice fishing is fair to good. Anglers take perch on teardrops and small jigs. Bluegill anglers have good results.

Insider tips: Bring your own bait; the nearest bait and tackle shops are on SR 101 south of the reservoir. Bring live minnows to Beaver Creek Reservoir. Fish the weeds at the southern end of the reservoir for excellent largemouth action. Some smallmouth are taken along the riprap shoreline.

OHIO

Belmont Lake

BELMONT COUNTY ■ 117 acres of fishing water

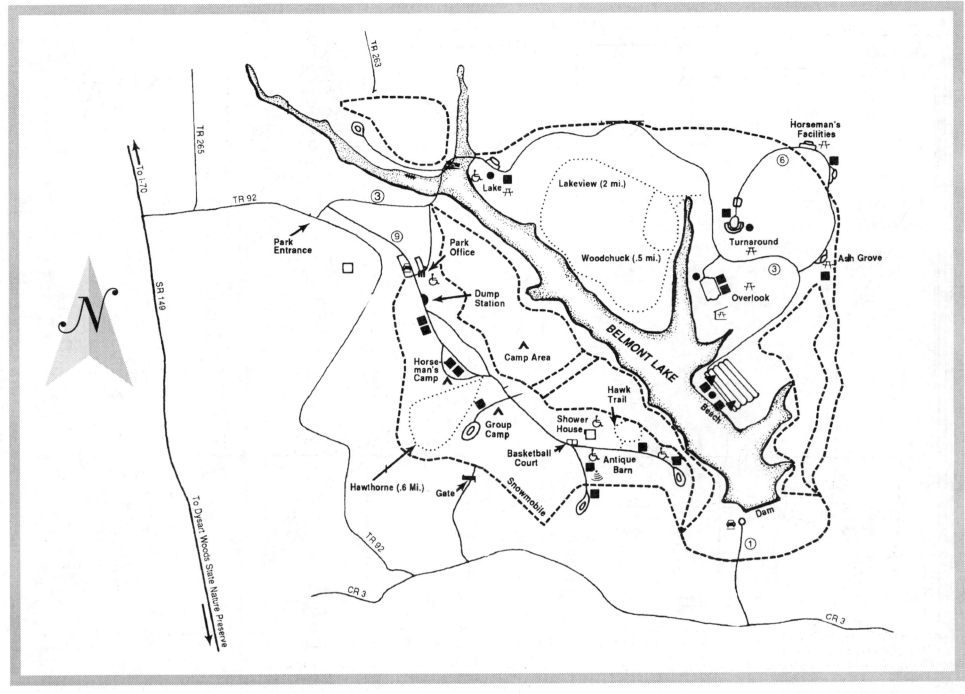

Location: In Belmont County, east of Cambridge and the I-70/I-71 interchange. Depart exit 208 off I-70 and proceed two miles south to SR 149 to Barkcamp Park Road.

Wildlife district office: (614) 594-2211.

Fishing opportunities: Bluegill, largemouth bass, crappie channel catfish and golden trout.

Water conditions: Relatively clear.

Bottom composition: Mud, firm.

Horsepower restriction: Electric motors only.

Stocking: Trout each spring; channel catfish.

Camping: 150 sites in Barkcamp State Park; call (614) 484-4064.

Bait and tackle are nearby.

Special regulations: Check the slot limit on bass.

Outlook:
Bluegill - very good
Largemouth bass - excellent
Channel catfish - excellent
Golden trout - excellent in spring
Crappies - good

Barkcamp was once the site of a logging operation, but that was a long time ago and the second-growth oak-hickory woods are back and crowding the creeks, lake shoreline and covering the rolling terrain. Today, Barkcamp State Park and Belmont Lake are one of the finest outdoor recreation destinations in the state, set between lush agricultural fields and nearby strip mining tracts. The sandstone hills of the region make it part of the Appalachian highlands where layers of coal were formed by decaying swamp vegetation millions of years ago during the Pennsylvanian geological period. The woodlands near Belmont Lake support good numbers of white-tailed deer, wild turkey and other wildlife.

Belmont Lake and the park are a gem, little known outside Belmont County.

How to catch 'em: The best plan of attack for largemouth on Belmont is to fish from a boat in the evening in front of the dam. Try nightcrawlers, flippers and spinners. Electroshock studies have determined there are a lot of big bass in Belmont, but anglers will have a tough time figuring out the formula to catch them.

Local experts say the fish in the relatively shallow 10-12 foot lake (up to 40 feet at the dam) will hit roostertails and nightcrawlers if presented correctly. Some nine-pound bass have been surveyed at the lake. As always, spring is the best time for bass and the many coves and bays are likely places to try plastic worms, poppers, deer-hair lures, small crayfish-colored crankbaits or minnow imitators.

Each year several thousand golden trout are stocked by April 1. The most popular and effective way to take the beautiful fish is using simple pasteurized cheese on a spinning rod. Bluegills are in average abundance with excellent harvestability. Ultralight tackle and small live bait can be fun from the shore or small boat. Channel catfish run 10-25 inches and are stocked regularly.

Hot spots: Trout are stocked near the boat ramp each spring, most of which are caught within weeks. Unlike many lakes, these trout quickly spread out in the lake. Typically, one week after the initial stocking, trout can be caught in front of the dam. Near the lake picnic area, which three fingers of

Barkcamp Creek converge, is a place of heavy cover, coves and shallow bays.

Underwater structure: About 150 Christmas trees were submerged in the lake in the late 1980s. Look for some stumps and light aquatic vegetation. Shoreline cover can be good in places.

Boat launching: The small ramp is at the north end of the lake, across the lake from the park office. Seasonal boat tie-ups can be rented from the state park.

Ice fishing: Bluegill fishing can be very good. Ice anglers typically start drilling holes near the fishing access at the north end of the lake, them move from there to find the fish.

Insider tips: There may be a boat rental concession operating on the lake in the near future. The state park has a wheelchair accessible fishing area at the lake picnic area. Some hunting is permitted in designated areas. The state park features a 700-foot beach, seven picnic areas, boat launch, campground, winter recreation and day-use areas that are heavily used.

Berlin Lake

■ 3,650 acres of fishing water ■ 68 miles of shoreline STARK, MAHONING & PORTAGE COUNTIES

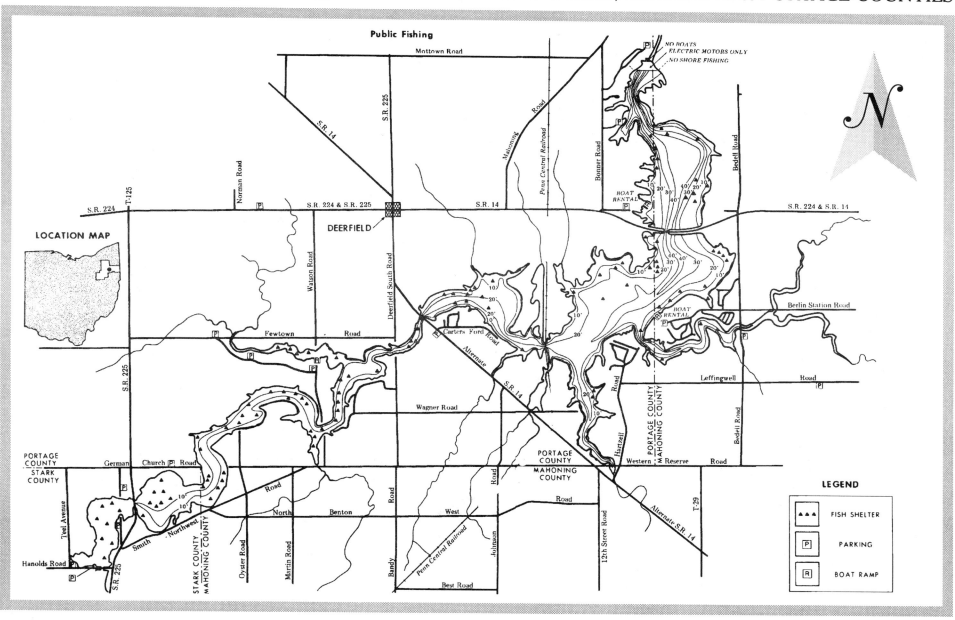

Location: In Stark, Mahoning and Portage counties, 60 miles south of Lake Erie and 25 miles west of the Pennsylvania border. The lake is accessible from U.S. Route 224 and SR 14 and 225.

Wildlife district office: (330) 664-2293.

Fishing opportunities: Walleye, black and white crappies, small- and largemouth bass, muskie, white bass, channel catfish, bluegills and yellow perch.

Water conditions: Colored.

Bottom composition: Mud, sand and gravel.

Horsepower restrictions: None.

Stocking: Walleye.

Boat rentals available.

Camping: Corps of Engineers operated.

Outlook:
Walleye - good, improving
Crappies - fair to good
Smallmouth bass - fair
Muskie - poor, but when you hook up it's excellent
White bass - excellent

The U.S. Army Corps of Engineers built the popular lake on the Mahoning River between Lake Milton and the city of Alliance in 1942 for flood control and as an industrial water supply. Because of the purpose of the lake, its level can fluctuate annually more than 50 feet. When the water is at low pool, rock outcrops, cliffs and ledges can be seen (remember the location of these structures!). The lake is surrounded by Corps of Engineers, state and private property.

How to catch 'em: Berlin Lake is a trophy muskie lake, with a 40-pound monster muskie taken each year. Most muskie anglers are trolling deep-running baits in the mid-summer over dropoffs. Largemouth anglers will want to fish during the spring and early summer among the stump and at streams. Casting, drifting or trolling spinners with a worm can be effective. Smallmouth, found in the north end, along rocky ledges, sandbars and small bays, can be taken by casting bright spoons, crayfish-colored plugs, minnow imitators and small diving crankbaits from a boat toward shore and retrieving in deep water. Also try still fishing and drifting soft craws and other live baits against a tight line.

Walleye fishing is improving and stockings have been restarted in Berlin Lake. Walleye anglers are seen using planner boards, trolling and casting crankbaits. Local experts say yellow is a hot color and tipping lures with pork or live bait is good insurance. Drifting or still fishing is still popular over reefs and just out of any moving water.

Look for white bass below the dam in fast water in April and May. Cast small spoons and bucktail spinners tipped with a live minnow. Crappie angling can be very good in the spring around fallen trees, brush piles and in the stumps. Local experts say live bait or jigs and small spinners work the best. As the water warms, catfish angling improves. Cats can be found in deep channels at depths of 15-20 feet where live bait and simple chicken livers are the preferred baits.

Hot spots: For walleye, smallmouth bass and muskie, try the wider, more open northern end of the lake. For crappies, largemouth bass or bluegill head for the narrow southern end of the lake where you will also find areas of flooded vegetation and long bays.

Underwater structure: Christmas trees and wooden pallet structures have been placed in the lake over the years and if anglers can find them they are good fish attractors. Some of the lake has submerged stump fields and old house foundations. Some small reef complexes are also in the lake and best found by watching local anglers or talking with area bait and tackle dealers. Walleye anglers will want to key on the reefs.

Boat launching: Powerboaters, waterskiers, pontoons and other recreational traffic is heavy on the lake. Several years ago the U.S. Army Corps of Engineers studied the recreation traffic on the winding lake and determined it is one of the most heavily used lakes in the country. Therefore, summer weekends are very difficult times for anglers. In fact, by early Saturday morning many of the boat launch parking lots are filled to capacity. The only public boat launch (no fee) is on Bonner Road at the north end of the lake near the SR 224 and SR 14 bridge. This launch has undergone nearly a million dollars in improvements in 1996. The launch has four lanes, courtesy docks and is accessible to anglers and boaters with disabilities.

Ice fishing: Walleye and crappies are popular ice fishing targets. Anglers typically pinch holes near access points and near the SR 224 and SR 14 bridge.

Insider tips: Berlin has many private docks and marinas. The lake is drawn down in mid-October. Although patience is the key element, trolling for really big muskie can be fun. Bring lots of sandwiches and try during mid-week.

Cutler Lake

MUSKINGUM COUNTY ■ 15 acres of fishing water

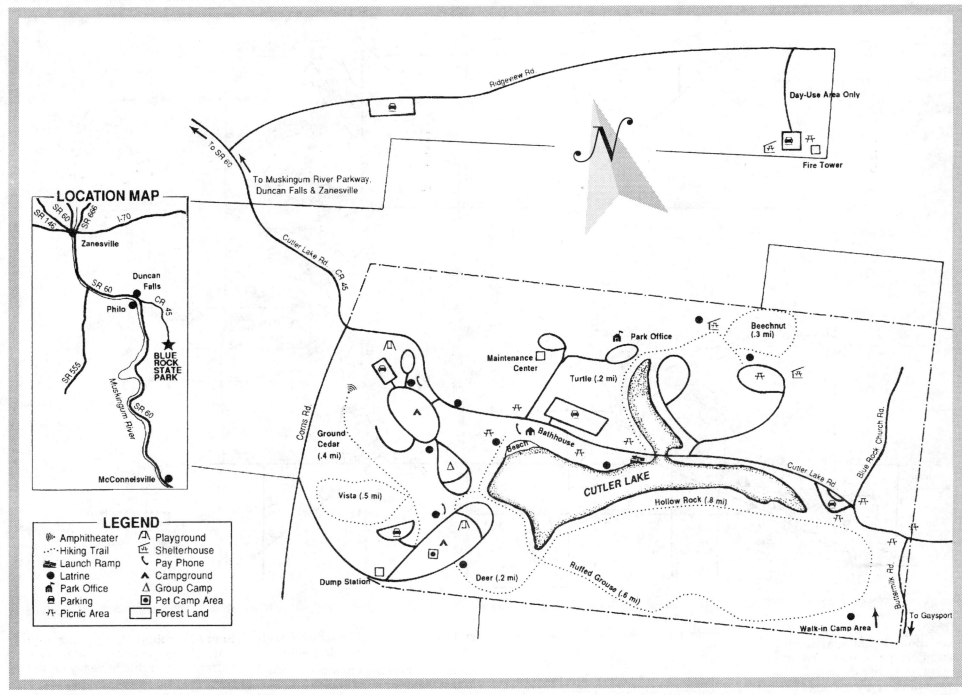

Location: Near Blue Rock State Forest, in Blue Rock State Park.

Wildlife Division office: (614) 594-2211

Fishing opportunities: Bluegill, redear sunfish, largemouth bass and channel catfish.

Water conditions: Clear

Bottom composition: Soft, mud, many pads.

Horsepower restrictions: Electric motors only.

Camping:: 101 sites in state park, call (614) 674-4794.

Boat rental: Canoes and pedalboats.

Outlook:
Bluegill - good
Redear sunfish - good
Largemouth bass - good
Channel catfish - good

Cutler Lake, also known as Blue Rock Lake, was drained and renovated in 1988. At this time fingerling largemouth bass, bluegill and redear sunfish were stocked. The small lake is in Blue Rock State Park.

How to catch'em: Surface lures, dragged over the pads bring up good catches of bass. Small and shallow, the lake is not a big-time destination, but a wonderful place to view.

Hot spots: Across from the swimming beach, on the south side of the lake, a shallow cove is considered to be the best spot on the lake to fish. It is accessible by boat. Other angler report good fishing near the small launching ramp at mid-lake on the north side.

Underwater structure: The lake is devoid of man-made structure, but there are lots of lily pads (American locus).

Boat launching: A small launching ramp serves the needs of electric-powered craft. Bring your canoe and topwater baits and spinners for some padding and casting in the broad expanses of lily pads.

Insider tips: The state park has three cabins, camping, wonderful shelter houses, liking trails, beach and day-use areas.

Bresler Reservoir

■ 610 acres of fishing water ■ 3.7 miles of shoreline ALLEN COUNTY

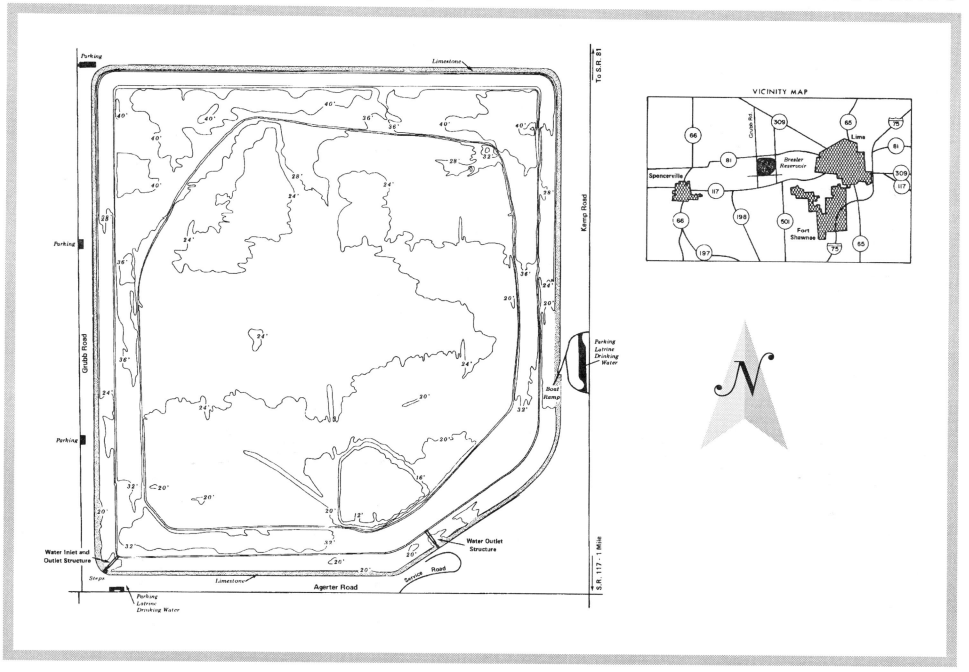

Location: In west-central Allen County four miles west of Lima, one mile south of SR 81 and one mile north of SR 117 on Kemp and Grubb roads.

Wildlife district office: (419) 424-5000.

Fishing opportunities: Small- and largemouth bass, bluegill, crappie, carp, walleye, yellow perch, bullheads. channel catfish (excellent) and rock bass.

Water conditions: Three to four feet visibility, good quality.

Bottom composition: Flat earthen, limestone rip rap shoreline.

Depth: 30 feet along the north shore, shallows (12-15 feet) along the south side.

Horsepower regulations: Electric motors only, no boat rental.

Stocking: Annually with channel catfish, walleye and perch.

Bait: Bring your own; no nearby shops.

Capacity: The reservoir has 5 billion gallons of water.

Bresler Reservoir, a water supply for

the city of Lima, sits four miles west of the municipality. It is a huge upground reservoir that was built in 1970. The reservoir is surrounded by farmland and has an average depth of 27 feet, with deep spots at the north end exceeding 44 feet. An underwater island at the south and (shallower) end produces food, which concentrates the fish. If you fish the open water, use heavy spoons and jigs and bait. Spring is the best time to fish Bresler.

Because of the flat, virtually feature-less bottom, fish suspend and relate to the shoreline and any contour or outlets. Spring is the best time to fish Bresler.

How to catch 'em: Unique to the almost square reservoir is using the balloon method for catfish. Local anglers tie their line to a balloon— some use a small beach ball—sus-pend their crawler rig, cut or stink bait under it, and let the wind blow the balloon way out into the reser-voir. Then the anglers use binocu-lars to watch the balloon. Some big walleye have also been taken using the drifting balloon trick and a nightcrawler harness.

Bresler has a very good bluegill population and the best places to find them are around the pump

houses (inlets and outlets). The pump house in the southwest cor-ner is the hottest spot. The average size of bluegills is 5.5 to seven inch-es. Try lively redworms, larval baits and mousies. Crappie fishing is good and they are found around any cover; local anglers say to use gold hooks.

Walleye have been caught up to 28 inches, but most are smaller (14-18 inches). Walleyes (and perch) are evenly distributed around the reser-voir and when water temperatures are right, they will chase crank baits. During the summer and fall, walleyes can be caught by drifting or trolling jigs and minnows, slowly worked spinners and bounced worm combinations.

Channel catfishermen do well in the flat reservoir. Plenty of 15-20 pounders are taken using the bal-loon method or on chicken livers and old gizzards under a bobber. When I fished the manmade body of water, I caught a 12-inch bullhead— my personal record!

The entire shoreline of the reservoir is protected by rocky rip rap. On the east side of the reservoir, which gets pounded by the prevailing winds, larger chunks of rip rap, up

to three feet in diameter, have been installed. About halfway down this shoreline is a dropoff to about 35 feet of water, which is well known locally as an excellent place to shoreline fish for smallmouth bass. White bass can be found in schools throughout the body of water. Try fishing evenings in May, using flashy spoons and beaded spinners.

Boat launching: A terrific ramp, complete with latrine, drinking water and plenty of parking, is on the east side of the lake off Kemp Road, just north of Agerter Road. There is no cost to launch. This is the only ramp on the reservoir.

Ice fishing: Bluegills and perch through the ice are fair. Ice out is the most productive time to jig small lures tipped with waxworms. Ice fishing for walleye with jigs with stinger hooks worked slowly on the bottom brings reasonable success.

Insider tips: Bring a balloon, binoc-ulars and crawler harness for some interesting shoreline catfishing. Work the shallow area of the south end of the lake for bass and panfish. Try catching your personal record bullhead using live-ly crawlers in the spring.

C.J. Brown Reservoir

CLARK COUNTY ■ 2,120 acres of fishing water ■ 10.5 miles of shoreline

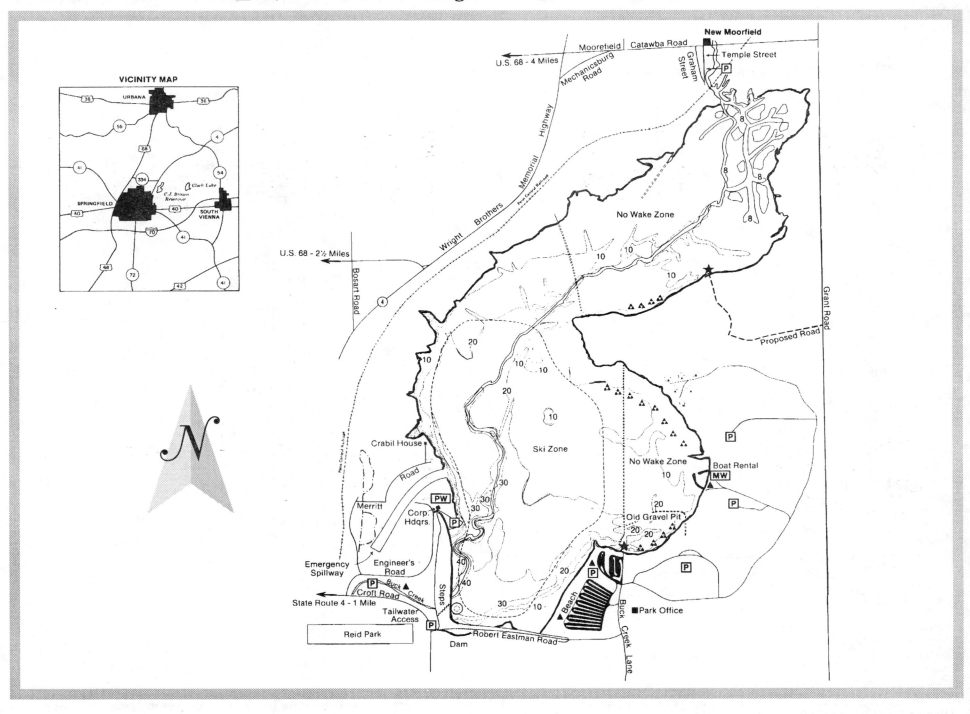

Location: In Buck Creek State Park, Clark County. Two miles northeast of Springfield, about one mile east of SR 4 on Croft Road, and three miles north of U.S. Route 40 on Bird Road and Buck Creek Lane.

Wildlife district office: (513) 372-9261.

Fishing opportunities: Largemouth bass, white and black crappies, bluegill, channel catfish, rough fish and walleye. Sunfish have entered the lake from Buck Creek.

Water conditions: Transparent one to three feet, changes seasonally.

Bottom composition: Fine, sand, silt and uniform; shallow and muddy upper end.

Horsepower restrictions: Unlimited horsepower. No wake zones are marked.

Stockings: Walleye (annually), crappies and catfish.

Dam: 6,600 feet long, 72 feet high, Corps Visitor Center.

Depth: Maximum of 40 feet.

Camping: 101 sites in the state park were built in 1987. Call (513) 322-5284.

Outlook:
Bluegill - fair
Channel catfish - good
Crappie - good
Largemouth bass - fair
Walleye - excellent

Clarence J. Brown Reservoir is a flood control and recreation reservoir in the Great Miami River watershed. It was finished in 1973 impounding Buck Creek. It drains 82 square miles. The eastern shore of the lake slopes gently, while the western shoreline drops off rapidly at 30 feet. The upper end of the reservoir, north of the Buck Creek Lane crossing, is very shallow. Standing trees in some of the coves along the western shoreline provide most of the fish cover in the lake.

The state park is one of the most modern and busiest in the state. All types of recreation take place on the lake, including water skiing, scuba diving, pleasure boating and very good fishing during weekdays.

How to catch 'em: Spring walleyes are taken along the rip rap shoreline with twister tails, jigs and twisters of white and yellow. Some anglers tip a bright-colored lead-head jig with a minnow and work the bait parallel to the bank. As the water warms, most local experts suggest that anglers troll or drift with deep diving crankbaits or spinners with trailing nightcrawlers. Drift across the old creek channel and in front of the Corps headquarters. Fish attractors north of the state park marina can also hold walleye and other species during every season. Check regulations on walleye. The average caught is 14 inches; the average kept is probably 16 inches in length. Some 10-pound walleye are taken. Some walleye are taken in the tailwaters below the dam.

Brown Reservoir is a good crappie impoundment April through June. Look for any brush or along the rip rap and still fish with live minnows or jigs tipped with bits of worm or larval baits. Bluegills will stay in the shallows much of the summer. Kids can have a ball fishing along the rip rap bank with redworms and a simple bobber. According to local anglers, the old channel is a decent largemouth hot spot in the spring.

Catfish can be found in the creek mouth at the upper end of the lake. Bring your oldest stinky baits.

Underwater structure: Some structure is in place, but as usual, it's hard to find. The lake is void of significant structure, making fishing tough much of the season. If you can, find the submerged roads, railroad bed and underway humps. This is a bathtub-like lake; you must find the underwater features to find the fish. Watch where other anglers are fishing; then try the area.

Boat launches: A modern launching ramp, with plenty of parking, is near the park office at the end of Buck Creek Lane. The beach and dam are near the launching ramp. The state park marina (513-322-5992) offers full services, boat rental, snacks, bait and tackle.

Ice fishing: Virtually none.

Insider tips: Brown is best in May and June when the walleyes are near shore. Evening fish along with the locals; many don't start fishing until 9 p.m. Night fishing around the marina in the summer can also be productive.

Buckeye Lake

- 3,600 acres of fishing water ■ 32 miles of shoreline FAIRFIELD & PERRY COUNTIES

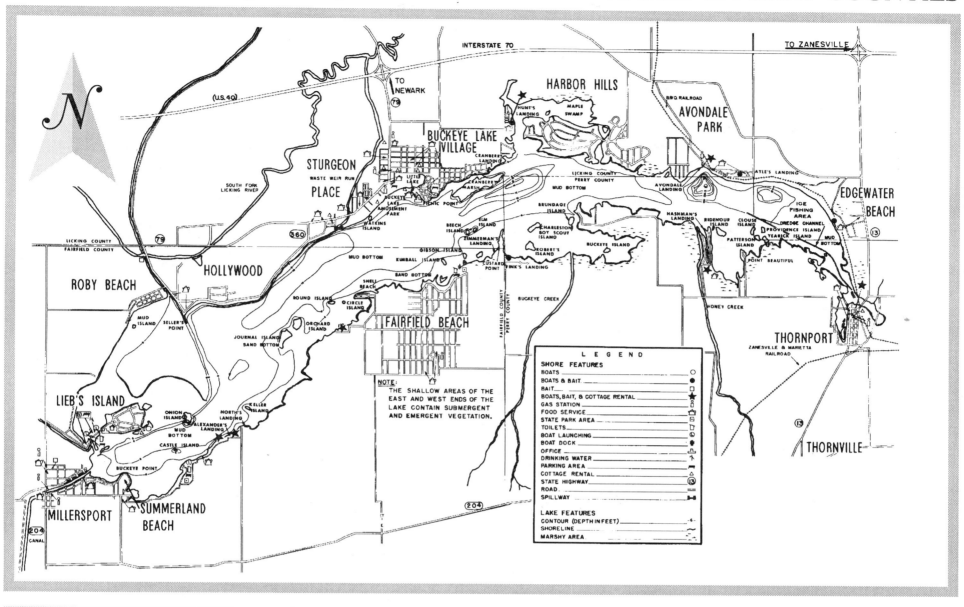

Location: About 20 miles west of Columbus. Take I-70 east from Columbus. Take any of the following roads south from I-70 to the lake: SR 37, SR 79 or SR 13.

Wildlife district office: (614) 644-3925.

Fishing opportunities: Buckeye Lake is an excellent warmwater fishery. Muskie (very good), walleye (good), catfish, bass (excellent), panfish (very good).

Water conditions: Murky and brown.

Bottom composition: Stumpy, muddy.

Bottom temperature (summer): 85-95 degrees.

Underwater structure: Narrow reefs, stumps.

Average depth: 4.5 feet.

Boating: Unlimited horsepower. There are more than 3,000 private boats on the lake.

Buckeye State Park: Park office is on Liebs Island, call (614) 467-2690. It's the 12th oldest park in U.S.

Characteristics: Many coves, islands, shallow flats, warmwater marshy areas at the east end.

Stocking: Because of the neighboring fish hatchery, the lake often gets surplus fish planted.

Camping: Two private camp-

grounds are nearby.

History: When the last glaciers retreated from Ohio some 18,000 years ago, they left in their wake innumerable lakes, kettles and wetland. One such shallow lake was at present-day Buckeye Lake, only the prehistoric lake was actually much larger than the present lake. By the 1700s when the first Europeans settlers were entering the region, Buckeye Lake had largely silted in and became a bog dominated by thick sphagnum moss and other northern plants. It was much like a Canadian lake.

Early settlers dubbed the area the "Great Swamp." The return of Buckeye Lake was not a natural, but a manmade occurrence. In the 1820s, Ohio caught canal fever and towns across the state fought to have a canal connecting them to important markets in the east and south. The result was a network of canals that didn't work and that needed feeder lakes to supply them with water. A dike was built at the west end of the Great Swamp to create a feeder lake. Cranberry Bog, which appears as an island east of Picnic Point, is a unique reminder of the thick sphagnum moss that was dense in the area. The bog is now a floating mat, unusual this far south.

How to catch 'em: Buckeye Lake is an interesting and productive fishery, except for mid-summer when water temperatures will require you

use creative techniques. The lake is popular with bass clubs. Bass anglers use standard techniques like rubber worms in the weeds and stumps, crankbaits and spinners in the spring and fall. Some local anglers recommend yellow-colored topwater frogs that can be jerked and worked over weedbeds and aquatic vegetation near the shore.

Muskie fishing is excellent. But, as always, you need to put in your time fishing the big predators. Having your jerk bait lure in the water when the muskies go on the bite is half the challenge. Try points along the south side of the lake; this is where members of the Huskie Muskie club have been quietly observed trolling and taking some good-sized fish.

Hot spot: The Cranberry Marsh, near Buckeye Lake Village, is highly recommended for panfish. Game fish are most often found along the docks and channels. Hunt's Landing and Maple Swamp are excellent bass angling areas where spinners can be buzzed in the shallows. Ice fishermen take good numbers of perch at Clouse Island. Shoreline anglers should try for catfish and crappies along the wall, next to the North Shore Ramp or on Lieb's Island. At Green Lake, a protected bay off the lake at North Shore, is a 10-foot square fishing pier accessible by persons with disabilities.

Boat launching: Four of the state

launching ramps are newer, while the other ramps were built in the 1960s. The North Shore Ramp at the village of Buckeye Lake is one of the busiest. Because the lake averages only 4.5 feet deep, boat size is limited. Slow-moving pontoons, sailboats, rowboats and canoes are common on the cove-filled lake. Don't take your boat where you don't see another one operating—the shallows will get ya! Nearly 1,000 acres of the lake are less than 1.5 feet deep. The lake can get rough quickly. If it does, head in or find a cove.

Ice fishing: Perch and panfish are taken on larval baits. The best ice fishing is just before ice-out.

Dredge: A large dredge does work on the lake and many local anglers fish near the unit that seems to attract fish and produce food.

Insider tips: The best fishing is from a boat. The lake is one of the best in the state at ice-off and ice-on times of the year (especially for crappie). Try spring and summer fishing Monday - Thursday, when recreational boating is at its lowest. Try to find the 4.5- miles-long dam—it looks like a levee, and has residential houses on it. The nearby Hebron Fish Hatchery at the north end of the lake is open to the public. Waterfowl hunters should keep this lake in mind. Buckeye State Park is the 12th oldest state park in the country.

Bucyrus Reservoirs

CRAWFORD COUNTY ■ No. 1–5 miles, Riley - 1.25 miles, & No. 4–2 miles of shoreline

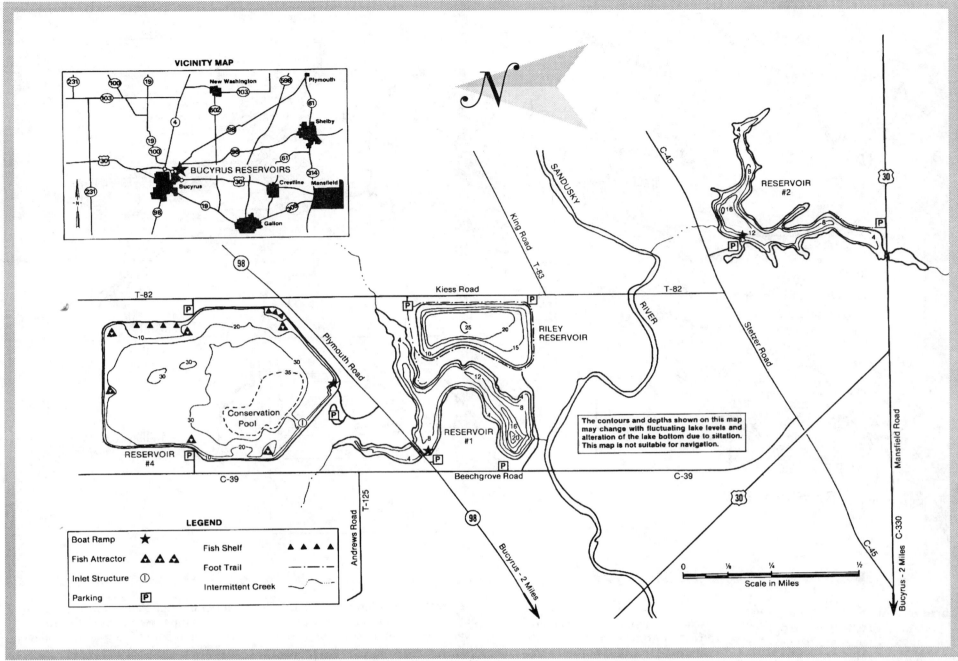

Location: Two miles northeast of Bucyrus along SR 98 and Stetzer Road (CR 45). Reservoirs No. 1 and No. 4 can be reached directly off SR 98. Riley Reservoir lies south of SR 98 on Kiess Road (Township Road 82). Reservoir No 2 lies on CR 45 east of Kiess Road; the upper end of Reservoir No. 2 can be reached off U.S. Route 30 to the south. The reservoirs are in Crawford County.

Fishing opportunities:

Reservoir No. 1 - Largemouth bass, northern pike (few), bluegill crappies, sun- and rough-fish.

Wildlife district office: (419) 424-5000.

Reservoir No. 2 - Largemouth bass, channel catfish, crappies, bluegills, sunfish and carp.

Riley Reservoir - Walleye, white bass, channel catfish, yellow perch, large- and smallmouth bass, bluegills and rock bass.

Outhwaite Reservoir No. 4 - Yellow perch, large- and small-mouth bass, channel catfish, walleye, rock bass and bluegill.

Bottom composition: Earthen, mud, some weedbeds in Nos. 1 and 2.

Horsepower restrictions: Electric motors only.

Stocking: Annually

Outlook Reservoir Nos. 1 and 2:
Largemouth bass - fair to good
White crappies - good, especially in No. 2
Channel catfish - good

Reservoir No. 1 is a shallow (and warm) on-stream impound with a mud bottom. The narrow reservoir has lots of cattails, and here you may find a few northern pike left over from plantings conducted years ago. Reservoir No. 2 is also an on-stream irregular-shaped impoundment with a small dam. Like Reservoir No. 1, this impoundment has a tree-lined shore, is a little deeper. Both of these older reservoirs are relatively shallow. They have a light current and there is a lot of cover, especially along the small bays and shoreline. They are pleasant places to fish.

Riley Reservoir is a small upground reservoir with a depth of about 20 feet. The shorelines are regular and treated with rip rap. Water is pumped into this impoundment and the water clarity is six to seven feet. Cool water species are in good num-bers, including saugeye, smallmouth bass, yellow perch, channel catfish, rock bass and crappies.

The newer Reservoir No. 4 is on SR 98 and often called the "arrowhead" reservoir because of its shape. This impoundment is deeper than the rest, about 25 feet. It has some rock and brick piles that the city of Bucyrus installed before filling the reservoir. The rubble reefs offer good cover and are a contrast to the flat, featureless earthen bottom. Here are walleye, smallmouth, chan-nel catfish, bullheads, rock bass and some carp. Walleyes run 16-18 inch-es. Perch move back to the cover in the late summer and fall; stick with live bait for the best perch action.

How to catch 'em: Spring is the peak fishing period for these neigh-boring reservoirs. Because Nos. 1 and 2 are shallow and offer good shoreline cover, run lures shallow. Buzz spinners or use live bait of minnows, redworms or night-crawlers along any structure. The best fishing tactics in these two impoundments is to work the dropoffs, any shoreline cover, stick-ups, fallen brush and points. Plastic worms and topwater propeller baits were recommended by one longtime local angler.

Reservoir No 4 and Riley are deeper and offer good summertime drift fishing or slow trolling opportunities using deep running artificials and active live bait. Drift for walleye near the bottom when the water temperature warms. Bounce or walk a crawler rig. Here you will also pick up a few perch and catfish. Small- and largemouth relate to the shoreline and will take correctly worked spinner baits. Walleye can be taken along the shoreline in the spring and will chase crankbaits and twister tails.

Boat launching: Reservoir No. 1 has a primitive gravel and dirt ramp for hand launching. Reservoir No. 2 has a good gravel launching ramp. Reservoir No. 4 has a two-lane hard-surfaced ramp with parking lot.

Ice fishing: Opportunities are good; fishing pressure is low. Local anglers report fair perch fishing using tear drops and larval baits.

Insider tips: Reservoir No. 4 is the best fishing impoundment. Boat fish Riley and Reservoir No 4. These two impoundments also pro-duce good to very good bluegill angling near any kind of vegetation, stumps or shoreline cover (try a slip bobber in the summer).

■ 664 acres of fishing water ■ 7.8 miles of shoreline ATHENS & MORGAN COUNTY

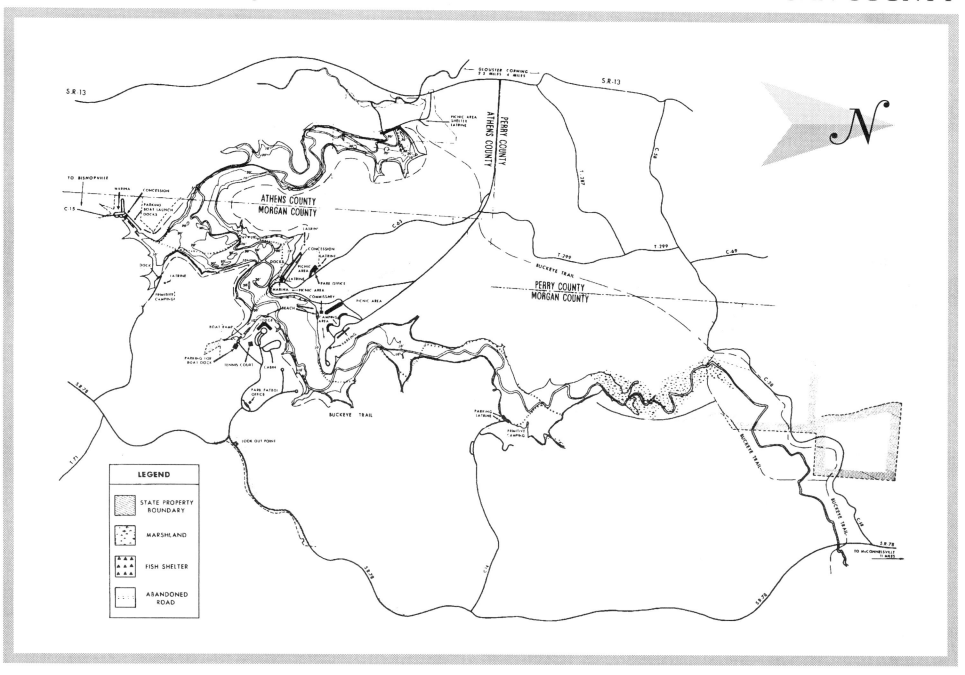

LEGEND

	STATE PROPERTY BOUNDARY
	MARSHLAND
	FISH SHELTER
	ABANDONED ROAD

Location: In Athens and Morgan counties, the dam is three miles north of Glouster on SR 13. The lake is 40 miles south of I-70. The state park office is one mile off SR 13 and CR 63.

Wildlife district office: (614) 594-2211.

Fishing opportunities: Largemouth bass, crappie, bluegill, saugeye, walleye, channel and shovelhead catfish, and rough fish.

Wildlife district office: In Athens, call (614) 594-2211.

Water conditions: In summer and fall it's fairly clear.

Average depth: 20 feet.

Bottom composition: Mud, some rock.

Horsepower: 10 hp limit.

Underwater structure: Beneath the lake are seven covered bridges and some timber and weedbeds.

Boat rental: Two locations, Dock No. 1 which has fuel and is off SR 78, and Dock No. 4.

Camping: Three public campgrounds (two are on the lake and other on a ridge) with 85 total sites.

Special restriction: Check regulations relative to slot limits.

Burr Oak Lake State Park: 3,265 acres, lodge, cabins, trails. Call (614) 767-7570.

Stocking: Saugeye.

Outlook:
Bluegill, redear - fair
Largemouth bass - excellent
Channel catfish - excellent
Saugeye - good

Burr Oak Lake is a mature, long, winding lake set in a deep hollow. Public lands surrounding the lake are rugged and rolling, covered by a dense oak-hickory forest. Unfortunately the only burr oak found in the area is at the R.J. Miller Memorial Grove near the state park cabins, planted in 1968. Because of the vast public lands that surround the lake, the fishing experience is pleasant and remote.

How to catch 'em: Four- to five-pound saugeye are common in the lake. Since being stocked, saugeye and improving bass production have put Burr Oak Lake back on the map. The lake was built in 1950 and has matured and improved since its fish production peak when it was 10 years old. Burr Oak Lake is much like Lake Logan, where the current

world record saugeye was taken. Fisheries biologists have great hope that the saugeye production will continue to improve rapidly.

Spring and early summer bass anglers should work lures and plastic worms slowly from shore to deeper water. From mid-summer to fall, work surface lures in a stop-and-go fashion around stick-ups, fallen trees, across weedbeds and over aquatic plants. When the water is warm, try spinners or bait crawlers. Heavy weeds will collect on spinners or crankbaits, so try running in pockets and gaps along aquatic beds. Many fall bass anglers slowly troll deep-running lures, crossing the channels and running along points. Lots of seven- to eight-pound largemouth are taken annually. Some local experts claim Burr Oak Lake is one of the best bucketmouth lakes in the state. It is, at least, one of the most pleasant lakes to fish for largemouth.

The upper end of the lake is terrific for bullhead fishing. Catfish are found throughout the lake. Catfish anglers often night fish using day-old shrimp, nightcrawler gobs and beef livers. These nocturnal anglers fish just off the bottom, slowly. Angler success is high for early spring largemouth bass and mid- to

late summer catfishing.

Bluegill are very abundant and very small. Ice fishermen occasionally find some good bluegills. Trees have been cut along the shore and concentrate most species of fish.

Hot spots: Dock No. 3 is well-known locally as an excellent place to catch catfish. Scented doughballs and various cut baits are used. Saugeye and big catfish can be taken in 35-foot-deep water in front of the dam.

Boat launching: There are four public ramps; one is at the state park's 60-room lodge with 30 cabins for guests. Two of the ramps have marinas. Dock No. 1 has gasoline. Be careful at the upper end of the lake, especially past Dock No. 3.

Ice fishing: When weather conditions permit, panfishing is fair. Local experts say you must find the old creek channel and use live minnows.

Insider tips: Bass production has been steadily increasing. The best fishing is from a boat, so you can get over weedbeds and drift across the channel or structure. Both bass and catfish tournaments are held on the long lake.

Caesar Creek Lake

WARREN, CLINTON & GREENE COUNTIES ■ 2,830 acres of fishing water ■ 40 miles of shoreline

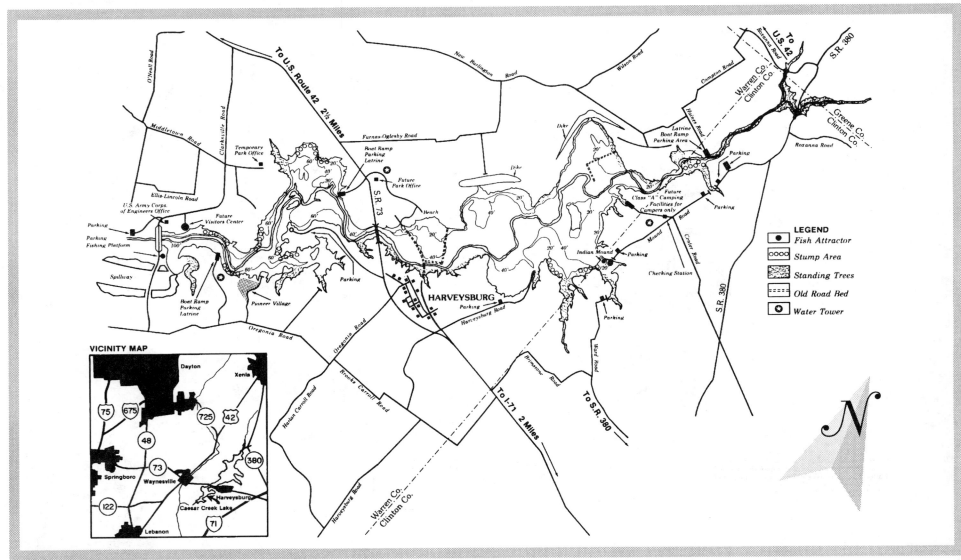

Location: In Warren, Clinton and Greene counties. Four miles east of Waynesville and two miles west of I-71 along SR 73, the lake is about 30 miles northeast of Cincinnati and 15 miles southeast of Dayton.

Wildlife district office: (513) 372-9261.

Fishing opportunities: Large- and smallmouth bass, crappie, bluegill and catfish.

Water conditions: Fair visibility, cold, deep.

Bottom composition: Mostly fine substrate (silt and sand), 20 percent rock.

Depth: Up to 150 feet, normal depth of 115 feet.

Horsepower restrictions: Unlimited.

Stocking: Both walleye and saugeye annually.

Special regulations: 15-inch size limit on black bass.

Drainage area: 237 square miles; the dam is three miles above the mouth of Caesar Creek.

Camping: Caesar Creek State Park, (513) 897-3055.

Outlook:
Bluegill - excellent
Crappie - fair to good
Largemouth bass - good
Saugeye - very good
White bass - very good

Caesar Creek Lake is the deepest lake in Ohio, steep-sided, and can be hard to fish. The lake is surrounded by state public lands cloaked in oak-hickory and beech-maple woodlands. The U.S. Army Corps of Army Engineers maintains an excellent visitor center near the huge dam.

State park facilities include a 287-site campground, Pioneer Village, 484-acre Caesar Creek Gorge State Natural Preserve, fossil observation areas, 32 miles of hiking trails, a 1,300 foot beach and a group lodge.

The diverse habitat and large size of the lake offer anglers many coves and bays, inlets and underwater structure (timber, roadbeds and stumps) to explore. White bass have exploded on the scene through feeder rivers (possibly threatening the walleye population). Crappie fishing is fair, but largemouth and smallmouth bass angling can be very good seasonally. Because of heavy recreational boating, weekdays are the most enjoyable times to fish the cold lake. On summer, weekends, anglers should plan on getting off the lake by 10 a.m. The lake quiets back down about 8:30 p.m. Caesar Creek Lake may be the busiest lake in Ohio. The 2,750-foot-long earth and rock dam was completed in 1978.

How to catch 'em: The lake fishery is very good, mostly because of the many small bays and inlets that vary from one to 70 acres. Most of the bays contain standing timber, brush and stick-ups that provide good fish habitat, especially during the spring and fall. Anglers should also concentrate on stumpy zones and patches of standing timber along the shoreline. The southwest end of the lake has several areas worth exploring. Local anglers suggest that serious bass fishermen try spinners around the timber and rocks that surround the islands, and near the old roadbeds by Harveysburg. The lake has lots of points, a wide creek channel and areas of firm, rocky bottom.

The lower end of the lake offers plenty of bays and coves near the shoreline. Toward the upper reaches of the reservoir, steep rocky dropoffs, flooded timber, old foundations, rocky bottoms and roadbeds are excellent areas for sport fish. In these areas you might also pick up smallmouth or spotted bass. Largemouths are typically 1-14 inches, with some weighing up to four pounds.

Some say the crappie angling is improving. The lake has a good population of 7-11 inch crappies that are best taken in wooded bays in April and May. Spring and summer, local anglers use live bait and bobbers around rip rap, the rocky shoreline and deep humps. You can also still fish live minnows over any type of structure in the coves and central lake. Drifting and trolling waxworms, minnows and small lures is a relaxing way to approaching angling on this deep body of water. Work slowly, use live bait, and you can pick up bluegills all summer in the deeper water and along the shoreline. Five- to eight-inch bluegill are the norm. In the summer many of the 'gills are taken in 10-20 foot water and around submerged humps at that depth.

Saugeye are heavily planted and there are good numbers of 13-18 inches fish, with some reaching 24 inches in length. Try the tailwater of the dam for some fast seasonal action. White bass move in April and May up the tributaries and can be seen chasing shad at the surface in late summer. Look for white bass fishing to continue to improve. Cast small spoons and crankbaits into the schools when they are moving.

Underwater structure: A large tire structure is on the south side of Old Indian Mound, near the campground. Check the map and watch other anglers who are working over roadbeds, substrate and the creek channel.

Boat launching: The lake is active with skiers and powerboaters. Five launches are scattered around the perimeter of the lake. The two largest ramps are near the state park office on SR 72, just south of Corwin. The main ramps are on the south side of the lake, with one serving the campground.

Insider tips: Fish spring and fall. Camp in the well-maintained campground and launch your boat from the campground. This is a very good bluegill lake. Bring a can of redworms and small hooks.

Clark Lake

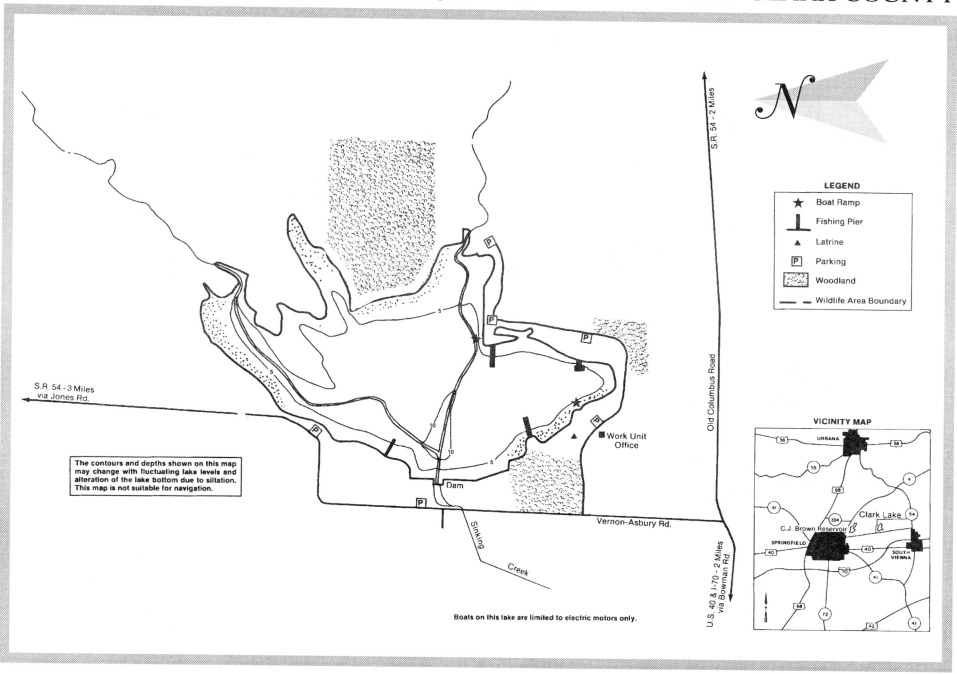

LEGEND

★ Boat Ramp

⊥ Fishing Pier

▲ Latrine

Ⓟ Parking

Woodland

— — Wildlife Area Boundary

The contours and depths shown on this map may change with fluctuating lake levels and alteration of the lake bottom due to siltation. This map is not suitable for navigation.

Boats on this lake are limited to electric motors only.

S.R. 54 - 3 Miles via Jones Rd.

S.R. 54 - 2 Miles

Old Columbus Road

U.S. 40 & I-70 - 2 Miles via Bowman Rd.

Vernon-Asbury Rd.

Sinking Creek

Dam

Work Unit Office

VICINITY MAP

Location: In Clark County, eight miles east of Springfield, northwest of Harmony, off U.S. Route 40.

Wildlife district office: (513) 372-9261

Fishing opportunities: Largemouth bass, crappies. bluegill and catfish.

Bottom composition: Mostly mud; some gravel and sand.

Water conditions: Low visibility, strong farm runoff.

Depth: Shallow, average of five feet.

Shoreline: Gentle, with vegetation.

Clark Lake is formed from the impounding of Sinking Creek in the 4,384-acre Great Miami River watershed. The earthen dam was built in 1958 and is owned and operated by the Ohio Division of Wildlife. The deepest spot in the lake is about 10 feet near the dam.

The remote little lake is not a great fishery, but it is a pleasant hideaway in this part of the state, not far from the much larger C.J. Brown Reservoir. This is a perfect place to bring your cartop boat, a bunch of kids to go crappie fishing.

How to catch 'em: From canoes and tiny boats, a few fly fishermen cast spider patterns and popping bugs for crappies and the many stunted bluegills that kids love to catch. The three eastern bays are shallow, but can be a lot of fun fly fishing during the spring. Your No. 5 eight-foot trout rod and some delicate patterns are all you need for an afternoon of fun.

Most of the shoreline is gentle, where young children can cast into the water. Bring a can of redworms or nightcrawlers and bobbers for lots of fun with the family. Some big rough fish are also known to grab a gob of crawlers which can give young anglers a tussle. Three fishing piers and a latrine are also near parking and the lake's edge.

Boat launching: A small launching ramp is available for electric boats.

Insider tips: For most of the lake's existence, it has been a poor fishery. But in the past few years it has blossomed as a very good crappie lake. This small lake is a terrific day-use lake; bring the entire family.

Clear Fork Reservoir

RICHLAND & MORROW COUNTIES ■ 944 acres of fishing water ■ 14 miles of shoreline

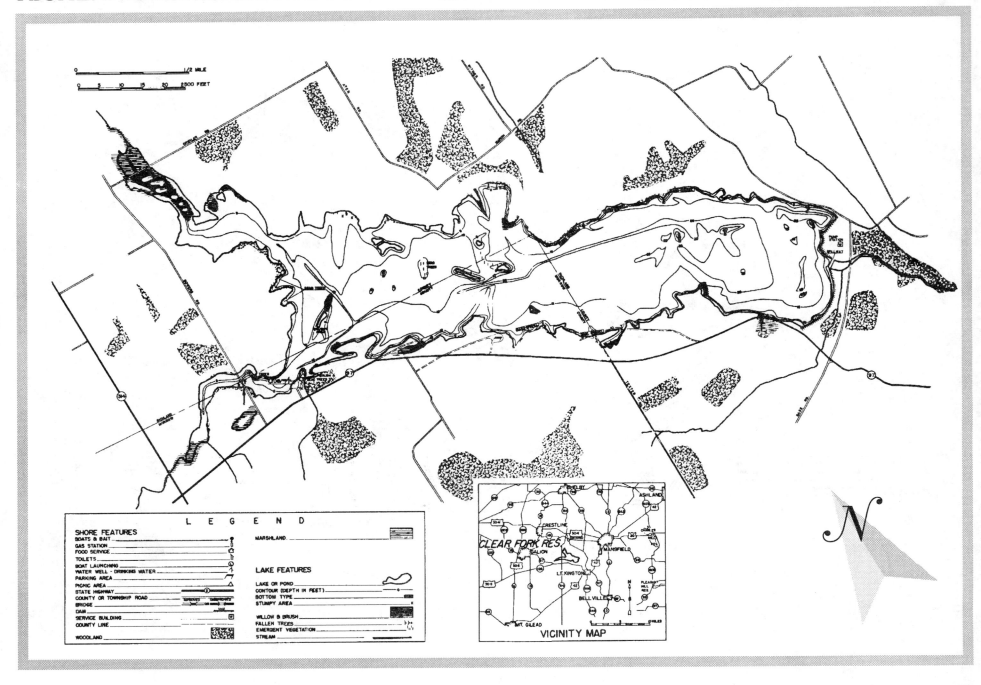

Location: In Richland and Morrow counties between the cities of Mansfield and Galion.

Wildlife district offices: (419) 424-5000.

Fishing opportunities: Muskie, crappies, largemouth bass, bluegill, yellow perch, white bass and channel catfish.

Water conditions: Medium to clear.

Bottom composition: Gravel, sand and mud.

Horsepower restrictions: There is an enforced speed limit of 10 mph.

Stocking: Muskie annually.

Boats are rented at the marina.

Camping is on the lake.

Outlook:
Muskie - excellent
Crappies - good
Largemouth bass - good
Bluegill - fair
White bass - fair
Channel catfish - fair
Yellow perch - fair

The city of Mansfield controls the well-known muskie lake and features a spanking-clean concession stand, campground, ramp and day-use areas. According to regional biologists, Clear Fork is the best lake in the state (maybe the nation, some say) to catch a muskie. The city's park and top fisheries management makes this a super destination lake, especially for muskie anglers.

How to catch 'em: The lake has a high-density muskie population, including many trophy-size individuals. There are about two muskies per acre in Clear Fork Reservoir. In fact, this is a brood lake where muskies' eggs are collected each spring for use in hatcheries. Some 40-pound fish are in the clean lake. Gizzard shad are the primary forage of the muskie, so many anglers use shad-like lures in the system. Because of the heavy forage base, muskie can reach 30 inches by age three. In northern states that rely solely on natural reproduction, fish would need five years to grow to this size.

For the most part, trolling is the best technique. Grandma, Grim Reapers and Believer lures are popular here, and many other big plugs and trolling baits are sold at the marina. Try shad mimics. When you cast for muskie, use jumbo spinners and crankbaits.

Clear Fork also has a fair population of 7-13 inch white bass and plenty of 5-6 inch bluegills. Both white and black crappies in the 8-13 inch size can also be found throughout the lake. Largemouth bass anglers can also expect very good fishing, often catching many 2-5 pound bass in the 12-20 inch range.

Hot spots: The campground on the lake often has some top muskie experts that are willing to offer some sage advice and tips on what to use and where to go. Local muskie experts fish heavily in the spring around the islands on the west end and the "humps," which are three little contours near the dam on the east end of the lake. Anglers also work near the row of buoys near the dam. Some also fish the "spring hole" at the eastern end of the bay where anglers will cast against the wooded shoreline and around fallen trees and branches. First-time anglers to the lake may want to watch the fishing action from a distance. Look for anglers with huge nets sticking up from their boats, and observe their trolling patterns, lure selection and so on.

Some of the downstream areas can be good for muskie lost over the dam. The south shoreline is open to bank fishing.

Underwater structure: From southern weedy bays to wooded shorelines and islands on the north, Clear Fork Reservoir has lots of natural structure that holds all types of fish. The park area also offers excellent shoreline angling and a nearby fishing pier accessible by fishermen with disabilities.

Boat launching: The marina, which sells bait and tackle, has a launching ramp off SR 97 at the southwest corner of the lake. The marina usually has good fishing reports and information.

Ice fishing: There is none allowed.

Insider tips: Leesville and Clear Fork are the two most productive muskie lakes in the state. Some years, more than 20 muskies 42 inches or more are caught. About 200 muskie each year are hooked that are between 30 and 42 inches. Remember to catch and release your muskie. The lake has a heavily enforced 10 mph speed limit. I'd like to see more lakes allow any size motor, but enforce a speed limit.

Clendening Lake

■ 1,800 acres of fishing water ■ 44 miles of shoreline HARRISON COUNTY

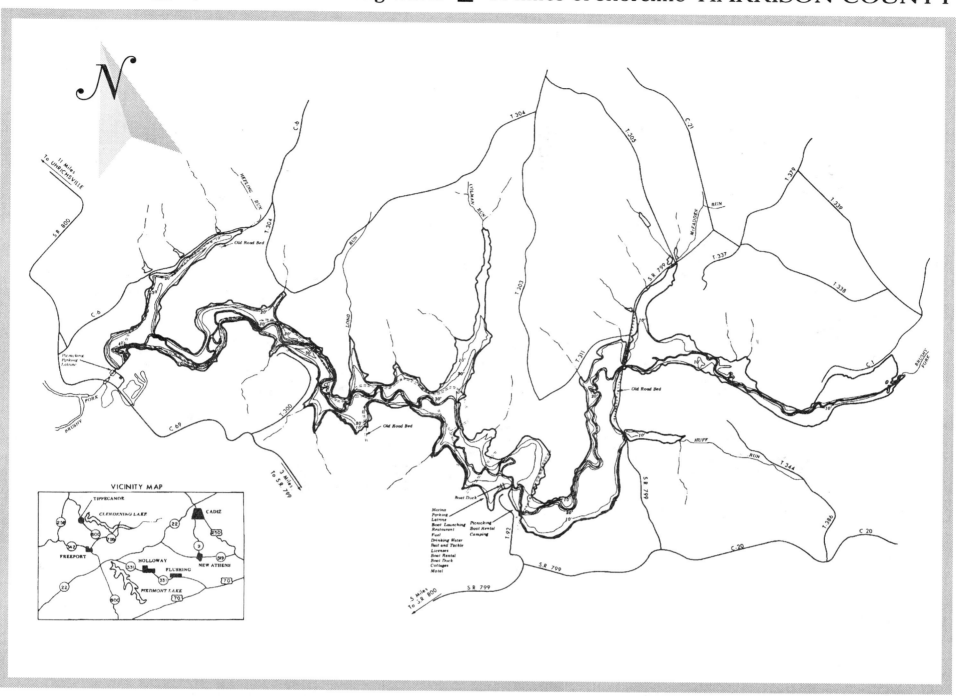

Location: In Harrison County. The dam is off SR 800, and SR 799 bisects the lake. New Philadelphia is about 25 miles north of the lake.

Wildlife district office: (330) 644-2293.

Fishing opportunities: Largemouth bass, crappies, bluegill, flathead and channel catfish, muskie, white bass and saugeye.

Water conditions: Clear and clean.

Bottom composition: Mud, some rock.

Horsepower restriction: 10 hp.

Stocking: Saugeye.

Maximum depth: 41 feet.

Camping: 80 sites at marina; call (614) 658-3691.

Boat rental at the marina.

Outlook:
Largemouth bass - excellent
Crappies - poor
Bluegills - fair
Flathead catfish - fair
Saugeye - good

Clendening Lake is in the scenic hill country, two miles from Deersville and southeast of New Philadelphia. It is a Muskingum Watershed Conservancy lake and is long, narrow and clear with lots of vegetation. It also has a lot of rock in it (but there are no smallmouth bass—sorry).

How to catch 'em: Clendening Lake is a superior largemouth bass lake. According to fisheries biologists, when they are asked by professional and semi-professional bass anglers where to go in Ohio, they are directed here. Largemouth anglers will want to bring along a box full of crankbaits, spinners and plastic worms. The clear water causes the fish to sight feed, so presentation is critical—use light line. Largemouth are typically 12-23 inches.

Due to the clean water, some anglers like to quietly wade the shoreline casting artificial lures. Try this technique in the evening for some refreshing fishing action.

Crappies and bluegills are undersized, usually about eight inches in size. Nevertheless, kids will enjoy catching them, and serious panfish-ermen can take good numbers using redworms in the early spring. There are good numbers of 15-24 inch saugeye in the lake, but they sometimes go unnoticed because of the excellent largemouth fishing. There are plenty of 10-pound saugeye in Clendening—so bring your night-crawler rig or try jigging up some of these fish. Huge catfish are frequently taken from the lake, many on set lines and cut bait. Rod and reel anglers should try standard baits of chicken parts, liver, scented doughballs and commercial baits. Some anglers also fish a big dead minnow weighted to the bottom. White bass school in April; the season is short and productive period. When casting bucktails, you can pop one of the silver fish on each toss.

Hot spots: Amazingly, the largemouth bass fishing is so good in the lake, you can start just about anywhere and catch old bucketmouth. You many want to start by fishing the shoreline—especially along the east—and around the rock lines that meet the water.

Underwater structure: Over the years Christmas trees have been submerged throughout the lake and a number of shoreline trees felled. Panfish love the downed trees.

Boat launching: One MWCD marina and launch is on the lake. The marina offers boat rental and sales, fuel, food, marine service and supplies. If you get frustrated with the fishing on a hot summer's day, you can always head for the designated boater's swimming area and take a dip. Call the marina at (614) 658-3691. A second ramp is off Country Road 6 near Tippecanoe.

Ice fishing: Very little ice fishing is done on the lake.

Insider tips: In the spring, anglers often hear turkeys gobble and grouse drum. A few sailboats ply the water on the quiet lake. The state record flathead catfish was taken from Clendening in 1979. The cat weighed a whopping 76 pounds and was nearly 54 inches long. Not many muskies are taken from Clendening Lake. The Buckeye Trail, which links all four corners of Ohio, passes by the lake. Near 5,000 acres of MWCD lands surround the scenic lake. Hunting is permitted in designated areas. Saugeye are under-fished.

Cowan Lake

CLINTON COUNTY ■ 692 acres of fishing water ■ 17 miles of shoreline

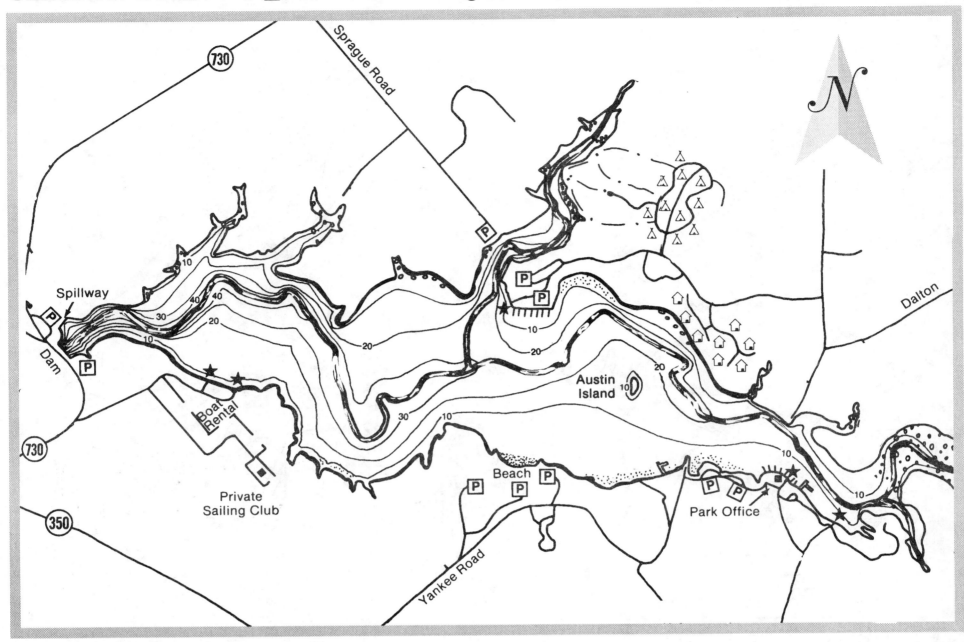

Location: In Clinton County, about seven miles southwest of Wilmington, 35 miles southeast of Dayton and 40 miles northeast of Cincinnati. The lake is accessible from U.S. Route 68 and State Routes 350 and 730.

Wildlife district office: (513) 372-9261.

Fishing opportunities: Largemouth bass, muskie, crappie, catfish, bluegills and rough fish.

Water conditions: Fair clarity, can be turbid.

Bottom composition: Mud, silt, some clay, a few rocky areas.

Horsepower restrictions: 10 hp and under.**Camping:** 237 camp sites, 27 cabins. Call the state park, (513) 289-2105.

Special restrictions: 15-inch minimum on bass.

Stocking: Muskies annually.

Bait: State park marina and nearby shops.

Shoreline: Plenty of areas in the park; try the tailwaters.

Outlook:
Largemouth bass - excellent
Crappie - good
Muskellunge - good

Catfish - excellent

The lands around Cowan Lake were shaped by the last glacier that receded through the region about 10,000 years ago. Once a shallow sea, shale deposits are vast, interesting and filled with fossils of the era. Both Liberty Shale and Waynesville Shale can be seen at the spillway near the Cowan Lake Dam. Fossil hunters comb this, and other bedrock areas, around the lake looking for prehistoric life forms. The 1,076-acre surrounding Cowan State Park opened in 1968 and the dam was built in 1950. The park has camping, a public beach, six picnic areas, marina with fuel, bait and boat rental, and scenic cabins.

Cowan Lake has a strong population of largemouth bass. It is one of the best bucketmouth fisheries in the state.

How to catch 'em: Bass are evenly distributed around the lake. Nevertheless, local experts advise anglers to work the many bays and coves, looking for underwater points and other fishing holding habitats. It's possible to catch 30-40 bass daily; most won't be keepers.

Largemouth populations are excellent, with most of them in the 12-15 inch range. Local experts says most common techniques work for the plentiful fish. Some recommend

grape-colored auger-tail worms, ripple rind, skirted jigs and small crayfish-colored crankbaits. Chartreuse-colored spinner baits and pig and jig combos also do the job. It's hard not to catch largemouth in this lake.

Crappies are very good in the spring. Action slows somewhat in the summer as the fish move into 8-15 feet of water. Look for brushy areas, points and dropoffs when the water temperatures increase. Marina staff says that October can be a killer month for crappies in all parts of the lake. Night fish for catfish all summer along the south shore or near the dam.

The muskie population is small, but growing. Veteran muskie anglers troll along points and dropoffs in the lower half of the lake, often near the north shore, crossing over the old creek channel. Staff says some muskies have been taken in the narrows in front of the park office slow trolling medium-sized and medium-depth cigar-shaped plugs. Keep your hooks sharp, and troll and troll and troll. You have to put your time in to catch muskie at Cowan Lake, or anywhere.

Unofficial lake records: Muskie - 23 pounds; largemouth bass - six pounds; smallmouth bass - four pounds, 14 inches; crappie more than pounds; shovelhead catfish - 50 pounds and 40 inches.

Boat launching: A private 151-slip sailing club and horsepower restrictions keep the lake pretty quiet Even on summer weekends, anglers can usually find peaceful areas and decent catches. The South Shore Marina (513-289-2656) sells fuel, bait, food, fishing tackle, licenses and rents boats and dock space. The largest ramp on the lake (eight lanes) is near the park office and features nearby shoreline fishing, parking and picnic tables. A smaller ramp is at the end of SR 730.

Hot spots: In most coves and bays, largemouth are best found along the south shore and the upper end of the lake near vegetation. Crappies are best near the dam with a grub jig.

Ice fishing: Very little activity, but fishing could be good to very good when conditions allow it.

Insider tips: The 10-horsepower motor restriction keeps the big bass boats and bass tournaments to a minimum, making this one of the best bass fishing experiences in the state. The South Shore Marina can offer excellent fishing reports; call (513) 289-2656. Ask about recent muskie catches. Some 30-pound muskie have been seen.

Deer Creek Reservoir

■ 314 acres of fishing water ■ 8 miles of shoreline STARK COUNTY

Water conditions: Muddy.

Bottom composition: Soft mud.

Depth: Ten-foot average.

Shoreline: One-third of shoreline is accessible.

The reservoir was constructed by the Army Corps of Engineers as a primary water supply for the city of Alliance. The water body is contained by an earthen dam with a concrete spillway across Deer Creek, a tributary of the Mahoning River. Finished in 1954 and filled in 1955, the reservoir has had both good and bad fishing. Today the angling is fair at best. But its location is good, and access is good for families living in the Alliance area.

How to catch 'em: The fish population is stunted, but kids can have fun at the old reservoir. The surrounding agricultural lands and occasional train that chugs by make for a quiet place for a picnic and fishing for pint-sized panfish. Few largemouth of any size are ever taken from the lake. Bring your brightest-colored lures and cast the shoreline, around undercut banks and the stream inlet. Rumors persist that there is a jumbo muskie lurking in the murky waters.

Hot spots: The small peninsula where the boat launch is located can yield a few decent crappies in the early spring. This is the best area for children to try their skills under mom and dad's supervision. A nearby latrine, drinking water, picnic tables and gentle shoreline can make for a fun afternoon near the lake.

Underwater structure: Christmas trees were sunk many years ago and are probably disintegrated by now. The lake is featureless and increasingly shallow.

Boat launching: The small launch is best for small fishing boats. An occasional canoeist with fishing rod may also be seen paddling through the mud-colored water.

Insider tips: You won't catch big fish here. In fact, avid anglers will want to seek out another nearby lake. Nevertheless, area families can have fun shoreline fishing Deer Creek using simple tackle and techniques. Bring a picnic, flying disc and a well-stocked cooler to ward off slow fishing frustrations.

Deer Creek Lake

FAYETTE & PICKAWAY COUNTIES ■ 1,277 acres of fishing water ■ 19.4 miles of shoreline

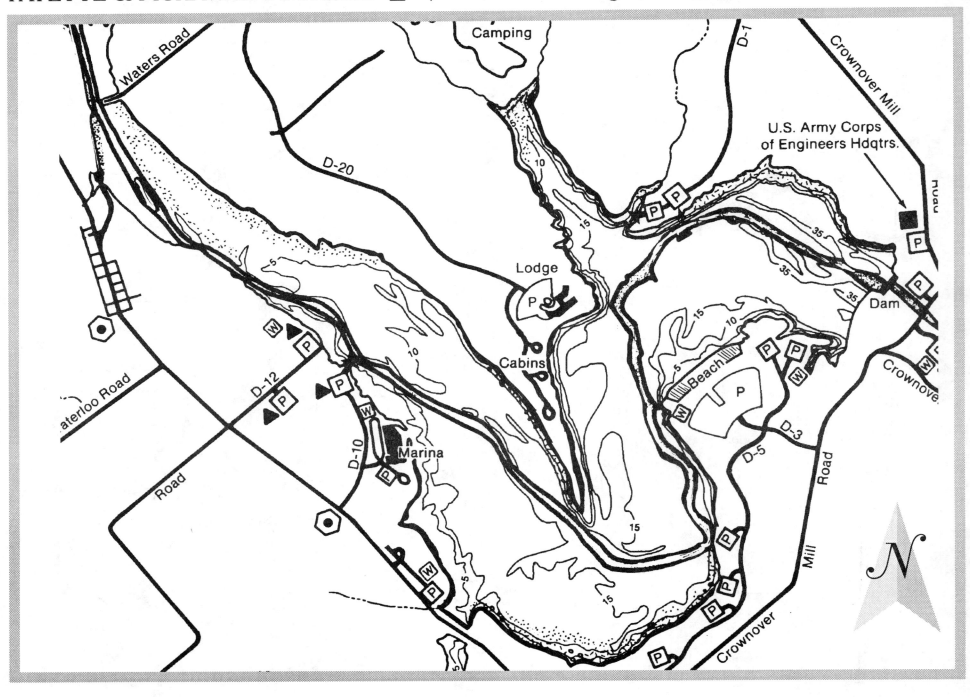

Location: In Fayette and Pickaway counties, four miles south of Mount Sterling on SR 207. The lake is 57 miles form Dayton and 35 miles from Columbus.

Wildlife district office: (614) 644-3925.

Fishing opportunities: Saugeye, channel catfish, largemouth bass, crappies and white bass.

Water conditions: Turbid, muddy, clears slowly.

Bottom composition: Mud.

Horsepower restrictions: None.

Stocking: Saugeye are heavily stocked.

Camping: 232 sites, 25 cabins at the Deer Creek State Park, call (614) 869-3508.

Boat rental at marina.

Average depth: 12-14 feet.

Bait and tackle shops in the area.

Outlook:
Channel catfish - excellent
Saugeye - excellent
Crappie - good

Largemouth bass - fair
White bass - excellent

The lake was finished in 1968 by the U.S. Army Corps of Engineers to help control floods. The terrain in the region is gently rolling to flat, with moist soils. The lake has shallow, gradual sloping shorelines. From the area of the marina to the dam, the old creek channel generally runs along the lake shoreline, providing deep-water habitat to bank fishermen. Shoreline access is excellent around the lake.

How to catch 'em: Saugeye are 10-26 inches and are stocked in Deer Creek Lake heavily and grow quickly. Small jigs, spinners, worms and minnows are all good baits to try. A former state record saugeye (9 pounds, 27 inches) came from the colored waters of the lake.

Largemouth bass are in fair to good population of 10-14 inches. Most of the bucketmouths are taken along the rocky shoreline and points, especially in the fall. Some of the best largemouth angling is during the annual flood control drawdown. White bass from 8-12 inches are in very good numbers and easy to catch in the spring and in Tick

Ridge in the summer.

Crappies average 7-9 inches. Fishing is good from spring well into summer with most caught on yellow and hot pink jigs with brightly colored plastic worms. Crappie fishing is best along the brushy shoreline in the creek channel above the lake. Look for channel catfish in the upper lake and in the stream channel. Bluegill fishing is very good along the deeper shoreline in the lower half of the lake, especially in June and July. No matter what the species, when using artificial bait, the brighter colors such as chartreuse and yellow generally work the best in the dark waters of Deer Creek Lake. Look for bluegills along the deeper shoreline in the lower half of the lake.

Hot spots: The No. 1 hot spot is at the tailwaters. Many quality fish are easily caught here, especially during the winter or early spring. Deer Creek, upstream from Yankeetown Rd. is productive for white bass in mid- to late spring, and for smallmouth and rock bass. In low water, old SR 207 below Pancoastburg is good for fishing smallmouth with crankbaits. Catfish are caught mainly in the upper reaches and the

stream channel as far upstream as Dawson Yankeetown Road. Try the two concrete access piers at the tailwaters for fast action on saugeye and other species.

Underwater structure: Little man-made structures have been placed in the lake in recent times. Due to water movement, there is little vegetation in the turbid lake.

Boat launching: Two improved ramps serve the lake. The most popular is at the Deer Creek marina off SR 207 and another is near the Harding Cabin, which is reached via Yankeetown Road and Township 197. A variety of boats can be rented from the marina by the hour, day or week.

Insider tips: The lake is drawn down each winter. In mid-September the Corps of Engineers drop the lake level by 15 feet. The state park has camping, 25 cabins, golf course, bridle trails, hiking, a large modern lodge, beach, hunting and naturalist's programs. December through March is the best tailwater fishing.

Delaware Reservoir

■ 1,300 acres of fishing water ■ 35 miles of shoreline DELAWARE, MARION & MORROW COUNTIES

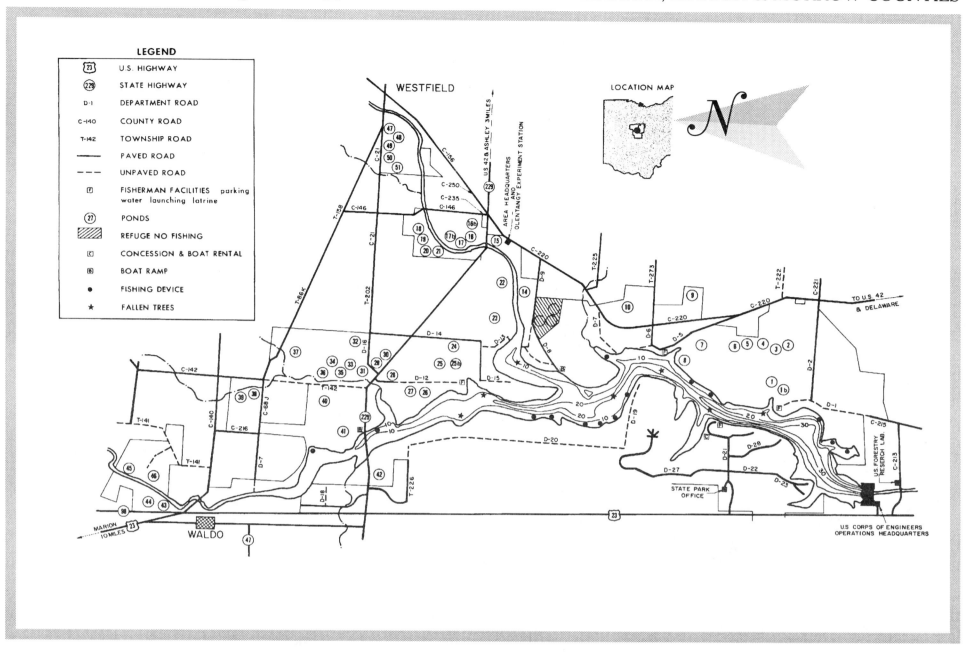

Location: About 20 miles north of downtown Columbus on U.S. 23, eight miles north of Delaware and east of U.S. 23 (Olentangy River).

Wildlife district office: (614) 644-3925.

Fishing opportunities: Largemouth bass, white bass, crappies (excellent), bluegills, saugeye, catfish, walleye and some muskie.

Bottom composition: Mud, some firm gravel points and old road beds.

Water conditions: Seasonal high water and muddy in spring, little underwater structure.

Camping: 214 sites (164 with electricity) in the Delaware State Park. Boat docking is available near camping sites. Call (614) 369-2761.

Stocking: Saugeye were introduced in 1989.

Bait and tackle: Something's Fishy near the dam and Norton Bait and Tackle near SR 229 and U.S. 23.

Delaware State Park: 1,815 acres, marina, campground, shoreline fishing, concession, docks.

Muskie were once stocked in the long reservoir that is surrounded by majestic hardwoods, lush croplands and old farms fields and the state park amenities along the west shore. Very few muskies are taken today, although some are reportedly caught below the dam and down through the low head system. Today, the lake sets on 350-million-year-old bedrock and is best known for its huge crappies (some have been taken more than 18 inches in length!). Most are black crappies, which are thicker and scrappier than whites. Check size regulations regarding crappies.

The dam was constructed by the U.S. Corps of Engineers in the late 1940s and filled to pool level in 1950. There are 55 ponds constructed by the Division of Wildlife for waterfowl and fishing purposes on the property. The ponds are occasionally stocked. The farm pond areas (on the east side of the lake) are terrific for spring fly rodding for panfish and bird watching.

How to catch 'em: Slab-sized crappies can be taken on minnows and bobbers in the brush in the spring or 1/32-ounce tube jigs set about two feet below your bobber. Throw your tiny jig and bobber out and jerk it a little bit, let it sit, then jerk it again. The crappies will take the jig between jerks.

Water levels can change rapidly on the lake, making bass angling difficult. Most anglers work the quiet bays and around stumps using top water plugs, spinners, nightcrawlers and other highly colored artificals.

White bass runs can be strong in the lake tributaries, the Olentangy River and Whetstone Creek. Use shinny spinners and rooster tails on white bass—move to find them, and the action can be fast.

Delaware is a very good to excellent catfish lake. Saugeye fishing is fair on the lake.

Boat launching: Inside the state park are two launching ramps; one just inside the gate and the other at the marina where boats are rented and bait is sold. A small launch on the east side of the lake abuts the Delaware Wildlife Area.

Ice fishing: Because it doesn't take much rain to move the lake, ice rarely gets stable.

Insider tips: Crappie fishing in early April is fantastic. Try a fly rod and tiny bug popper to raise the chunky black crappies. The small east launch is near some excellent brushy areas filled with crappies.

Delta Reservoirs 1 & 2

FULTON COUNTY ■ No. 1–30 acres, 11 miles of shoreline ■ No. 2–50 acres, 11 miles of shoreline

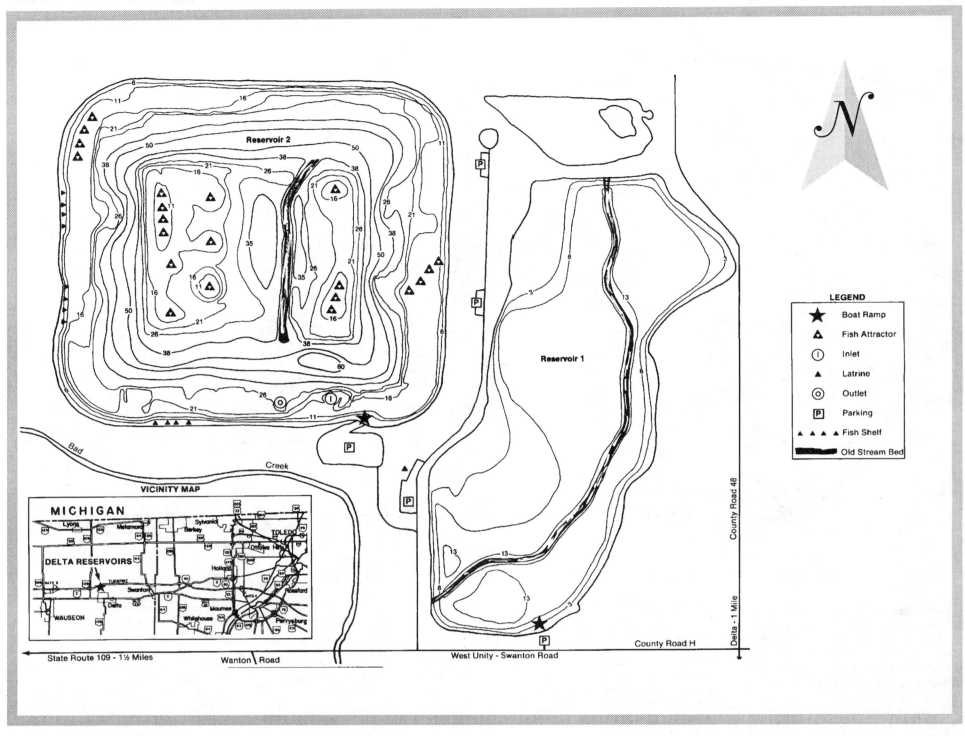

Location: Both reservoirs are one mile north of the village of Delta on County Road H, 1.5 miles east of State Road 109. They are 22 miles from Toledo, 65 miles from Findlay and 35 miles from Defiance.

Fishing opportunities: Large- and smallmouth bass, saugeye, bluegill, crappie, a few northern pike.

Water conditions: Both are quite clear.

Bottom composition: No. 1 has gravel and mud; No 2 is mud.

Boat rental: None.

Horsepower restrictions: Electric motors only.

Average depth: Reservoir No. 1 is 10-12-feet deep.

Stocking: Various species at No. 1 since 1940.

Camping: Harrison Lake State Park, about 8 miles away.

Reservoir No. 1 is an on-stream impoundment (or semi-upground reservoir) with a lot of shallow water. The bottom composition is varied and there is some cover along the shoreline. This reservoir was built in 1933 by the village of Delta as a municipal water supply. Depth ranges from 3 to 12 feet. The warm, shallow water provides good shoreline fishing and aquatic plant growth. Some areas of the shoreline are rip rap.

Reservoir No. 2 was built in 1984 and is an upground reservoir with a depth of 8 to 60 feet. Typically, upground reservoirs have cooler water temperatures, which extends the season. There is a lot of varied depth in the center of the square-shaped reservoir. The fish population in this reservoir is saugeye, smallmouth bass, yellow perch and channel catfish. Fish are not huge in the reservoir, but the catching is steady. The average saugeye is about 14 inches; smallmouth are usually two pounds or less. This reservoir was stocked in 1984 with largemouth bass, rock bass, crappies, walleye and saugeye.

How to catch 'em: Bring the kids.

Shoreline fishing can be very good to excellent in the spring. Bluegill, although small, can be taken easily on redworms, small jibs, and hook and bobber. Catfish angling is productive. Many anglers night fish using stink baits and bobbers.

Bass anglers will need crankbait in the cover in Reservoir No. 1 during the spring. In the much deeper No 2 pool, many local saugeye and small-mouth anglers use live bait and lead-headed jigs with tails while drifting. Good numbers of large-mouth are found along the shoreline in No. 2. Try evening fishing for bass.

Try for saugeye along the shoreline in the spring using spinners and worm rigs.

Hot spots: The northwest corner of Reservoir No. 2 is excellent, although over populated by anglers from spring to ice-up. Bank fishing around the entire shoreline is very good on Reservoir No. 1.

Underwater structure: Delta Reservoir No. 2 has numerous locations where Christmas trees have been bundled and sunk to provide cover. The clear water and sparse natural cover concentrate fish in the manmade cover. Both bodies of water offer significant shoreline fishing. No. 2 also has a tire-pile reef and fish spawning shelves on the west and south dikes.

Boat launching: An old, narrow gravel ramp serves the shallow Reservoir No. 1. It's an adequate launch for canoes, cartop boats and rowboats. A double lane, concrete launching ramp with parking serves Reservoir No. 2.

Ice fishing: Generally, it's only fair. Some ice fishermen do well jigging a minnow in the deepest parts of No. 2.

Insider tips: These are lightly fished reservoirs, offering very good spring and early summer angling. Bring the kids for fast shoreline fishing action in the early summer. Some local anglers report taking lots of small panfish on tiny jigs tipped with waxworms. A rare northern pike is taken from Reservoir No. 1.

Dillon Lake

■ 1,325 acres of fishing water MUSKINGUM COUNTY

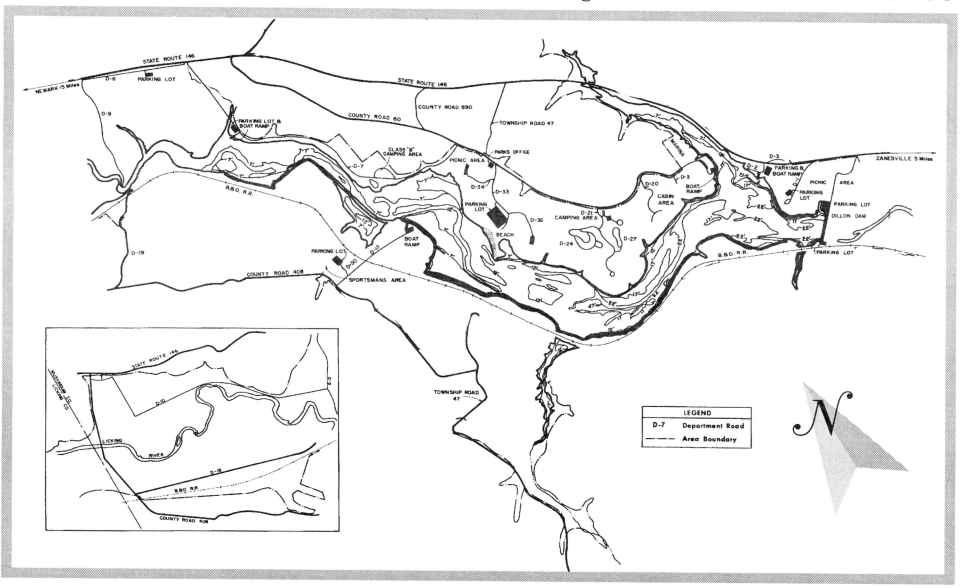

Location: In Muskingum County. The area lies six miles northwest of Zanesville, off SR 146; it may be reached by driving southeast from Newark on SR 16 to SR 146.

Wildlife district office: (614) 453-4377.

Fishing opportunities: Muskie, crappie, bluegill, largemouth bass, saugeye, northern pike, walleye, striped bass and chan-

Water conditions: Rain determines color, which constantly changes.

Bottom composition: Good spawning beds; silt.

Average depth: 13 feet, reaching 33 feet deep at the dam face.

Horsepower restrictions: Unlimited.

Camping: 192 sites in Dillon State Park. Call (614) 453-0442.

Stocking: Largemouth, saugeye and some tiger muskie.

Shoreline access is limited; high banks.

Boat rental: At state park marina.

Drainage area: 748 sq. miles.

Outlook:
Bluegill - good
Largemouth bass - excellent
Channel catfish - excellent
Saugeye - excellent
Crappie - good

Dillon sits on the edge of the

Appalachian Plateau in an area on the verge of deciding whether it wants to be hilly or flat. It's neither, yet it's both. The hills are well-rounded and the valleys broad and gentle. This is a pleasant and productive fishing lake that is surrounded by 300-million-year-old black hand sandstone. The lake is close to many interesting things. Bring the entire family for a long weekend. The lake is a flood control reservoir and was completed in 1966. The lake is 730 feet above seas level. The main leg is about 2.5 miles long.

Dillon was a top muskie lake until the early 1970s when the lake level was rapidly lowered to work on the state park marina. Many walleye and muskie departed out the spillways. Muskie are making a minor comeback according to staff, but they aren't being fished much.

How to catch 'em: Dillon is a very good fishing lake all summer, except, of course, when a prolonged heat spell depletes the oxygen and the fish become sluggish. Fish are often seen barely moving along the surface. Black-colored bottom jig and pigs and plastic worms are suggested by local experts for bass. All-color plastic plugs and spinner baits can also be effective the lake. Determining the mood of the bass will help you choose a color. On any day of the week, you can go out and catch what's locally called "Dillon bass," which, of course, are just barely under legal size. There

are a ton of these scrappy 10-11 inch bass. Staff says that many tournament anglers concentrate their efforts in the Big Run and Poverty Run embayments using rubber worms and medium-running lures cast at the shoreline.

In general, anglers should concentrate on the dam, shorelines with structure and the area known as Dillon Falls (a large rapid run over limestone), about one mile from the dam where northern pike and walleye can be taken. Try bucktails for pike.

A good sonar unit is probably the most important piece of equipment on Dillon Lake. Once you find the narrow channel and multiple pockets, you'll catch fish. Many successful pan fishermen concentrate on the brushy shoreline using live bait in the spring and early summer. Some anglers also drift near the shoreline or cast at eddies in an effort to locate fish. Others fish trailwaters for year-round action.

Boat launching: Four ramps serve the busy lake. Two improved launches are near the dam, one at the marina at the end of Dillon Hills Drive and the other, Big Run boat ramp, off SR 146. The Nashport ramp on Road 7 on the shallow no-wake section of the upper lake and the Pleasant Know Launch are both more suitable as small boat drop-soffs. The marina, on the small leg of the lake, rents pontoons, canoes, pedalboats and runabouts.

Underwater structure: Natural dead falls and a few old sunken Christmas trees make up most of the structure. There are a few areas where some old stumps are still left, but after 30 years, much of the natural structure is gone. The channel is easily defined by your depth finder and continues to be one of the most productive strips in the narrow reservoir.

Shoreline: Although bank fishing is sometimes difficult from the varied shoreline, it does make for fun hiking and trying. Some of the shoreline is gentle and sandy; other sections are mud embankments, rocks or tree-lined.

Hot spots: Fish the shoreline from a boat; drift the channel. The best fishing for all species is when the river is on the rise.

Insider tips: The lake has from 15-20 bass tournaments each summer. The high banks make for poor sailing, but do keep some of the wind off anglers making delicate boat handling possible. Thirteen-inch black crappies are common. The Dillon State Park has a sandy beach, seven miles of hiking trails, 29 cabins and a marina with 70 seasonal docks. Most of the areas north of the beach are only three to four feet in depth. You may bow fish for carp in the backwaters and marsh areas in the vicinity of the Irville boat ramp.

Dow Lake

ATHENS COUNTY ■ 153 acres of fishing water ■ 7 miles of shoreline

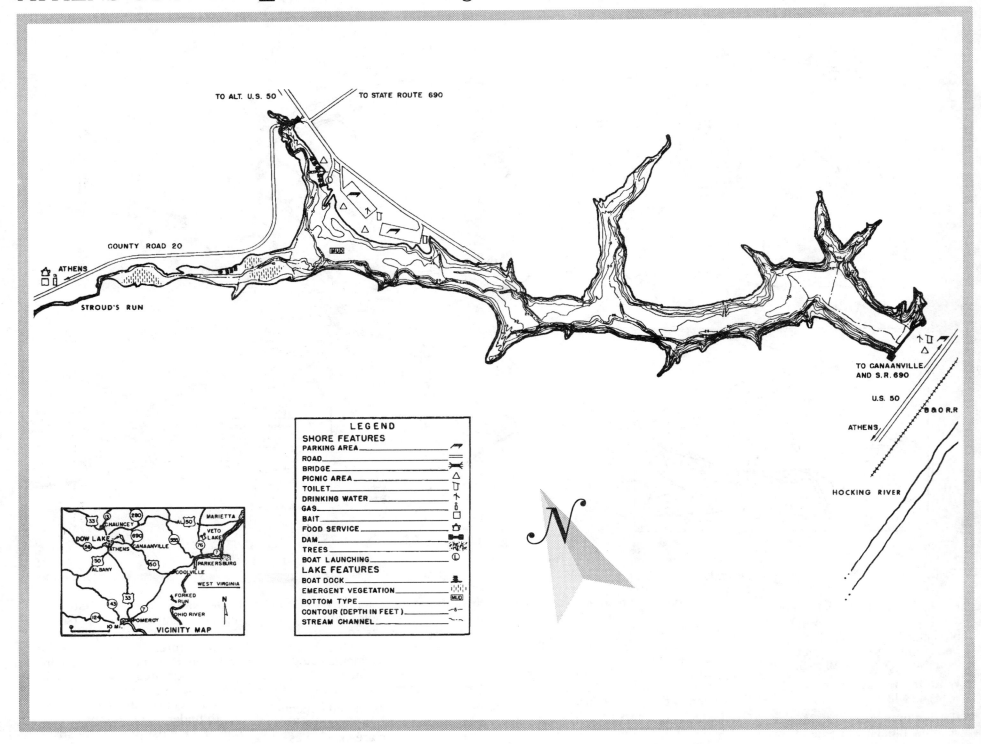

Location: In Athens County, Canaan Township, northeast of Athens on CR 20, south of U.S. 50.

Wildlife district office: (614) 594-2211.

Fishing opportunities: Bluegill, redear sunfish, largemouth bass, golden trout and channel catfish.

Water conditions: Medium clarity.

Bottom composition: Mud, some shoal outcroppings.

Horsepower restriction: 10 hp.

Stocking: Trout, channel catfish.

Special regulations: Check the slot length limit.

Depth: Dropoffs to 25 feet.

Outlook:
Bluegill, redear - fair
Largemouth bass - excellent
Channel catfish - excellent
Golden trout - excellent

Dow Lake has responded wonderfully to the Division of Wildlife's management strategy to improve the bass fishery. It is not uncommon for bass anglers to catch a dozen fish in the protected slot size range or larger in a typical day. The lake is formed by the damming of Stroud's Run Creek. Don't tell too many people about this interesting lake.

How to catch 'em: The quick dropoffs acts as feeding shelves for largemouth. Finding the dropoffs and bouncing and cranking across and over them is a productive method suggested by several local anglers. Try crayfish colors and brights. The lake is fairly protected and boat handling is usually easy, so drifting over the ledges and dropoffs is simple. Fishing the vegetation in the spring for bass can be a blast. Topwater lures and plastic worms can be productive. Jerking topwater lures over standing and floating vegetation might produce some thundering and exciting hits. Local anglers say you must remain extra quiet when topwater fishing the shallows and vegetation in the spring. Try jerking a plastic frog over the plants to make the bass really mad. Don't forget to work baits in and around the pockets and edges of weedbeds.

Thick aquatic vegetation makes for difficult fishing in the upper reaches and bays, and along the shoreline during mid- to late summer. Bluegill and redear sunfish are of average quality and are most often found in the deeper sections of the lake. Some brushy areas hold good numbers of bluegills. Look for fallen shoreline trees. Catfish are found in multiple-year classes with many fish up to 24 inches and seven pounds. "Whisker" anglers will find excellent conditions, access and fishing for the big cats.

Hot spots: After the trout have been released, concentrate your efforts at the dam. Find the humps and quick dropoffs and fish over them. Shoreline access is excellent; some bank anglers stay near the boat launch.

Underwater structure: The lake is fairly deep and there are some productive quick dropoffs. About 200 Christmas trees have been placed in the lake. One bundle of submerged trees is off the boat ramp and other locations are along the north shore of the middle northern bay and along a bend near the dam.

Boat launching: The ramp is on a bay at the north end of the lake. Adequate parking, drinking water and picnic areas are nearby.

Ice fishing: It's fair. Not much ice fishing is done on the lake.

Insider tips: The April trout festival follows a 3,000-5,000 fish stocking each year. There is parking at the dam. Bring your own bait.

26

East Branch

■ 420 acres of fishing water ■ 7.5 miles of shoreline GEAUGA COUNTY

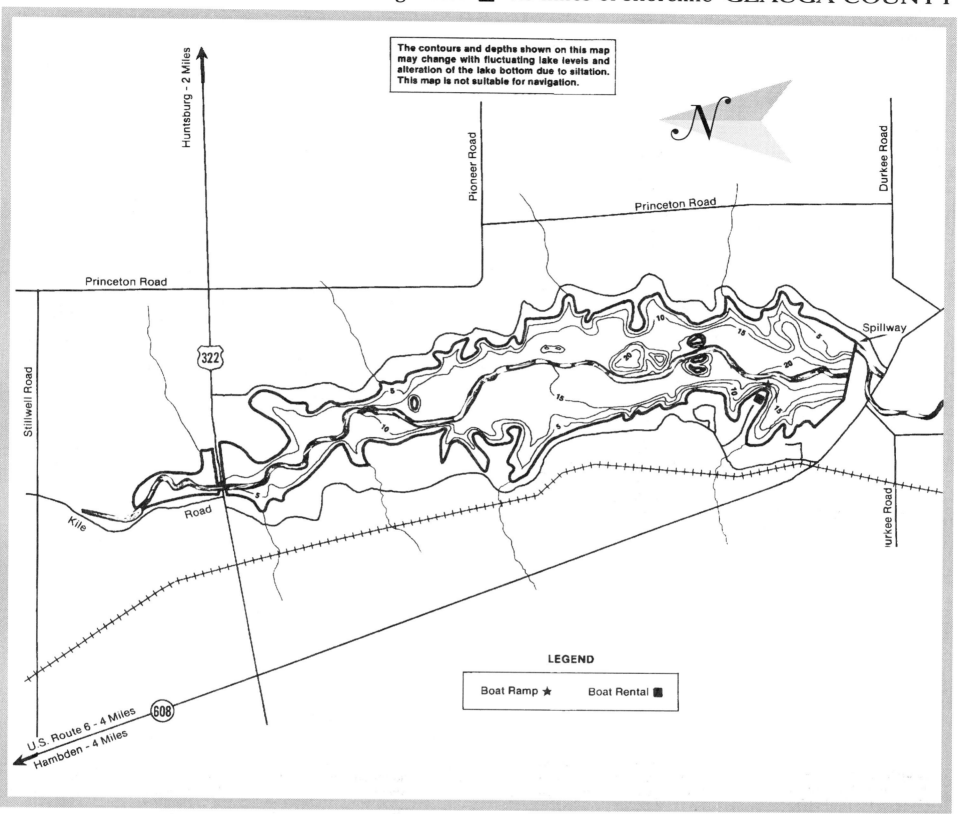

The contours and depths shown on this map may change with fluctuating lake levels and alteration of the lake bottom due to siltation. This map is not suitable for navigation.

LEGEND

Boat Ramp ★   Boat Rental ■

Location: In eastern Geauga County, 40 miles east of Cleveland, near the intersection of SR 608 and U.S. Route 322, which cross the reservoir. 55 miles from Akron and 65 miles from Canton.

Wildlife district office: (216) 678-0077.

Fishing opportunities: Largemouth, bluegill, crappie, catfish and northern pike.

Permit needed (small fee).

Water conditions: Medium clear.

Horsepower restrictions: Electric motors only.

Bottom composition: Firm, earthen.

The quiet reservoir is used to tem-

porarily store water then released on an as-needed basis through the Cuyahoga River to the final impoundment at Lake Rockwell. The reservoir supplies water to the city of Akron and 300,000 customers daily and surrounding areas, a total of 350,000 during the summer. The system pumps 46 million gallons per day. The reservoir was constructed in 1939 and is recreationally managed by the Geauga County Metro Parks District. The parks district is undertaking a variety of shoreline and public access improvements.

The surrounding lake has many small glacial kames and relict, including a glacial lake and pond. Also in the area are plenty of habitat-rich marshes, meadows and mixed woodlands.

How to catch 'em: A few intrepid fly fishermen cast streamers at northern pike in the early spring;

some anglers choose to toss spoons along the brushy edges, shallows and tributary streams. Local experts recommend using large gold shiners and still fish for the best results on pike during the pre-spawn/spawn (until the first of May) period. By mid-summer, pike fishing shuts off.

Look for largemouth bass along the shoreline cover in the spring. During summer, the bucketmouths move to deep water and often suspend near humps, dropoffs and the old creek bed. Look for bluegills near any weedbeds in the central section of the lake.

Hot spots: For pike, target the very up-stream (north) end in the early spring. The rest of the year, key on largemouth bass, which are under-fished.

Underwater structure: North of the three small islands near the boat

launch is a winding creek channel and a 20-foot-deep hole that you can hole fish during the summer. There are several humps in the reservoir. Most anglers rely on shoreline structures. Aquatic vegetation consists mostly of milfoil and pondweed.

Boat launching: A single launch serves the underused lake. The best access to fishing is with a boat.

Ice fishing: It's on the increase as the lake becomes more recreationally managed.

Insider tips: Look for improvement around the lake by the metro parks district. East Branch is one of the few lakes in the region that has natural reproduction of northern pike. Look for shoreline access to improve.

27

East Fork Lake

CLERMONT COUNTY ■ 2,160 acres of fishing water ■ 35.8 miles of shoreline

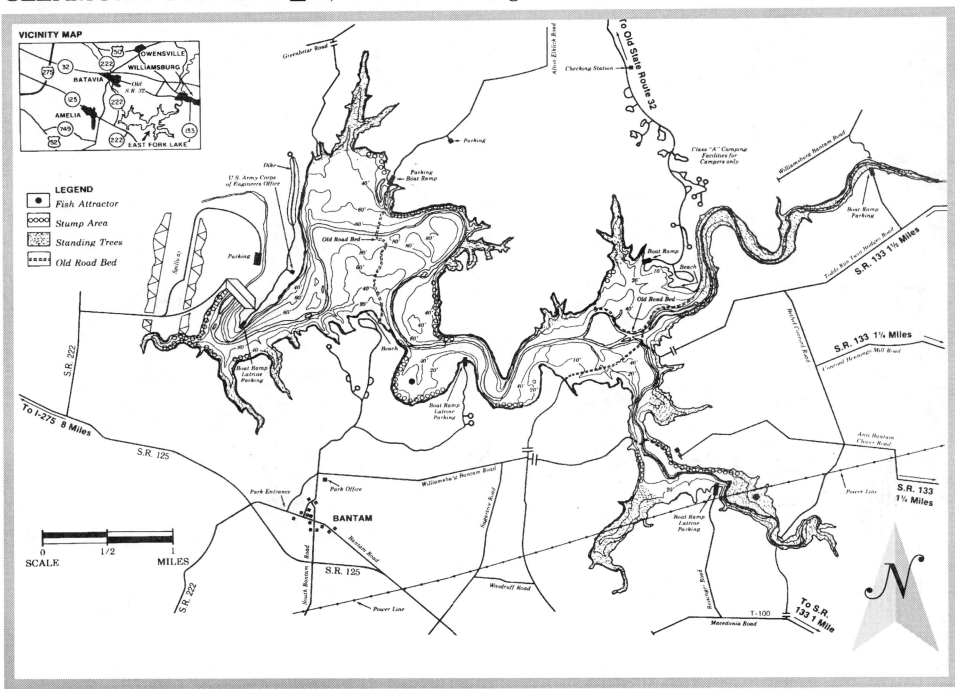

Location: In Clermont County off SR 222, two miles south of Batavia and 25 miles west of Cincinnati.

Wildlife district office: (513) 372-9261.

Fishing opportunities: Large- and smallmouth bass, black bass, sunfish, crappie, bluegill, channel and flathead catfish, and hybrid striped bass.

Water conditions: Colored.

Bottom composition: Varied from muck to gravel and sand.

Horsepower restrictions: Unlimited.

Stocking: Hybrid striped bass.

Special regulations: Check current bass rules.

Depth: Up to 80 feet; 100 feet at the dam.

Camping: 416 sites in the state park. Call (513) 724-6521.

Outlook:
Channel catfish - excellent
Crappie - excellent
Largemouth, Kentucky spotted bass - very good
Hybrid striped bass - excellent

The scrappy hybrid striped bass planted in East Fork come from taking the eggs of a striper and fertilizing them with a white bass. This cross produces a tough fish that does well in these conditions. The lake was raised to a full pool in 1979 and has some steep shorelines. The upper reaches of Cloverlick and Poplar creeks, along the main stem, were left uncleared to provide fish habitat. Intense fish habitat work before impoundment has made the reservoir an excellent fishery. There are stumpy zones, standing timbers, old road beds and a few tire structures that do an excellent job of holding fish.

How to catch 'em: Striped bass are best taken on three- to five-inch live gizzard shad. Earlybird anglers usually get their gizzard shad by cast netting for them (check rules). Some guides on the lake keep gizzard shad by using custom round aerated tanks. The biggest striped bass reported are in the 12-pound range. Hybrid striped bass are best taken in the early morning and evening until sunset. You'll need a

boat to catch them. Softcraws are also used in 10-20 feet of water. Some local experts say to cast jigs and surface plugs when you see shad at the surface. Lake guides use live gizzard shad for consistent fishing success.

Hot spots: For hybrid striped bass try the west side of the island off the boat ramp at the end of Afton-Elklick Road and over the old road beds with flats nearby. Striped bass are also taken in good numbers at the mouth of the two coves west of the state park beach at the west end of the lake. About the only place to shoreline fish for hybrid stripers is west of the beach on the south side of the lake at the end of South Bantam Road.

Largemouth bass run 10-14 inches, with some up to 21 inches. A fair number of spotted bass are in the two-pound class. Crappies average 8.5 inches and are always in the brushy main lake shoreline areas. April and May are the best months to take big crappies. Try drifting over old road beds with minnows.

Underwater structure: Most of the bay on the lake has standing timber. Learn where the old road beds and

creek channel are located. Significant stretches of the shoreline are stumpy with some fallen trees, vegetation and brushy areas near the banks. Watch other anglers, or use your fishfinder to determine dropoffs and points.

Boat launching: Five good-quality ramps surround the lake, with the biggest east of the state park office. The launches are well marked.

Ice fishing: Once you get south of I-70, it's only during the most severe winters when safe ice is formed.

Insider tips: More than one million striped bass are planted annually from the upper ramp south of the campground ramp at the end of SR 32. Biologists are working to increase the striped bass fishery. The lake gets heavy recreational boating traffic. Local bait shops have information about guides who work on the lake. The huge state park has 57 miles of bridle trails, Rent-A-Camps, 55 miles of hiking trails, a 1,200-foot beach and nature programs.

Ferguson Lake

■ 305 acres of fishing water ALLEN COUNTY

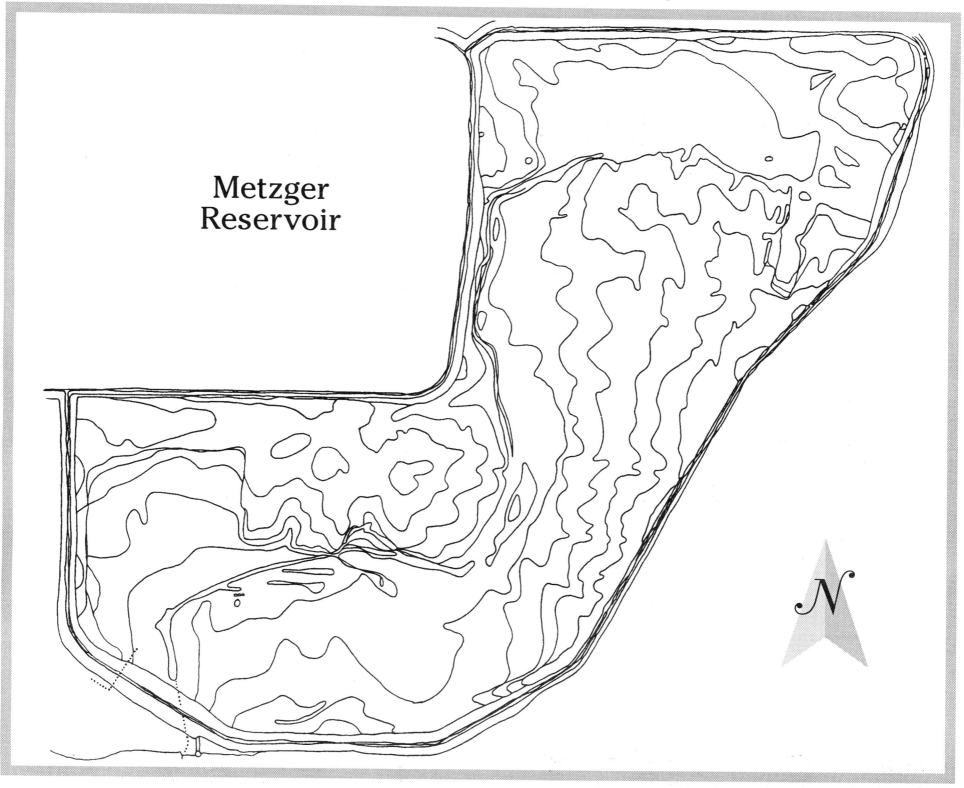

Metzger
Reservoir

N

Location: Near Lima. South of SR 81 on East High Road.

Wildlife district office: (419) 424-5000

Fishing opportunities: Walleye, yellow perch, channel catfish, white bass, smallmouth bass and bluegill.

Water conditions: Green and cool.

Bottom composition: Clay, firm, some silt.

Horsepower restrictions: Electric motors and cartops boats.

Stocked: Walleye and channel catfish.

Average depth: 25 feet.

Outlook:
Walleye - good
Yellow perch - good
Channel catfish - good
White bass - good
Smallmouth bass - good
Bluegill - fair to good

The upground reservoir for the city of Lima originally was stocked with walleye, yellow perch, bluegill, yellow perch and channel catfish. The lake is a very good walleye and perch fishery. Ferguson backs up against Metzger Lake and an urban area.

How to catch 'em: Good populations of 15-29 inch walleye can be taken by drifting or balloon fishing using weight-forward spinners tipped with nightcrawlers. Yellow perch in the seven-to 12-inch size are common and taken from any brushy area and off dropoffs. Channel catfish average in the 14-28 inch size, with many 20-pounders caught annually drift fishing or with a balloon and gobs of crawlers or cutbaits. Fish for big cats on the bottom in any part of the lake during the summer and fall.

The white bass run can be fast and furious. The old reservoir has a sizable population of 8-15 inch white bass that run in surface-popping schools offshore in May and June. Casting jigs and spoons or ice fishing, will take the silver-colored fish. Smallmouth bass often keep to the shoreline and rocks. The lake has a good population of 14-19 inch smallies, with some up to four pounds. The bass can be spooky, but careful casting of small spinners or jigs and tails worked gently can bring in a creel full.

Bluegills caught from the shore are great fun. From cane pole and a can of worms to ultralight tackle and fuzzy grubs, the lake has a fair population of eight-inch fish.

Hot spots: The central part of the lake has some significant depth changes and patterns that would hold fish. Some structure is in the lake.

Boat launching: Cartop boats and canoes with electric motors only are used on the reservoir.

Underwater structure: A few Christmas trees have been placed, mainly to encourage yellow perch to start spawning.

Ice fishing: Consider the cool-water reservoir a good ice fishing destination for walleye and perch. Walleye anglers jig ice fishing spoons on the bottom and tip with a minnow. Some angler say they like wide fluttering-type jigging spoons with lots of action. Others use small jigs and minnows and stinger hooks

Insider tip: There is no good state-produced fishing map for the reservoir. The state plans on having an accurate topo map out in the next couple of years. Keep in touch with the wildlife district office for an improved map.

OHIO

Findlay Reservoirs 1 & 2

HANCOCK COUNTY ■ No. 1 - 187, No. 2 - 640 acres of fishing water ■ 7.5 miles of shoreline

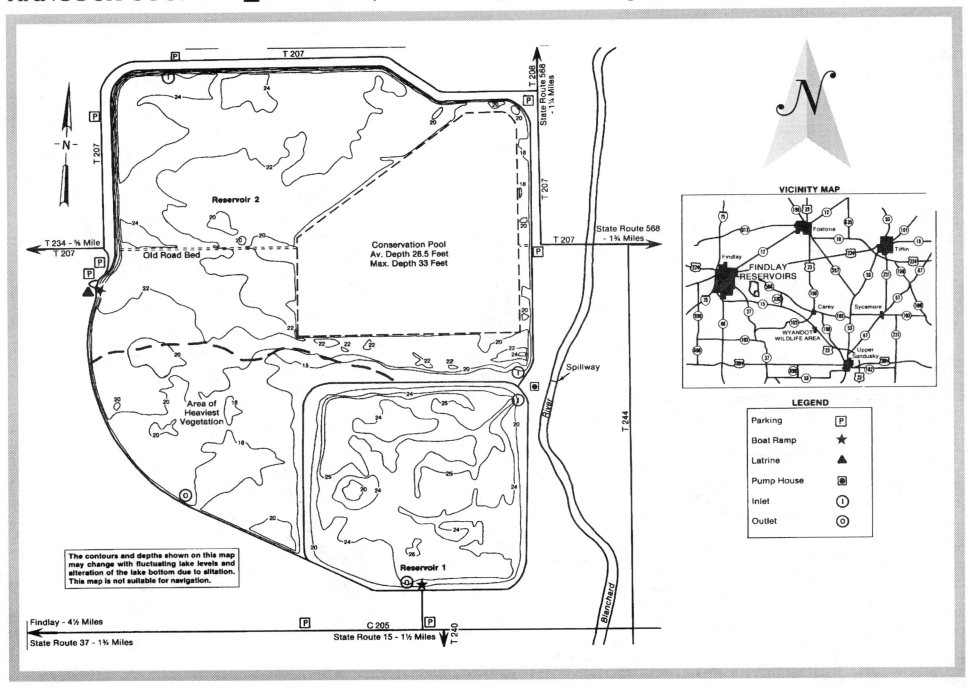

Location: Southeast of Findlay. They can be reached by traveling 2.5 miles southeast from Findlay on State Road 37 to Hancock County Road 205, proceeding east one mile to CR 234, north to Township Road 207, then east to the boat ramp on Reservoir No. 2. Reservoir No. 1 can be reached by continuing on CR 205 one mile east past County Road 234.

Wildlife District office: (419) 424-6000.

Fishing opportunities: Large- and smallmouth bass, bluegill, yellow perch, white and rock bass, walleye, crappies, carp and channel catfish. Both reservoirs have the same species.

Water conditions: Visibility three to four feet, fairly clear.

Bottom composition: Earthen, one old road bed, little aquatic vegetation cover.

Depth: Up to 24 feet in both.

Horsepower restrictions: No. 1, you may use electric motors only; No 2 allows up to 10 hp motors.

Outlook - Reservoir No. 1:

Walleye - good
Yellow perch - fair
Channel catfish - good
White bass - good
Smallmouth bass - good
Bluegill - fair

Outlook - Reservoir No 2:
Walleye - good, 18 - 20 inches, up to 10 pounds
Yellow perch - good
Large- and smallmouth bass - good
Bluegill - fair
Channel catfish - very good
White bass - good
Bullhead - good

The two side-by-side reservoirs share a common one-mile-long dike. The most popular fishing reservoir is the newer No. 2, which was built in 1968 as an upground water storage reservoir for the city of Findlay. The entire shoreline is open to bank fishing, but you'll be climbing around rip rap in most places. Reservoir No. 2 has a capacity of 5 billion gallons and is the largest upground reservoir in Ohio.

How to catch 'em: Ten-pound walleye are often taken on lead-head jigs, weigh-forward spinners (Lake Erie spinners) and live minnows. The best walleye angling is spring/summer and then again just before winter freeze-up. Drift for walleye in the summer using jigs with plastic tails or nightcrawler rigs. Some local anglers say they use a bouncing worm rig, worked slowly along places where the depth changes. Small-, largemouth and rock bass are taken along the shorelines. Bluegills are common at inlets and around any wood or plants.

Bluegill anglers are advised to try Reservoir No. 2 and fish around the in- and outlets. Tiny poppers and flies can be fly cast, or use live bait. Try a slip bobber over a minnow, varying depth frequently. Quite a few 20-pound catfish are taken annually, according to the wildlife district biologist. Reservoir No. 2 produces good catches in the early summer on cut bait. Try the balloon method, suspending a nightcrawler rig under it, in Reservoir No. 1.

White bass school in good numbers and are easily taken at the surface in open water or near the shore in the summer. Early-season white bass are firm and tasty; the flesh gets mushy later in the season, but they are fun to catch anytime. Try casting small colorful spoons and spinners with willow blades.

Underwater structure: Because of changes in water quality, significant weed beds are no longer present in the reservoirs. However, the state has installed a considerable number of Christmas trees over the last few years. Most of the trees have been sunk along the edges of both reservoirs in about eight feet of water.

Boat launching: A crude, steep ramp is on the south side of Reservoir No. 1, and a two-lane, concrete launching ramp is on the west side of the No. 2 reservoir.

Ice fishing: Pan fishermen do well during the winter. Ice fishing is restricted to periods when the city of Findlay says the ice is safe. Some walleye are taken off the bottom. Use a jigging spoon tipped with a minnow. Some anglers also attach a stinger hook and sometimes use a Fire Eye jig and minnow on the bottom.

Insider tips: Bring your fly rod in the spring and early summer for fast action on panfish and shoreline-hugging bass. Cricket-type flies are reported to bring up some big 'gills. The reservoirs are good place to bring children.

Findley Lake

■ 93 acres of fishing water ■ Four miles of shoreline LORAIN COUNTY

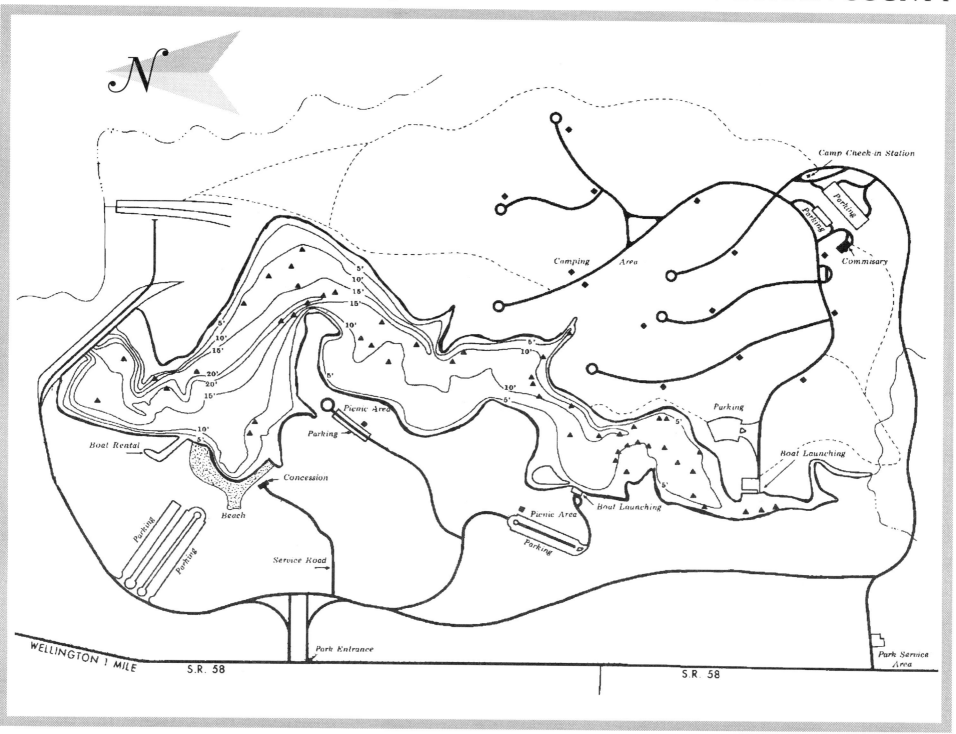

Location: In Findley State Park, Lorain County, 1.4 miles south of Wellington on SR 58.

Wildlife district office: (216) 644-2293.

Fishing opportunities: Largemouth bass, bluegill, crappie, bullhead, channel catfish and northern pike.

Fishing information: State park, (216) 647-4490.

Water conditions: Fair amount of runoff. Cloudy after rains.

Bottom composition: Many stumps, mud.

Horsepower restrictions: Electric motors only.

Boat rental: State park operated.

Camping: 275 sites in the state park; call (216) 647-4490.

Deepest areas: 25 feet, mostly shallow lake.

Stocking: Mostly self-reproducing, catfish are sometime stocked.

Bait: At the boat rental, a tackle shop one mile south of the park, and at the campground.

Outlook:
Bluegill - excellent
Largemouth bass - good
Crappies - very good
Catfish - good

The area was purchased in 1936-37 by Guy Findley, a Lorain County judge, who donated the lands to the state to be maintained as a state forest after the Civilian Conservation Corps planted a variety of pines and hardwoods in the tract. Findley Forest was transferred to the parks division in 1950 and six years later an earthen dam was completed across Wellington Creek, creating the 93-acre lake. The manmade lake has a good bluegill and largemouth bass population.

Intimate Findley Lake is an excellent place to introduce young anglers to bass fishing. There are lots of easy-to-catch small bass evenly scattered around the placid lake.

How to catch 'em: A slot limit (between 12-15 inches) on the lake

has helped the population of largemouth bass. Today, many four- to six-pounders are taken. There may be more shoreline fishing than from a boat on the lake. There are lots of gentle access points around the lake. Children will be able to take spring largemouth bass using minnows, worms or combination worm and spinner/artificial lures. Small hooks and a can of lively worms are all your family will need to shoreline fish for bluegills and crappies. Have the kids be as patient as possible and work around any stumps, sunken brush or logs you can find.

A few small northern pike are taken in the spring using spinners.

Boat launching: The main boat ramp is south of the peninsula, near the beach, and has a boat rental concession. It has a cement surface, parking and is near a picnic area. The other smaller ramp is for campers use.

Underwater structure: Pallets are sunken periodically on each side of the peninsula on the western half of the lake. There are a number of

clay tiles in the lake, most of which are near the dam. The south end of the lake is shallow and filling in with vegetation.

Ice fishing: Most anglers come out for bluegill and crappie using small jigs and minnows. Like open water angling, ice fishermen need to look for depth changes and structure. The west end of the lake is sometimes an excellent area, especially early and late in the winter.

Insider tips: The state park has excellent camping, 10 miles of hiking trails, three main picnic areas, a 400 foot sand beach, two public boat launches and day-use areas. At the north end of the state park is the Duke's Skipper Butterfly Sanctuary, a small preserve for the extremely rare insect. Butterfly collecting is prohibited. Bring the entire family to this quiet lake and state park.

Forked Run Lake

MEIGS COUNTY ■ 107 acres of fishing water ■ 107 miles of shoreline

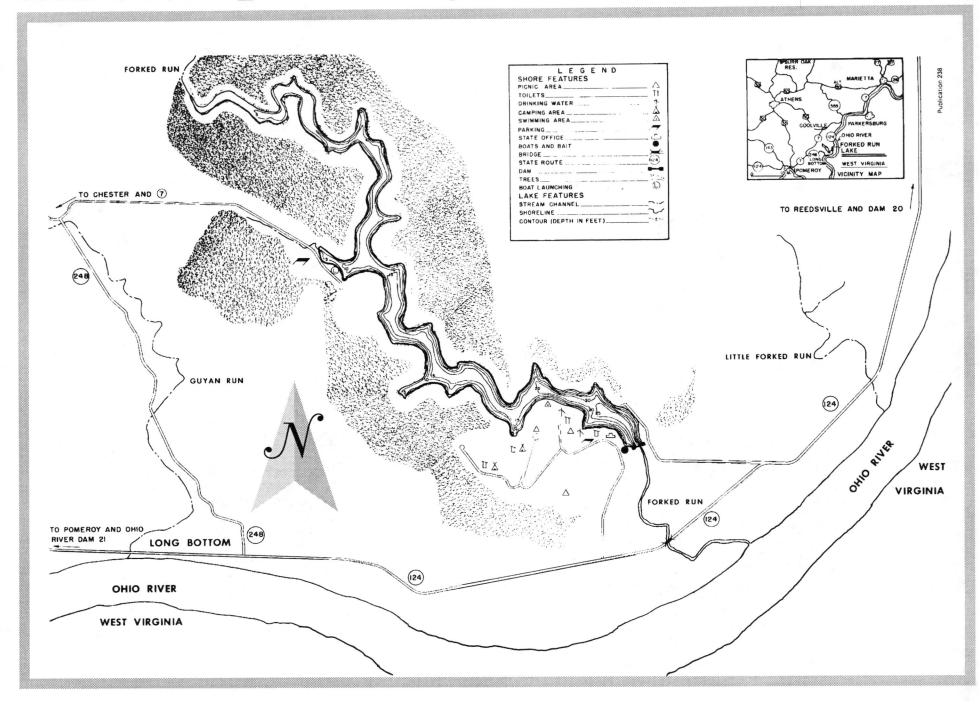

Location: In Meigs County, next to Ohio River and West Virginia border, north of SR 125, off SR 248. It's as far wousheast as you can travel in Ohio.

Wildlife district office: (614) 594-2211.

Fishing opportunities: Bluegill, channel catfish, golden trout saugeye, largemouth and spotted bass.

Water conditions: Clear.

Bottom composition: Mud.

Horsepower restriction: Electric motor.

Stocking: Trout and saugeye.

Deep at the dam.

Camping: 198 sites at the Forked Run State Park; call (614) 378-6206.

Outlook:
Bluegill - fair
Largemouth, spotted bass - good
Channel catfish - good
Golden trout - good
Saugeye - fair to good

Catchable yearling golden trout are stocked in late March annually at Forked Run Lake. The trout are typically 12-14 inches in length and weigh about one-half pound. The fishing pressure for the first few weeks after the stocking is heavy, but as the fish distribute, trout anglers have to hunt them our the remainder of the season. Saugeye are also stocked annually, after the initial stocking in 1990. Twenty-plus inch fish are reportedly taken.

How to catch 'em: Early season trout fishing is low tech. Anglers often adorn their hook with Velvetta cheese, marshmallow, Powerbait, larval baits like wax- and meal-worms. The trout will also hit small spinners. Local anglers challenge the saugeye with twistertails tipped with minnows. about 65 percent of the largemouth bass in Forked Run Lake are 12 inches long, yet quite a few five-pound individuals are taken annually. Bluegills are undersized (about 5 inches) but abundant while saugeye are in the 20-inch range and improving. Catfish are abundant and planted every other year. Some lunker catfish are caught on bank lines and jigs. Crappies are big in the spring, and kids will love catching the profuse bluegill along the shorelines in the state park.

Hot spots: The winding lake doesn't have the narrow, intimate bays that many impoundments have, making fishing good in most locations. Most of the bank fishing is concentrated near the dam. The upper end of the lake can be turbid, but generally the water conditions are constant.

Underwater structure: About 250 Christmas trees used to concentrate fish have been placed in the lake since the late 1980s. There are many fallen trees along the shoreline.

Boat launching: Two launches are on the lake. One is a paved ramp at the dam with a concession area (boat rental), and a small gravel ramp is on T-272 that serves the upper lake. The state park also manages a two-lane concrete launch on the nearby Ohio River. This is the only access to the Ohio River for miles.

Ice fishing: Some anglers venture out on the ice when conditions warrant, but the lake is not known for ice fishing.

Insider tips: Early in the spring there is a good to very good tailwater fishery for saugeye. The large pool below the dam fills at this time where fish tend to hold. Saugeye also stage in here from the Forked Run tributary. The state park has two hiking trails, camping, Ohio River access, a 500-foot swimming beach, two picnic shelters and an occasional bear (last seen in 1990). Locals pronounce the lake "For-ked Run." George Washington once called this area the "long bottom."

Fox Lake

■ 48 acres of fishing water ATHENS COUNTY

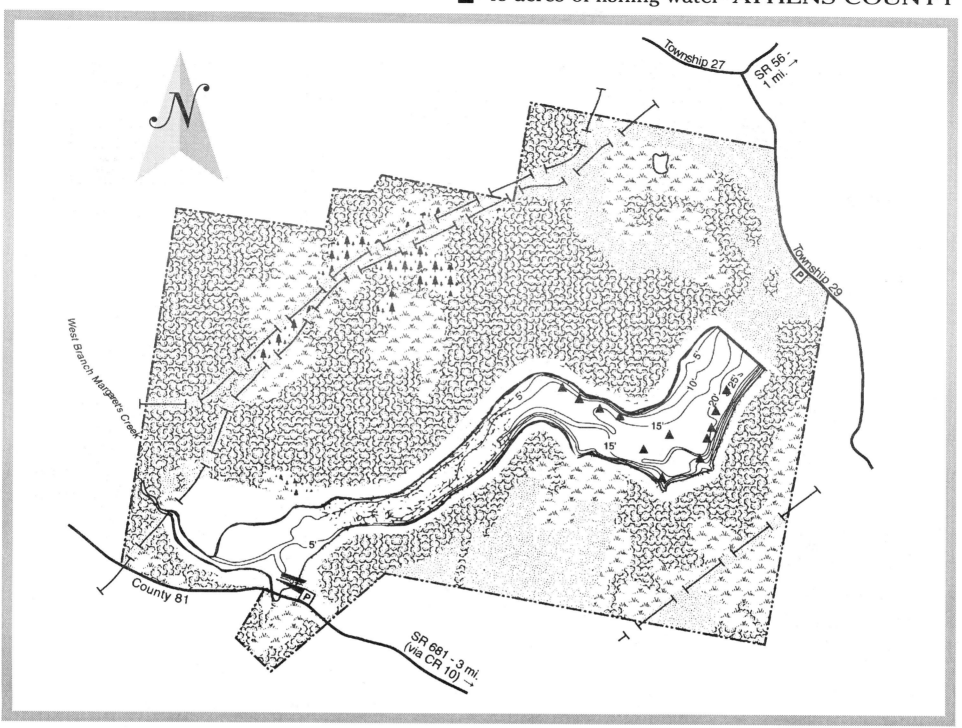

Location: In Athens County. County and township roads provide access from U.S. Route 50 and SR 56 and 681. The wildlife area and lake are 75 miles from Columbus, 148 miles from Cincinnati and 183 miles from Cleveland.

Wildlife district office: (614) 594-2211.

Fishing opportunities: Largemouth bass, channel catfish, bluegill, rough fish and redear sunfish.

Water conditions: Colored.

Bottom composition: Soft, mud.

Horsepower restrictions: Electric motor only.

Stocking: Channel catfish on alternate years.

Two parking lots.

Outlook:
Bluegill, redear - fair
Largemouth bass - fair to good
Channel catfish - excellent

The lake is in the middle of a 421-acre wildlife area that is rolling, wooded and spotted with open lands. The quiet lake is among wooded hillsides of oak and hickory and is not heavily fished. Fox Lake is an average fishing lake for most species, but a pleasant destination for a family fishing and nature-related outing.

How to catch 'em: Fox Lake is a topnotch catfishing destination during the entire season. Locals tend to fish the southern end using commercially prepared catfish bait or livers, chicken necks and fat nightcrawlers. A few grass carp have been stocked in the lake and are often seen gulping at the surface and munching vegetation. If you catch a grass carp, release it.

Largemouth bass fishing is fair to good in the early season in the upper part of the narrow lake. Try the stumpy areas flipping plastic worms and running small-bladed spinners. Try bouncing the spinner off the sides of the stumps, imitating insects or frogs hopping into the water. Night fishing with topwater

lures can also be fair to good in the upper end. Later in the year, move to the mid-lake and deeper water, over the old stream channel and near the dam. Bring the kids and some live bait for bluegills that are found evenly distributed throughout the lake. Youngsters love fishing from the floating pier.

Hot spots: Excellent channel catfishing is in the upper end of the lake, in the shallows and from the accessible fishing pier near the boat ramp. These areas can also be a hot spot for bluegill, depending on the time of the year. The dam area is also productive.

Underwater structure: About 300 Christmas trees, in bundles of three to five trees, have been submerged in the lake to improve habitat near the dam. The lake is stumpy and the south end is shallow. The shoreline has several fallen trees. Many Christmas trees are within casting distance of the accessible fishing pier.

Boat launching: The ramp is on a wide cove off from Country Road

81, three miles from SR 681. The ramp, with small parking lot, is adequate for small fishing boats and has access to the southern, shallow section of the lake.

Ice fishing: Limited.

Insider tips: Grass carp were introduced in the early 1990s to help control aquatic vegetation. A new floating accessible fishing pier is near the boat launch. Largemouth bass growth in the lake has been poor.

The 421-acre Fox Lake Wildlife Area surrounds the lake and is managed for rabbit, gray and fox squirrel, ruffed grouse, woodchuck and deer. Some waterfowl and woodcock are also in the tract. The north end of the lake has a cave-type shelter and large rock outcropping known as the "cradle in the rock" by local residents. These Buffalo sandstone outcroppings, which overlays upper and lower Brush Creek limestone, are more than 300 million years old.

Grand Lake St. Marys

MERCER & AUGLAIZE COUNTY ■ 13,500 acres of fishing water ■ 14,362 miles of shoreline

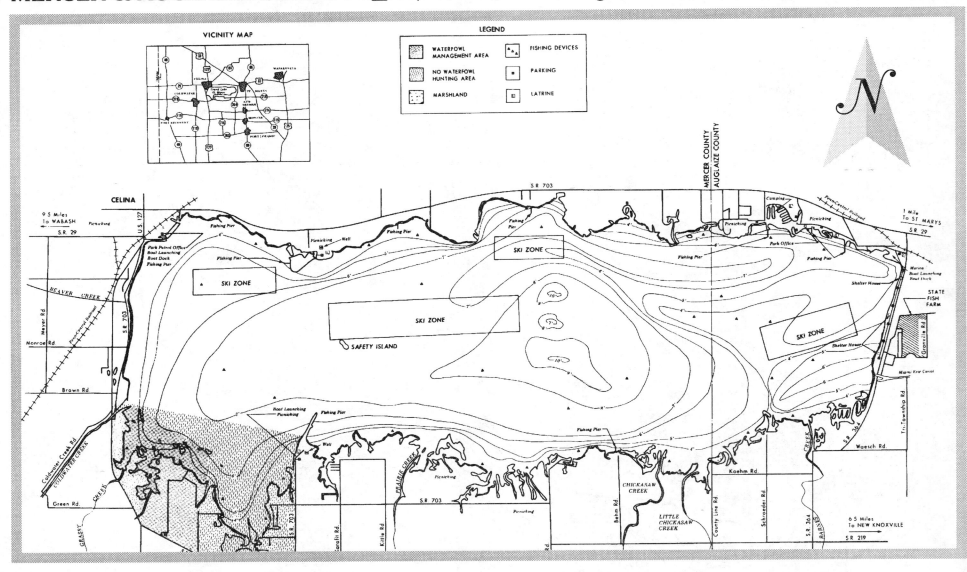

Location: In central Ohio's Mercer and Auglaize counties, 10 miles west of Wapakoneta. The city of St. Marys is at the northeast corner of the lake. State Route 29 lies to the north.

District wildlife office: (513) 372-9261.

Fishing opportunities: Largemouth bass, bluegill, crappies, channel catfish, bullheads, yellow perch, northern pike and striped bass.

Bottom composition: Mud, a dishpan lake.

Horsepower restrictions: Unrestricted.

Bait: Nearby, plenty of marinas, etc.

Water conditions: Murky, shallow.

Deepest spot: Ten feet (where the dredge was finished).

Horsepower restrictions: Unlimited, lots of ski zones and powerboats.

Stocking: None.

Camping: 206 sites in the 500-acre state park; call (419) 394-2774.

Boat rental: Call St. Marys Marina at (419) 394-2198 and others in the area.

Outlook:
Largemouth bass - good
Crappies - excellent
Catfish - excellent
Bullheads - excellent
Yellow perch - good

If you want to have fun on Grand Lake St. Marys, go crappie fishing from February to June, seek perch from October to the ice comes on, and ice fish through January. Catfish are good in the heat of the summer (dog days?).

The lake was constructed to store water for the Miami-Erie Canal. Two earthen dams were built on the headwaters of two major drainage systems. The lake, completed in 1845, is Ohio's biggest inland lake. It was the world's largest manmade lake until Hoover Dam was built. Grand Lake St. Marys was constructed by 1,700 German laborers for 30 cents a day and a jigger of cheap whiskey (about the same wages as fishing book writers). For a time, the lake helped to keep the five-foot depth in the 300-mile-long canal that had 106 locks, 19 aqueducts and 32 miles of feeder streams. The state park was one of the first 10 built in Ohio. The state park office has lots lake information.

For a big lake, it's an excellent crappie fishery.

How to catch 'em: This is a panfish lake. Avid perch anglers use minnows, waxworms and ice flies almost exclusively. The best perch time is at ice-out. Smart crappie anglers probe the feeder streams and channels after ice-out, and during April and May. The action heats up again in mid-autumn. Locals use a simple lead-head jig with a bobber and walk the shoreline. Tip the small hook with a waxworm or min-now. Fish slow.

Ten times more crappies are caught than largemouth bass in the dishpan-shaped lake. Some of the shoreline access points can product hookups. The lake's large population of crappies are mostly 8-11 inches, with some up to 15 inches. Largemouth bass run 10-14 inches, but there are good numbers of 2-4 pounders. The best time to fish largemouth is June - August along the rocks on the east and west shores, or in woody channels and small bays. Some striped bass are caught on flashy lures during the summer, and on large minnows around warmwater outlets during the winter.

Catfishing is great in the summer. Local experts use a trotline (in the restricted area) or worms. Certainly many more catfish could be taken on smelly shrimp or chicken innards. Bluegills are fun to catch in the clearer backwater, and depending on the time of year they will hit dry flies, small worms or tiny fuzzy lures. A few northern pike are caught, most while fishing for other species. Intrepid pike anglers may want to try the channels, marshy edges and backwater pools in the spring. Pike are tough to come by in the lake.

Hot spots: Canals. The handicapped accessible fishing pier can be a good site.

Boat launching: Many of the narrow channels around the lake are busy with local boat traffic. The St. Marys Marina, (419) 394-2198, sells supplies and fuel. Any of the state and national routes that circle the lake will have signs and access roads to the many launching ramps that serve the lake.

Shoreline: Several fishing piers are scattered around the lake, which offers good shoreline public access. The many narrow, stumpy coves provide for good crappie action, especially in April and May. The lake association has been active in placing brush piles and other structure.

Ice fishing: Perch through the ice is excellent through January. It has improved dramatically since new sewer lines were installed around the lake in the mid-1990s.

Insider tips: With few trees to protect it, the lake can quickly gather three-foot waves when the winds begin to blow. Watch the weather and for the posting of small-craft warnings. Lots of sailboats and windsurfers use the lake. A state-operated fish hatchery is at the east end of the land where long rearing ponds produce saugeye, northern pike and bass (none are planted in the lake). The lake also has Ohio's only inland lighthouse in Celina. Consider the above map only a guide as to depths. A pair of resident bald eagles can sometimes be seen flying over the shallow lake.

Griggs Reservoir

■ 364 acres of fishing water ■ 15 miles of shoreline FRANKLIN COUNTY

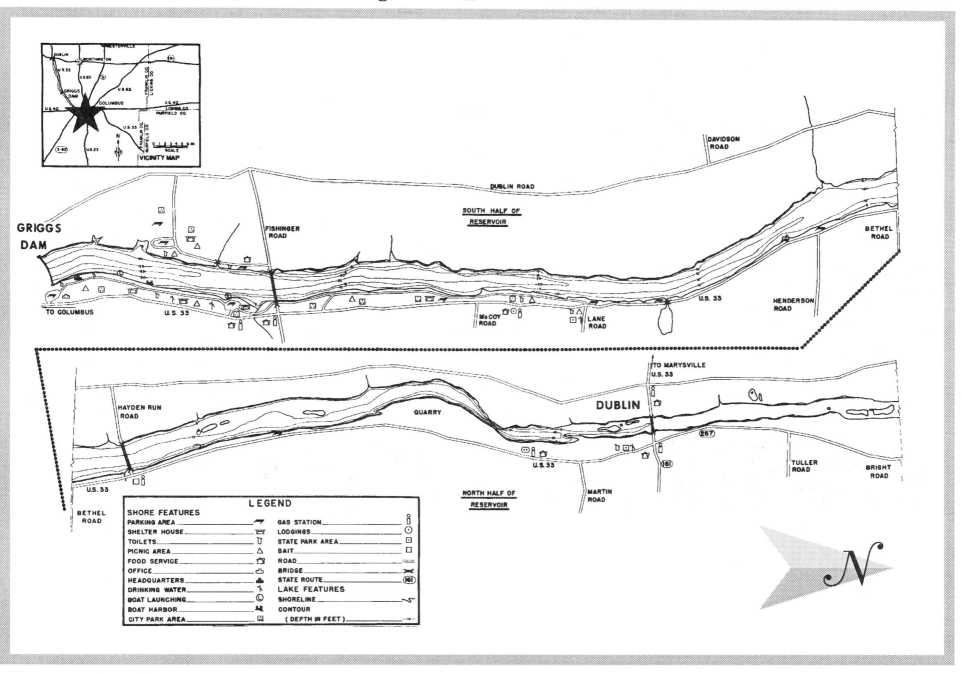

Location: In Franklin County, between Columbus and Dublin.

Wildlife district office: (614) 644-3925.

Fishing opportunities: Large- and smallmouth bass, channel catfish, crappies and saugeye.

Water conditions: Colored.

Bottom composition: Silt over limestone.

Horsepower restrictions: None.

Stocking: Saugeye annually.

Special regulation: Check minimum size limit on bass.

Outlook:
Largemouth bass - good
Channel catfish - excellent
Saugeye - excellent

How to catch 'em: Because of lower than average fishing pressure, some good-sized bass are in the urban reservoir. Being narrow and having significant recreational boat traffic, the reservoir is hard to fish. Largemouth are found in good numbers. Early season anglers will want to cast against the shoreline with spinners and plastic worms.

Griggs Reservoir is one of the top locations for excellent season-long catches of catfish. Commercially prepared baits seem to be preferred and nighttime angling is the rule. Fish slowly along the east shore after sunset. Saugeye are not heavily fished in the ribbon-like reservoir. A good population of 12-26 inch fish are in the system and local experts say to fish the tailwater one week after a storm for the best action. Drift fishing a jig and minnow or a light-weight bottom bouncer is common. If you drift against a tight line and have a good feel, you will catch saugeye.

Panfishing is fair on live bait and small hooks. Shoreline anglers can do well in the spring from the day-use areas at Griggs Dam.

Hot spots: The east side of the lake is owned by the city; the west side is private property. Plan to fish at the east side during the off hours. For bass, try the upper and north ends of the island.

Underwater structure: The underwater structure is limited in the river-like reservoir.

Boat launching: The two main launches are in the developed east side of the reservoir near the dam, accessed from Fishinger Road from either U.S. 33 or Dublin Road. A small harbor area is also near the dam.

Ice fishing: Very little is done.

Insider tips: The lake is an urban setting, crowded and heavily water skied. Sometimes fishermen get crowded off the reservoir. Consequently, not much fishing takes place during the day. The city park along the east bank has picnic areas, toilets, a shelter house and drinking water. Food service, lodging and bait are nearby.

Guilford Lake

COLUMBIANA COUNTY ■ 390 acres of fishing water ■ Six miles of shoreline

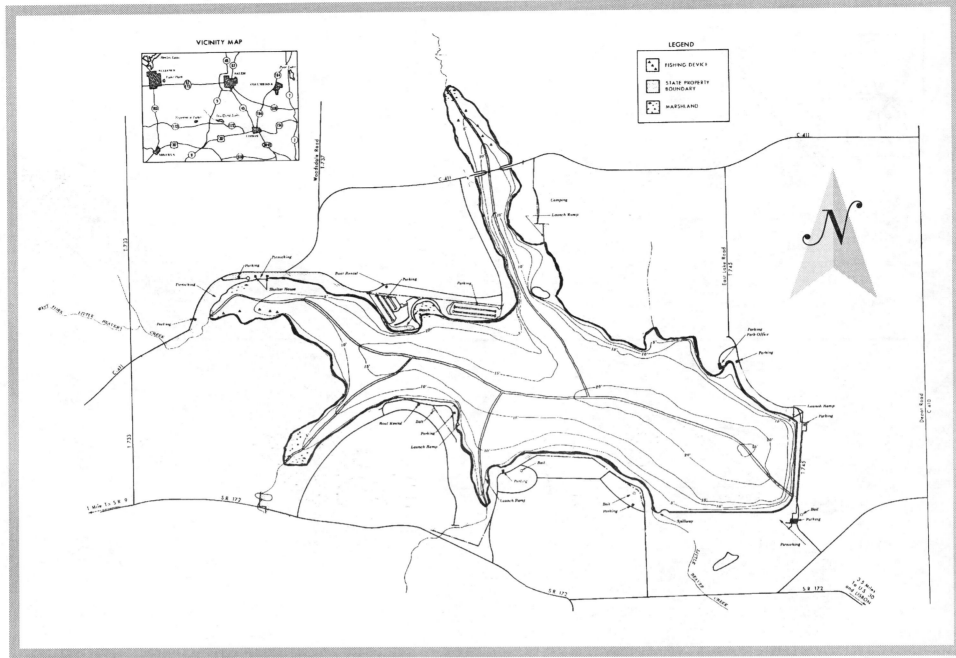

Location: In Columbiana County on the West Fork of the Little Beaver Creek, it is south of SR 172, which joins U.S. Route 30 near Canton and Lisbon.

Wildlife district office: (216) 644-2293.

Fishing opportunities: Largemouth and striped bass, channel catfish, northern pike and bluegill.

Fishing information: Hilltop Bait, (216) 424-5760.

Bottom composition: Sand, small stone.

Stocking: Channel catfish.

Horsepower restrictions: 10 hp limit.

Boat rental: At the small marina on the south side of lake.

Camping: 42 sites in Guilford Lake State Park; call (330) 222-1712.

Handicapped accessible fishing pier, off Hannah Drive.

Outlook:
Largemouth bass - good
Bluegill - fair
Channel catfish - good
White crappies - fair
Black crappies - good

Guilford Lake, on a glacial plateau near the Appalachian foothills, was constructed as a canal feeder reservoir for the Sandy and Beaver Canal in 1834. In 1927 the state purchased the area with the intent of developing it as a public area and fishing lake. In 1933 the dam was rebuilt.

Guilford Lake State Park was one of Ohio's original 13 state parks. The 500-acre park has a 900-foot beach, three launching ramps, a dock and boat rental. Areas surrounding the lake are swampy, indicating that the entire area may have been a remnant of a glacial lake.

How to catch 'em: Early spring brings an excellent crappie run. Both crappie and bluegill anglers might try fly casting spiders, bugs, crickets and poppers along the shore during the spring and early summer. Low-tech anglers can bring out their old cane pole and load-up a hook with worms for fast panfish action. Bluegills are small at Guilford Lake, few reach eight inches in length.

Largemouth bass love cover. A favorite local technique is to quietly drift along the shoreline (where there are many small boat docks) and cast to the shore and under wooden docks. 40 percent of all largemouth bass are at least 17 inch-

es long. Other anglers search the lake for the installed structure and cast action-type lures or work plastic worms in vegetation. The North Bay is a favorite spring fishing area. Some pike are taken in the marshy areas using plated spoons and patience. Don't forget to explore the shoreline of tiny Pine Island and the submerged Grass Island that are straight south a few hundred yards. Some manmade structure is also off the west end of the submerged hump.

Interestingly, catfish caught during the day are usually 16 inches or shorter, while cats taken at night average 25 inches in length. Catfish are stocked regularly.

Hot spots: Campground Bay (north of the campground, C-411 crosses it) is the lake's most popular spot for crappies and bass. Some eight-pound largemouths are taken from along the natural shoreline. Local anglers fish around the many small docks, buzzing spinner baits near the piers, docks and boats. Try the fishing dock in the campground, too.

Boat launching: Trailer boats should be launched at the modern ramp off Hannah Drive on the south side of the lake. Campers have their own small boat launch.

Underwater structure: The state park and citizen groups have installed a number of artificial reefs. Stop by the park office and pick up a photocopied map that details the location of these many reefs and other fish holding structure. The map indicates where Christmas tress, stump beds, the sunken island, lily pads and fallen timber are located. The park office is at the end of East Lake Road, near the dam, on the northeast side of the lake.

Ice fishing: Ice fishermen flock to the lake each winter finding good catches of panfish. Some ice fishermen claim to catch 100 small crappies an hour using minnows.

Insider tips: The second weekend in June is the annual youth fishing derby. The state park also conducts several catfish derbies throughout the summer. Also, model airplanes use the lake for amphibious fly-ins. Upon completion of a comprehensive dredging program, saugeye may be introduced into the lake in the near future. Two restaurants are on the lake. The lake has no water skiing or personal watercraft operation.

Hargus Creek Lake

■ 146 acres of fishing water ■ Five miles of shoreline PICKAWAY COUNTY

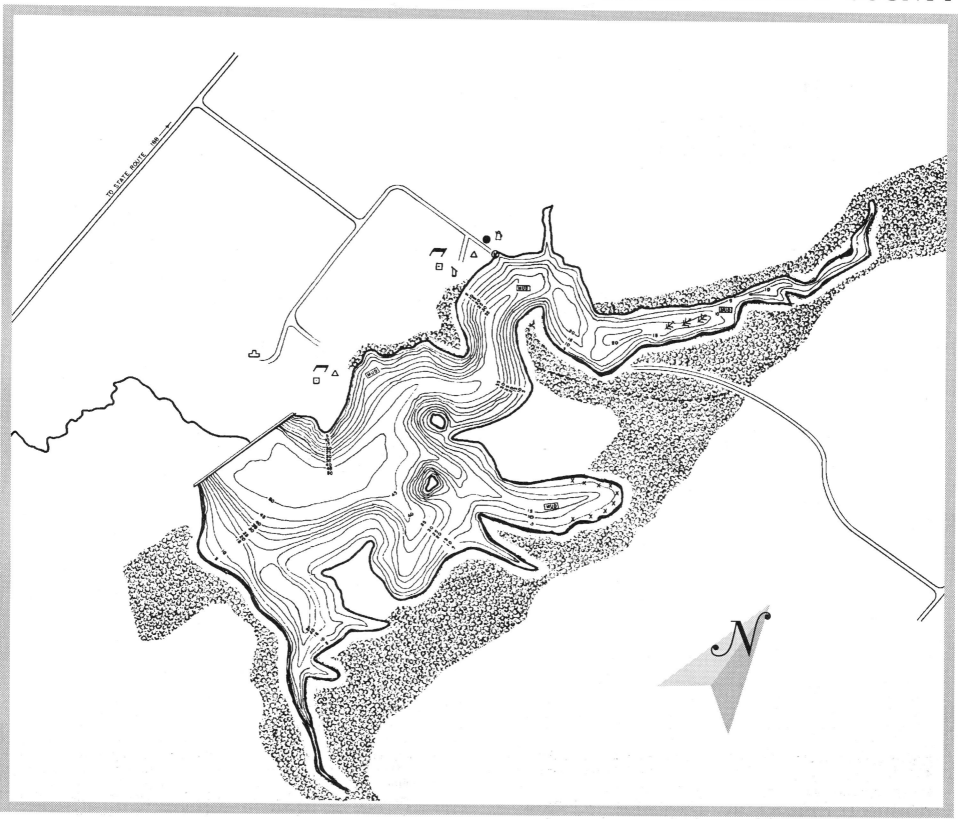

Location: In Pickaway County, northeast of Circleville, just north of SR 22.

Wildlife district office: (614) 644-3925.

Fishing opportunities: Largemouth bass, bluegills, crappies and catfish.

Water conditions: Medium colored.

Bottom composition: Rock, shale and mud.

Depth: 5-50 feet.

Food service available.

Boat rental.

Horsepower restriction: None.

Zebra mussel warning: Thoroughly dry your boat after use.

Bait and tackle are nearby.

Outlook:
Bluegill - fair
Largemouth bass - good
Channel catfish - improving
Crappie - poor
Muskie - poor

In 1986, Hargus Lake was drained, and fish were removed. The lake was restocked with largemouth bass, bluegill and catfishing. The lake has no recreational traffic, offering a peaceful fishing experience. The lake is improving, and increased management efforts are helping fishing quality. Crappies have gotten into the small lake and temporarily upset the largemouth bass/bluegill balance.

How to catch 'em: Head for the brushy north end of the lake in the spring as the waters warm for good bluegill action. As the water temperatures warm up, move toward the deeper parts of the lake.

Catfishing along the mud banks are good to excellent using gobs of worms on the bottom or still fish smelly cutbaits. Local experts say the crappies and bluegills chase live minnows and jigs and colored jigs and flashy grub bodies. In mid-summer many largemouth bass hold in the medium depths of 20-25 feet, often off the two islands in the central part of the lake.

Largemouth have a dense population of 8-13 inches in Hargus. A few are bigger. An occasional muskie is taken today. Muskie stocking was discontinued in the early 1980s.

Hot spots: The best around the islands and about halfway down the bay immediately east of the southern island. This stumpy area is bass heaven. Use crankbaits, dark plastic worms and small willow-blade spinners.

Underwater structure: The north end of the lake has good stretches of flooded timber.

Boat launching: Two modern ramps are on the west side of the lake.

Ice fishing: Most ice fishermen drill holes in front of the southernmost boat launching ramp. Poke holes along the dropoff and look for panfish. A good live minnow on a tiny colored jig head or a fat waxworm can bring in good numbers of bluegill and a few crappies.

Insider tips: Here's a chance to fish deep by early summer. Try between the island and buzz spinners around the bay east of the islands.

Harrison Lake

FULTON COUNTY ■ 105 acres of fishing water ■ 3.5 miles of shoreline

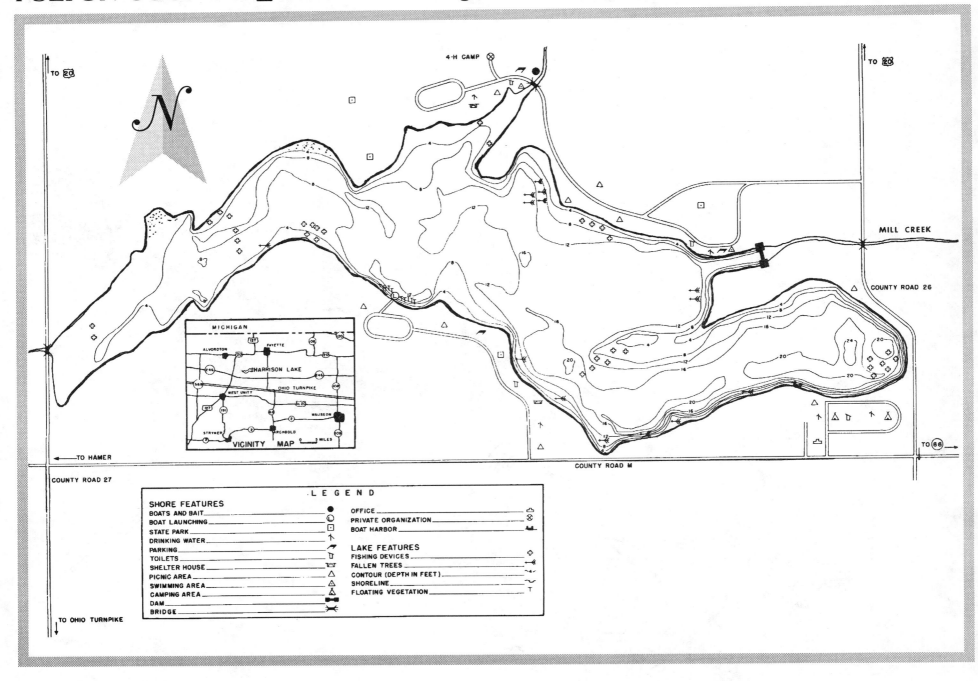

Location: In Fulton County. Two miles south of U.S. 20/127 and two miles west of SR 66, the lake is four miles south of the Michigan-Ohio border.

Wildlife district office: (419) 424-5000.

Fishing opportunities: Crappies, largemouth bass, bluegill, some pike and bluegills.

Water conditions: Turbid, lots of sediment.

Bottom composition: Sediment and mud.

Horsepower restrictions: Electric motors only.

Camping: 178 sites in the state park; call (419) 237-2593.

Stocking: Catfish.

Shoreline: Varied; steep in places, fallen trees.

Outlook:
Largemouth bass - good
Bluegill - fair
Channel catfish - very good
White crappies - very good
Bullheads - good

Harrison Lake may have been in Michigan, but in 1836, Congress agreed with Ohio's claim for the current border location. For years Ohio and Michigan argued over—and both claimed—the 11-mile strip of land that extends from the mouth of the Maumee River to the Ohio-Indiana line.

Today, Harrison Lake is an island of recreation opportunity amid lush farmlands that track to the horizon. The area is lightly populated, in part because of massive efforts to reclaim and drain what used to be called the "Great Black Swamp." Once wet, virtually impassable and mosquito infested, the lake and state park now serve fishermen from southern Michigan, Ohio and the rest of the Midwest.

How to catch 'em: Harrison Lake typically has lots of downed trees along its shoreline which holds good numbers of largemouth bass and crappies. The lake has high numbers of smaller-sized largemouth. Most of the fish are 12-21 inches. Bluegill run five to seven inches and white crappies seven to 10 inches. Crappie fishing in the spring is excellent around submerged pine trees and any other structure. Catfish anglers will find a healthy population of fish 12-20 inches in length.

Check with the state park staff for information on structure locations and fishing updates.

Hot spots: Vegetation on the south side of the lake holds all species of fish. Some anglers report that the point near the mouth of Mill Creek can be productive. Others prefer the southeast shoreline. Campers enjoy excellent shoreline fishing near their sites.

Underwater structure: The state park staff and others have strategically placed what they call "fishing devices" around the lake. The devices are tree structures. The structure shows up well on a depth finder and also are found by watching where the local anglers are drifting and jigging.

Boat launching: A single launching ramp is near the 4-H camp.

Ice fishing: One of Ohio's northernmost lakes, Harrison Lake can be busy with ice fishermen.

Insider tips: The state park has a 50-yard-long beach, 370 picnic tables and 70 grills scattered around the day-use areas. Catfishing is terrific at night on the lake. Films and nature demonstrations are shown in the state park's campground on Saturday nights.

Highland Lake

■ 170 acres of fishing water ■ 6.5 miles of shoreline COLUMBIANA COUNTY

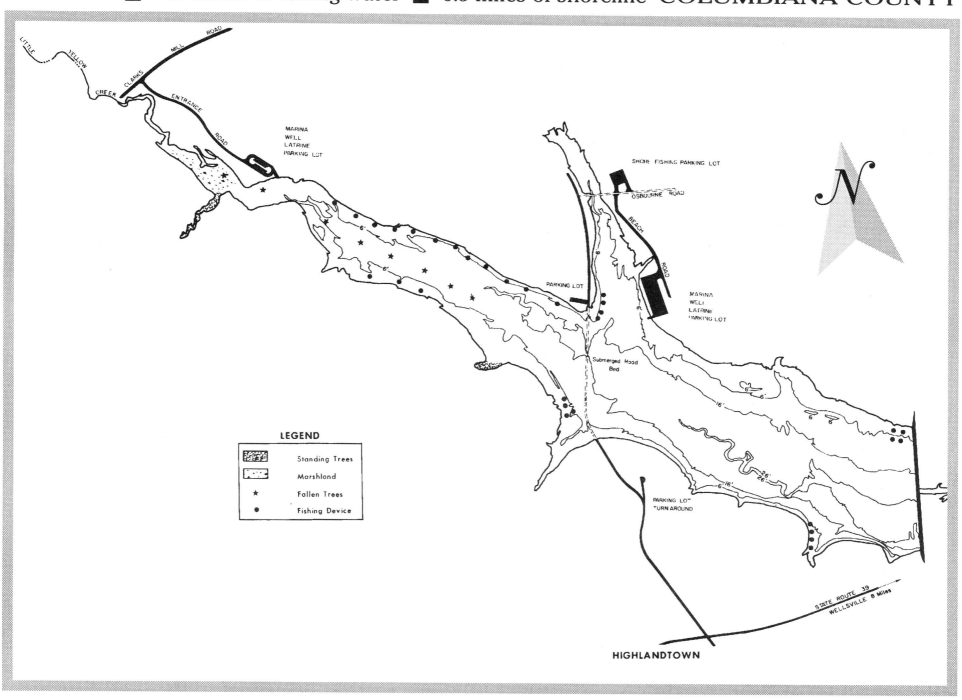

LEGEND

	Standing Trees
	Marshland
★	Fallen Trees
●	Fishing Device

HIGHLANDTOWN

Location: In Columbiana County, 4.5 miles northeast of Salineville off SR 39, nine miles south of Lisbon off SR 164.

Wildlife district office: (330) 644-2293.

Fishing opportunities: Channel catfish, brown bullhead, bluegill, crappie, largemouth bass, yellow perch and a rare muskie.

Water conditions: Clear.

Bottom composition: Heavily vegetated; sand silt, muck.

Horsepower restrictions: Electric only, under four horsepower.

Special regulation: 15-inch bass.

Stocked: As needed; once heavily stocked.

Bait: None nearby.

Outlook:
Channel catfish - good
Brown bullheads - excellent
Bluegills - excellent, large
Largemouth bass - very good, small size
White crappies - good
Black crappies - very good
Yellow perch - fair

Highlandtown Lake (built in 1966), surrounded by a large wildlife area, is a pretty lake managed specifically for bluegills. Therefore, a high bass size limit is in effect (currently, all largemouth must be at least 15 inches to keep). The lake has the highest average size (seven inches) for bluegill in the district. One of the biologists we talked with said this is the first lake in the state he would go to for a day of fast action and jumbo panfish. The shoreline is treed or covered with chest-high brush. The shoreline also has a heavy growth of cattails.

Plan to be on the lake early to get over the old bridge abutment mentioned below. The lake has fair shoreline access. Because the lake is in a valley, protected from the wind, a lot of belly-boaters use the lake and boat handling is easy. Fly fishing in the still air for bluegills is also a strong recommendation.

How to catch 'em: On a good day, anglers can catch 100 bass in an afternoon—but the biggest one you might see is eight inches. This size limit, of course, keeps the bluegill size large. Crappie fishing is also excellent. Still fish the lake with

maggots and waxworms for panfish. The west end of the lake is a very good bass fishery where small spinners, jigs and twister tails, rubber worms and other artificals work. Crappies are found in the mixed brush and vegetation throughout the lake. White crappies average nine inches; black crappies about 8.5 inches. Highlandtown is one of the best bluegill lakes in the state. Huge 'gills can be taken throughout the lake. Night fish for catfish using scraps of semi-spoiled meat, a gob of worms and a stout hook. The average catfish is 16 inches. A few nine-inch yellow perch are taken at the lake.

Hot spots: First-time fishermen to the lake should head for the mid-lake, over the old road. The bridge abutments are still there, and this is by far the hottest spot on the lake. Fishing along the old creek bed is also an excellent plan of attack. At one time, the wildlife division used to send divers to place a buoy over the old roadbed and bridge abutments. They no longer place the marker because anglers cut off the buoy, not wanting anyone to know about "their" hot spot. This spot is great either winter or summer.

Underwater structure: In part because the lake is owned by the wildlife division, plenty of quality fish-holding structure is placed in the lake each year. The devices are scattered around the lake, near the shorelines and along deep sections, off flats. They are easy to spot on a sounder or from the map.

Boat launching: The two concrete boat launching ramps on the north side of the lake are busy. A fishing pier accessible to persons with disabilities is also on the lake.

Ice fishing: Ice fishing is excellent for panfish. Dense populations allow anglers to use simple techniques of larval baits, small minnows and tiny jigs. Get your shanty over the old roadbed at mid-lake.

Insider tips: Bring your own bait and a belly-boat. This is a dandy panfishing lake. Try fly fishing at dusk in the shallows for bluegill. The placid lake is in a 2,105-acres public hunting area. Bring a No. 5 or 6 fly rod and some yellow or white popper bugs for panfish fun.

Hoover Reservoir

DELAWARE & FRANKLIN COUNTIES ■ 3,300 acres of fishing water ■ 45 miles of shoreline

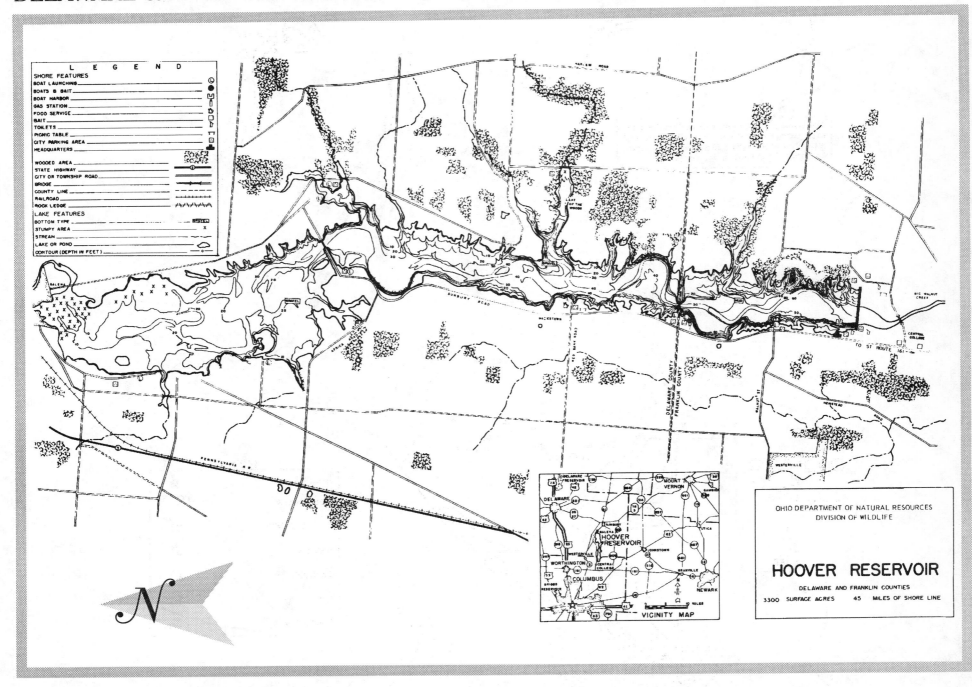

Location: North of Columbus in Delaware and north Franklin counties. Take SR 161 to Sunbury Road.

Wildlife district office: (614) 644-3925.

Fishing opportunities: Crappies (good), saugeye (very good), catfish.

Water condition: Muddy.

Bottom composition: Old gravel roadbeds, mud channels and murl.

Boating: Six hp and under.

Sailboats and boards are popular. No water-skiers allowed.

Bait and tackle: Several in the area, including a shop at the Red Bank Road ramp.

Stocking: Saugeye annually, fair natural reproduction of saugeye.

The quiet lake is municipally operated and is considered a very good saugeye lake. Because of boat motor size restrictions, the lake is the most peaceful fishing lake in Delaware County. Private lands surround the lake, limiting shoreline fishing to city parks. The best park is one on the county line on the west side of the lake. Many of the lake's coves are deep, with sharp shoreline drops.

How to catch 'em: The best saugeye fishing is at the dam using jigs (try tipping with a minnow and use stinger hooks), white and yellow twister tails and minnows, nightcrawler rigs and small crankbaits. Bass fishing is good along dropoffs (at the end of Africa Road, for example), coves and along points.

Local anglers like to cast against shorelines that have rock ledges. Bass anglers flip worms in stumpy areas near the town of Galena at the north end of the lake. The larger of the two islands at the north end of the lake is a popular fishing area that gives up some good catches in the spring before the water warms.

Boat launching: One of the most popular launching ramps is at Red Bank Road. Most others are small and scattered along the west side of the lake on Sunbury Road.

Insider tips: Saugeyes are good in front of the dam in spring and early summer. Locals says bright colored twister tails slipped against any current will work well.

Lake Hope

■ 120 acres of fishing water   ■ 5.7 miles of shoreline   VINTON COUNTY

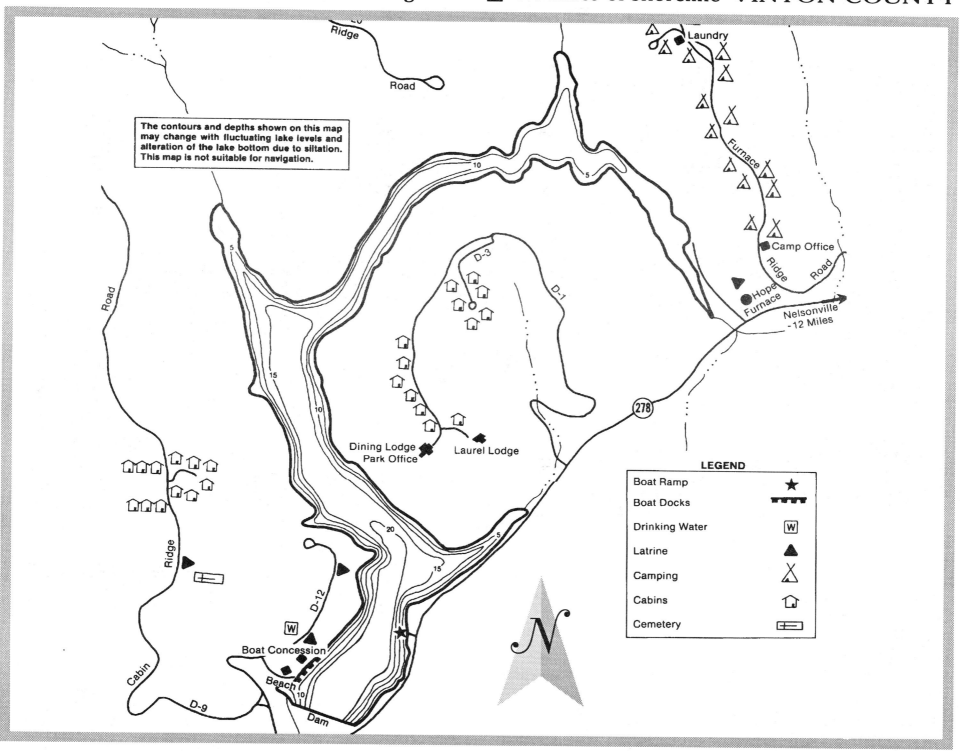

LEGEND

Boat Ramp	★
Boat Docks	▄▄▄
Drinking Water	W
Latrine	▲
Camping	X
Cabins	⌂
Cemetery	⊟

The contours and depths shown on this map may change with fluctuating lake levels and alteration of the lake bottom due to siltation. This map is not suitable for navigation.

Location: In Vinton County, about 15 miles west of Athens and 10 miles southwest of Nelsonville, with access from SR 278.

Wildlife district office: (614) 594-2211.

Fishing opportunity: Largemouth bass, crappies. channel catfish and bluegill.

Water conditions: Emerald green, fairly clear.

Bottom composition: Muddy and soft.

Horsepower restriction: Electric motors up to three hp.

Stocking: Channel catfish on alternate years.

Camping: 223 sites in Lake Hope State Park; call (614) 596-5253.

Bait at beach concession/boat launch area.

Outlook:
Bluegill, redear - good

Largemouth bass - good
Channel catfish - good

The area has lots of natural beauty and is in the region geologists call the "maturely dissected Allegheny Plateau." Translated, that means millions of years ago Lake Hope was a plateau but streams have cut extensive valleys creating the hills we have today. The rugged area is popular with backpackers (23 miles of hiking trails) and other outdoor lovers. The lake and neighboring state park are terrific places to bring the family. The region is quiet and secluded, no big boats roar on the lake—and the fishing is improving as water quality gets better.

The Big Four Hollow Project sealed off most of the iron and sulfur contaminants draining from some area coal mines, improving the lake's water quality. Since the cleanup began, some 20-pound catfish, several eight-pound largemouth bass and good numbers of panfish are being taken.

The lake was built in 1939 and impounds Sandy Run, a tributary of Raccoon Creek.

How to catch 'em: Bass average one to three pounds. Local experts say using a minnow or purple plastic worm along the banks and hollows works well on bass much of the year. The best largemouth bass fishing is in the early season. Many fish are taken over deepwater structure on lures of jigs and pigs or deep-diving crankbaits. The bass move to shallow water to feed when the temperature reaches about 70 degrees. At this time, cast buzz baits and spinners along the shoreline, over shallows and around weedbeds.

Bluegill tend to hang around structure if the water temperature is 55 degrees or cooler. Locals says deep water bluegills are fussy, but will take waxworms on small hooks if presented gently. The fish tend to suspend in mid-depth ranges in the half of the lake near the dam. They might also be caught near the surface when the water temperatures are suitable, or near spawning beds.

Most serious channel catfish anglers work the shoreline access points near the dam all summer when the water is 60-90 degrees. The lake has a good harvest of 20-inch catfish, most of which are taken on cutbaits and stout line. Bring your can of chicken livers, too.

Hot spots: The launch ramp shoreline, on to mid-lake is a hot spot. For catfish try along the dam access points. The upper lake has weed and lily beds.

Underwater structure: The lake is lightly vegetated due to alkaline water.

Boat launching: One primitive ramp serves the lake near the dam off Route 278. A small boat rental concession and beach are nearby.

Insider tips: The Lake Hope State Park has a large campground, lodge and restaurant, 69 cabins, bridle and hiking trails and boat rental. Look for signs of beaver around the lake. Largemouth bass have been stocked in the past.

Indian Lake

LOGAN COUNTY ■ 5,800 acres of fishing water ■ 29 miles of shoreline

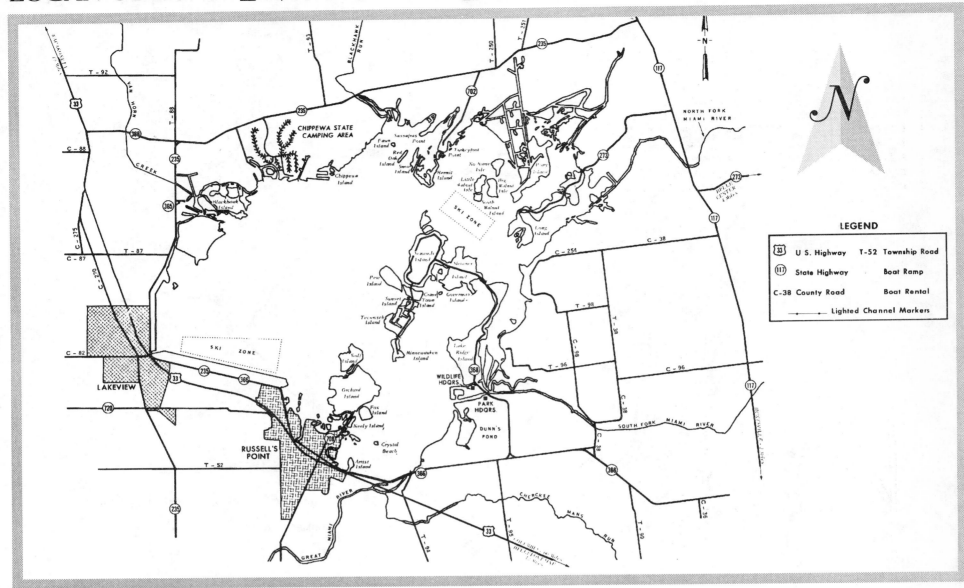

Location: In Logan County, 15 miles northwest of Bellefontaine on SR 235N. There is also an access from I-75 by taking the U.S. 33 exit east.

Wildlife district office: (614) 644-3925.

Fishing opportunities: Crappies, bluegill, channel catfish, yellow perch, white bass, some walleye and some rough fish.

Water conditions: Turbid.

Bottom composition: Lots of vegetation, muddy, some sand.

Horsepower restrictions: None.

Special regulation: Minimum on bass.

Stocking: Saugeye annually since 1988.

Average depth: Eight feet.

Boat rental and season docking: (513) 843-2717.

Camping: 443 sites in the state park, call (513) 843-3553.

Nearby bait and tackle.

Outlook:
Largemouth bass - good
Crappies - good
Channel catfish - excellent
Saugeye - excellent
White bass - fair

Indian Lake is an old canal feeder lake, first impounded in the 1850s.

It was originally only 1,000 acres and has been enlarged to about 5,800 acres today. The lake is shallow, fertile and busy. It supports a strong saugeye population, as well as channel catfish, crappies and improving largemouth bass. Water quality is getting better, and the lake is a success story relative to active managment and cleanup efforts.

At one time, Indian Lake was known as the "Midwest's Million Dollar Playground." Today, the area is still a popular resort and visitor destination. Nearby are caverns, shopping, cottages, golf, power boating and restaurants.

The bulk of the fishery is saugeye, catfish and crappies.

How to catch 'em: Indian Lake has several bait and tackle shops that specialize in up-to-date information about fishing, places to go and how to catch them. Most tackle shop experts suggest morning or night fishing, or visiting during the spring and fall, skipping the hectic summer.

Saugeye are evenly distributed and can be taken by trolling or drifting with a jig minnow/twister tail and spinners in deep water. Vertical jigging is an excellent technique. Largemouth bass are in good numbers from 12-18 inches, with some larger. Channel and vegetated areas are best in the spring, while the rip rap is a good bet during the summer.

As always, look for underwater logs and stumps, or around any of the 68 islands in the lake. Most largemouth are taken from boats using plastic worms, weedless spoons, crankbaits and spinners around weed pockets and around the islands. Dipping softclaws and nightcrawlers also a local favorite. The lake has many 7-12 inch crappies that can be taken on small jigs or live minnows form the shoreline. Locals like to use bologna for catfish (try Oscar Meyer). Softcraws and shrimp in deeper water also work well at night for channel catfish. Tributary streams after ice-out are also hot spots for big cats.

White bass can run in schools near the South Bank during April. Night fishing near the bridge with minnows during the summer can also produce the silvery-colored bass. Don't forget to cast spinners and jigs at surface-breaking schools and in the deep water. Head for the lily pads with a light action rod and a can of worms for chunky bluegills.

Hot spots: Try the spillway, tributary (where there is deep water from dredging) and the South Bank area for saugeye. Moundwood, North Fork, Old Indian Lake (the old natural lake with depth to 18 feet) are excellent areas. Try any rip rap shorelines for saugeye (largemouth and panfish, too). The northeast section of the lake, called the game reserve, has a lot of aquatic habitat and vegetation. Many of these channels are great for bluegill and largemouth.

Underwater structure: The lake has good natural underwater structure including old stumps, rooted weedbeds, points and many island shorelines. Try the game reserve for good natural structure in the northeast corner of the lake. The lake has plenty of stick-ups and pads.

Boat launching: Watch for ski zones. Public ramps are at Lakeview Harbor on U.S. 33, Moundwood (near the state park headquarters), Blackhawk near the state park campground and Chippewa Marina. There are some large full-service marinas on the lake. In the shallows, watch for stumps.

Ice fishing: This can be very good for panfish. Late fall and winter fishing is popular. For saugeye, use heavy jigs on the bottom.

Insider tips: Surrounded by many cottages, recreational boating on the lake is high. The lake is constantly dredged. The state park offers camping, two swimming beaches, four miles of hiking trails and various day-use amenities. Bow fishing for carp is done at the lake, mostly in the shallows in May. As many as 45 bass tournaments are held on the lake each year. The lake has 68 islands. A few muskie have been caught.

Jackson Lake

■ 242 acres of fishing water ■ 11 miles of shoreline JACKSON COUNTY

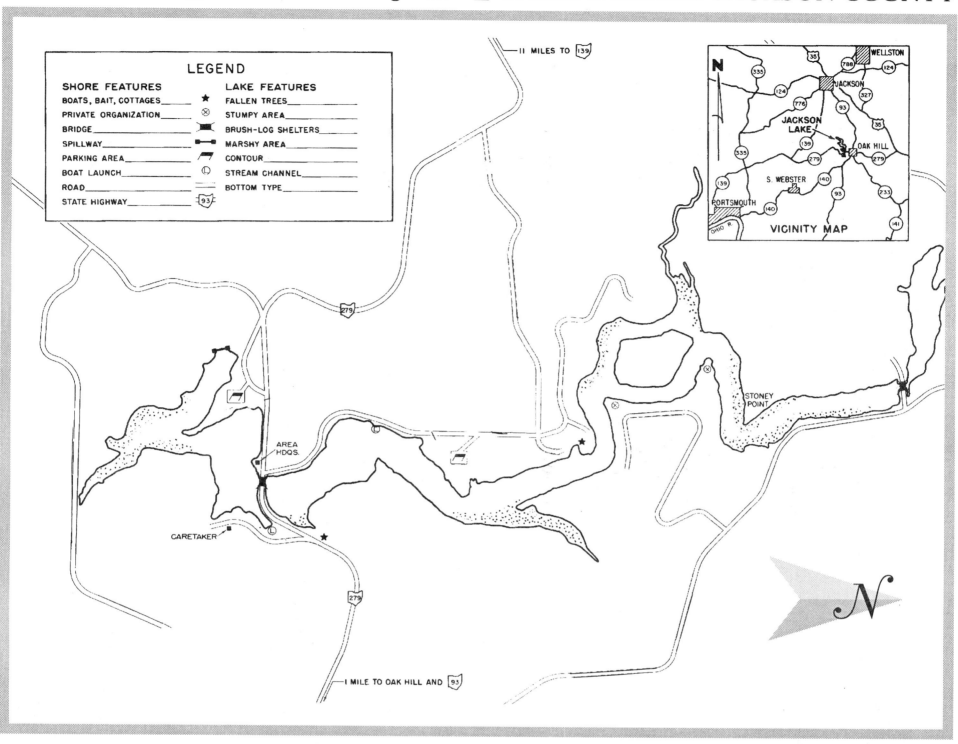

Location: Take U.S. 23 to U.S. 35, east to SR 93, then head west to SR 279 out of Oak Hill.

Wildlife district office: (614) 594-2211.

Fishing opportunities: Largemouth bass, channel catfish, panfish and a few northern pike and muskie.

Water conditions: Murky .

Bottom composition: Mud, soft.

Horsepower restriction: Electric motors only.

Stocking: Catfish on alternate years.

Boat rental: Johnboats nearby.

Camping: 36 sites in the state park; call (614) 682-6197.

Outlook:
Bluegill, redear - fair
Largemouth bass - good
Channel catfish - excellent

Jackson Lake is a quiet place, a getaway lake where family camping, a small beach and reasonable fishing

are popular. Jackson Lake is in the famous Hanging Rock Region, a region of rich iron ore deposits which coupled with vast stands of hardwood forests was once used to fuel huge iron-making operations. In fact, the remains of Jefferson Furnace, which produced iron for the Monitor, the Union's ironclad that met the Confederate ironclad, the Merrimac, is at Laurel Point.

How to catch 'em: Channel catfish is the emphasized species here. A steady stocking program keeps the nutrient-rich and heavily vegetated lake filled with good-sized channel catfish that are easy to catch. The cats are evenly distributed around the lake and standard cutbaits and prepared baits work well, especially at night in the summer. Bass fishing can be good to very good in the spring, with four- to five-pounders abundant. Some eight-pound bass have been taken in the past. The bass fishery is improving. Try your luck in the spring and late fall when the fish hit lime-tailed spinner baits around the old stream bed and around Rhodes Island. The large

island at the upper end of the lake is owned by former Ohio Governor James Rhodes.

A few muskie and northern pike are taken, but they are rare. The shoreline access at Tommy Been Road is a popular area for many anglers to try for sport and rough fish. Bluegills are moderately abundant, but of low quality (5-6 inches) and redear sunfish are typically 6-9 inches.

Hot spots: On the north side of the bridge, not far from the area headquarters building, is a cluster of submerged Christmas trees that savvy anglers sit over and jig. Directly north of there, off a point where state park day-use amenities are situated, also is a hot spot filled in with some old trees. Much of the action is north of the bridge.

Underwater structure: About 500 Christmas trees have been bundled and submerged to concentrate fish in the narrow lake over the years. Sections of the lake are heavily vegetated and shallow. About 250 trees were strategically planted in 1993

along points and depth breaks in the bays and coves near and north of the bridge. Additional Christmas trees in this area were added in the mid-1990s. The narrow lake is bathtub-like, with the deepest area about 15 feet.

Boat launching: A newer two-lane launching ramp and improved nearby shoreline fishing area are off SR 279. If water levels are high, the small bridge under SR 279 can be a tight squeeze.

Ice fishing: Weather permitting, the lake is ice fished, but reports are poor.

Insider tips: The lake has quite a bit of private property developed at the shoreline, but there is a 50-foot fishing easement around the lake. The state park has camping, a swimming beach, large day-use areas and a historical area. Between the park office and camp are a half-dozen apples trees that produce what locals call the "best cooking apples in the state."

Jackson City Reservoir

JACKSON COUNTY ■ 190 acres of fishing water ■ 8.4 miles of shoreline

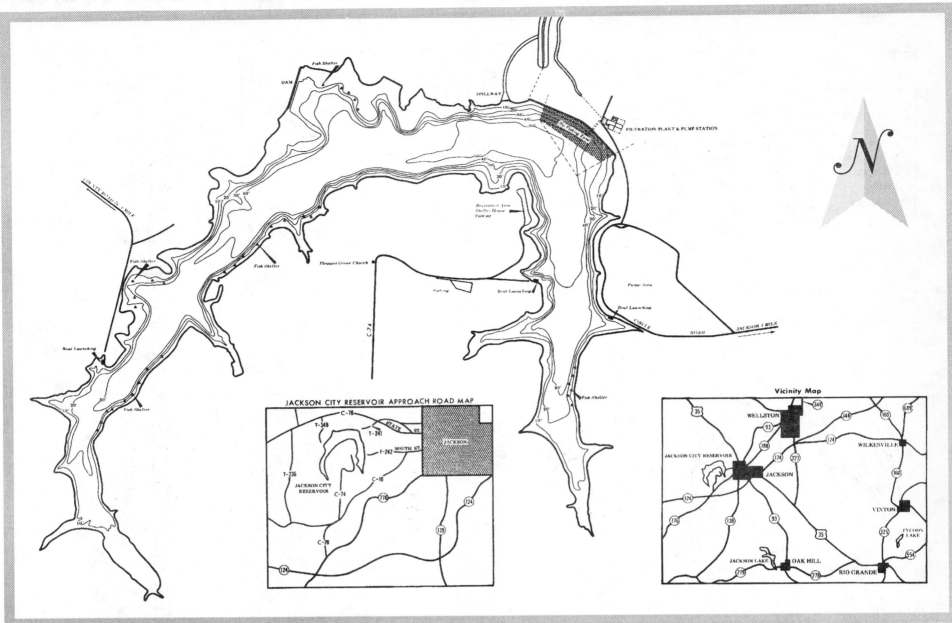

Location: In Jackson County, 1.5 miles west of Jackson. CR 76 (State Street) out of Jackson goes around the north side of the lake and CR 10 (South Street) travels around the south side of the lake.

Wildlife district office: (614) 594-2211.

Fishing opportunities: Bluegill, golden trout, largemouth bass, crappie and catfish.

Water conditions: Clear, few nutrients.

Bottom composition: Mud, some rock.

Horsepower restriction: Electric motors only.

Stocking: Trout and saugeye; channel catfish in alternate years.

Special regulations: Check slot limit rules on bass.

Depth: Up to 40 feet.

Outlook:
Bluegill, redear - excellent
Largemouth bass - excellent
Channel catfish - very good to excellent
Golden trout - excellent
Walleye, saugeye - good

Also known as "Hammer Town Lake," the lake was built in 1955 and is managed for fishing by the Ohio Wildlife Division. The lake was formed by a dam across a branch of Buckeye Creek. From the quiet horseshoe-shaped lake are beautiful vistas, very good fishing and city-owned day-use facilities. Several times during the last 20 years, the biggest bass taken in Ohio came from Jackson City Reservoir. Saugeye have been planted since the late 1980s.

How to catch 'em: Because of water clarity, Jackson City is difficult to fish. The big fish that are harvested from the lake are typically taken in February and March or October. Saugeye, which are more catchable than walleye in these conditions, are taken in good numbers and planted annually in the city-owned reservoir.

Jackson City Reservoir is deep enough to support a two-story fishery. The top story supports a good warm-water fishery, while the middle layer and deeper level possess the correct temperature and oxygen level to support cold-water species like rainbow trout. Rainbows are taken in good numbers in early March, especially after a few warm days and raising water temperatures into the high 50s. Bring light line and a lightweight spinning rod to fish the clear waters.

Largemouth bass congregate in the shallow coves close to deep water in the spring and can be encouraged by lively nightcrawlers. As the water warms, switch to spinners and work hard. Post spawn bass will suspend near long sloping points where deep-diving lures can get their attention. Local experts say topwater lures can produce exciting bites in the early morning or evening along the shoreline. If you are a midday angler in the summer, fish deeper, such as off dropoffs and rock shelves and bounce bottom lures and spinners along the humps and drops.

Jackson has excellent catfishing using the standard shrimp cutbait and crayfish in the shallower sections of the lake. Night fishing is considered the best time for catfish. Eight- to ten-pound catfish are common. Walleye are diminishing in numbers, but there are individuals up to 30 inches and 14 pounds. Saugeyes were introduced in 1991 and are in good numbers of up to 15 inches. Bluegill are above average in size (7-11 inches) and will take worms from May to July.

Hot spots: With good shoreline access, the steep shores have of vegetation along many areas. Work the rock shelves and sharp dropoffs with small spinners, spoons, cheese balls, roe or worms. As the water temperatures increase, fish deeper.

Look for water temperatures in the 60-degree range and below. Seven triangles and four squares of PVC-type devices near the west boat launch hold fish. Also try the PVC structure near the entrance to the large bay south of the boat ramp that is on the west side of the east curve of the horseshoe.

Underwater structure: In cooperation with the city of Jackson, some trees have been felled to add shoreline cover. Also, some interesting PVC pipe devices have been fabricated into Christmas trees and crib shapes in an effort to increase habitat. Because of the water clarity, you can easily locate the manmade structures. Biologists have surveyed the unique structures, and fish are holding and using the devices.

Boat launching: Three launches around the lake are useful for small, electric motor powered boats.

Insider tips: The Trout Festival is the second weekend in April. Early season trout fishing can be excellent; wait for those first warm days to trigger the fish in early March. Use light tackle and line in this clear lake.

Killdeer Reservoir

■ 285 acres of fishing water ■ 2.2 miles of shoreline WYANDOT COUNTY

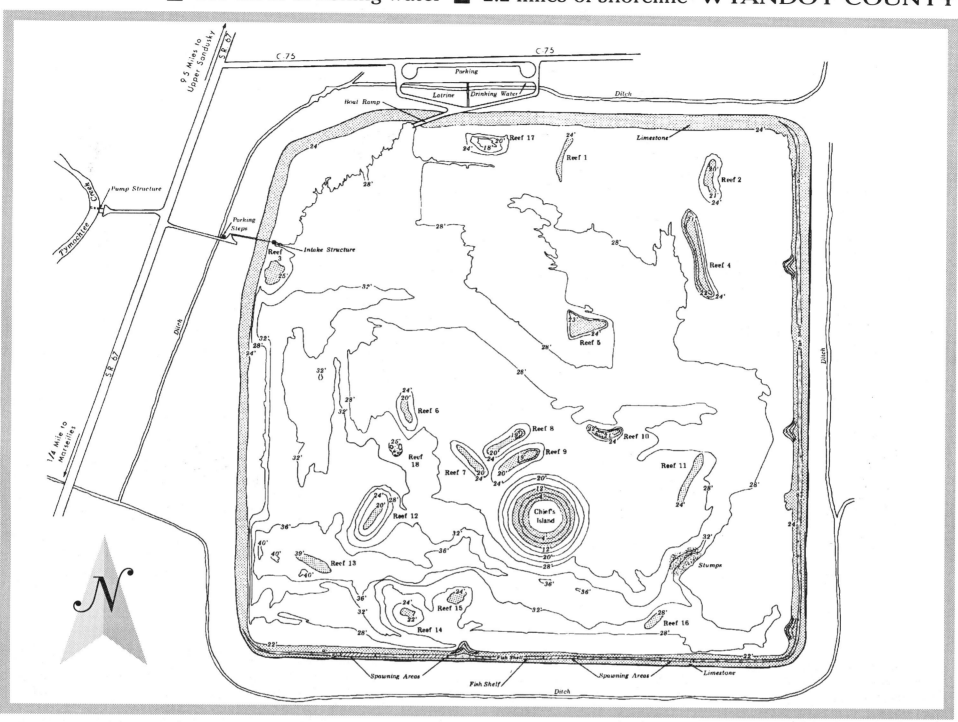

Location: In Wyandot County in the Killdeer Plains Wildlife Area off SR 67 near Marseilles.

Wildlife district office: (419) 424-5000.

Fishing opportunities: Bluegill, large- and smallmouth bass, walleye, channel catfish, yellow perch, bullheads, crappies and green sunfish.

Water conditions: Medium clear.

Bottom composition: Varied, clay, silt, reefs.

Horsepower restrictions: Electric motors only.

Stocking: Alternate years, catfish and walleye.

Depth: 16-37 feet.

Underwater manmade reefs.

Outlook:
Walleye - fair to good
Smallmouth bass - fair
Bluegill - fair
Channel catfish - fair

The square 2.3-million-gallon upground reservoir has a series of 18 reefs built into the bottom. They have a variety of cover on them such as gabion piles, rip rap rock cover, 22 tons of old tires and other devices. Fishery biologists have constructed the various reefs in an effort to learn more about which types of reefs are the best habitat and preferred cover. Scuba diving scientists have surveyed the man-made cover many times to determine which types are most effective. A few Christmas tree piles have also been placed along the edges, holding mostly yellow perch.

The unique reserve gets good natural reproduction on all species except yellow perch and walleye.

How to catch 'em: White twister tails are a favorite jig used around the many reefs for walleye and yellow perch. Spring is the best time to fish the reservoir that was built in 1971. Since most of the fishing reefs are in deep water, anglers get a chance to use weighted live bait and deep running lures, bright jigs and tails and even spoons. Smallmouth bass (average size 10-17 inches) hold mostly to the stone covered reefs, while bluegills congregate on the tire reefs and other devices. Bluegill (average size 6-8 inches) and crappies like the south shore and will hit minnows, small jigging spoons, larval baits and redworms most of the year.

Walleye fishing can be very good. Local experts recommend spinner and worm combinations along the shore in the spring and drift fishing crawling rigs and bottom bouncers in the deeper waters during the summer and fall. Largemouth often hang near the island and shorelines of the reservoir, especially along the shelves.

Hot spots: Spawning shelves are built into the reservoir along the east and south shores. These shelves are from 10 to 48 inches deep at normal pool. Bluegills and bass spawn here. Reef No. 17 is considered an ice fishing hot spot.

Underwater structure: They include 18 reefs and construction roads that were built and used as the reservoir was being built. These gravel roadbeds offer interesting cover. The bathtub-like reservoir is actually filled with many types of fish-holding cover that agrees with the fish population. Reef 17 is a topsoil reef and 18 is a boulder pile reef, while reefs 2 and 6 have stone-filled gabion baskets that extend four feet above the reef surface. Reefs 4, 7, 8 and 12 have tires installed in various designs on top of the stone surfaces. A few of the tire-based structures extend six feet above the surface of the reef.

Boat launching: The two-lane concrete boat ramp with tie-up docks and hard-surfaced parking lot is at the north end of the reservoir off C-75.

Ice fishing: This is good to very good for panfish. Walleye through the ice can be taken with a fluttering jigging spoon tipped with a minnow and trailing stinger hook. Some anglers recommend a treble hook as the stinger.

Insider tips: The adjacent green marsh gets it water from the reservoir. Use the map to fish the many reefs. Watch local anglers to determine which reefs are hot.

Kiser Lake

CHAMPAIGN COUNTY ■ 396 acres of fishing water ■ Five miles of shoreline

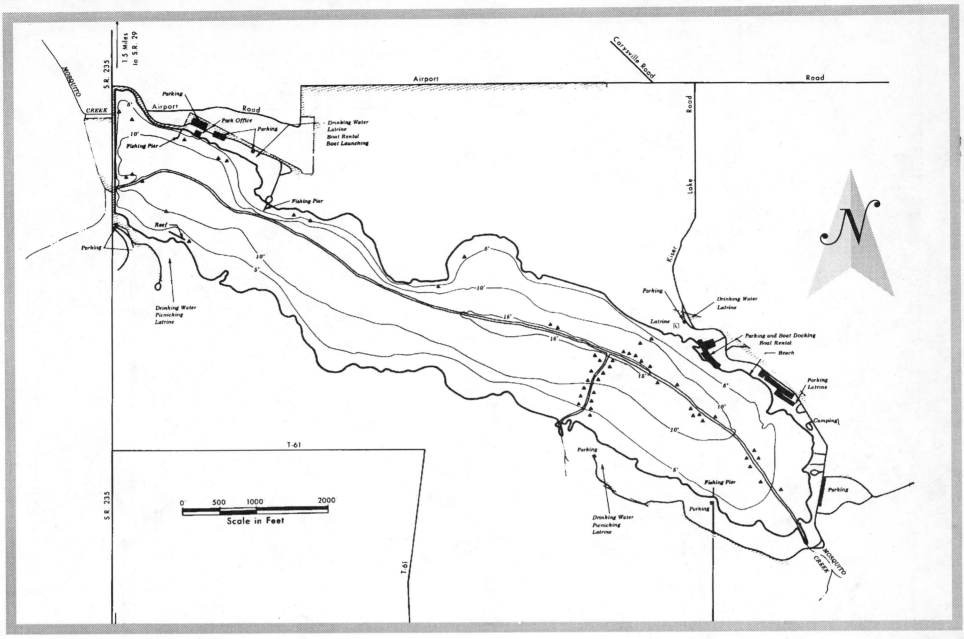

Location: In Champaign County, four miles northwest of St. Paris, 34 miles north of Dayton on SR 256. One hour west of Columbus.

Wildlife district office: (614) 481-6300.

Fishing opportunities: Hybrid striped bass, largemouth bass, channel catfish, crappies, bluegills and some walleye.

Water conditions: Average clarity, medium colored.

Bottom composition: Mud, vegetation.

Horsepower restriction: No motors

Stocking: Hybrid striped bass, saugeye and channel catfish.

Camping: 115 sites in the state park; call (513) 362-3822.

Two boat rental concessions.

Outlook:
Hybrid striped bass - good, improving
Crappie - good
Bluegill - excellent
Largemouth bass - good
Channel catfish - very good

Hundreds of proud workers from the WPA and Civilian Conservation Corps cleared the land which was to become the lake bottom. Unlike most dams in the state, the Corps of Engineers didn't build this one. The former State Highway Department constructed the dam, altered roadways and installed the spillways in the late 1930s. The 2.5-miles-long lake is named for John W. Kiser, who donated much of the land to develop the state park.

The lake is fished primarily for crappies and bluegill. The hybrid striped bass (sometimes called "whippers") fishery is improving as annual stocking continues and the shad population comes under control. Once the shad population is under control, other fish will bite better. The lake is well-known for bluegill and crappie fishing.

How to catch 'em: If you are a shoreline angler or a state park visitor, try the long manmade piers that get you into deeper water. From the piers, cast spinners and jigs with tails. From a boat, try to drift over the channel.

Hybrid striped bass are a schooling fish that move throughout the lake, rarely holding to structure long enough to fish. Local anglers are having success using chicken livers fished on the bottom for hybrid bass—as a bonus, you'll pick up a few catfish too. Largemouth bass can be taken from the bank or a boat. During the spring anglers can try small topwater and light-colored spinner baits around the stumps. In the summer or fall, concentrate on working around vegetation and in pockets between weedbeds. Largemouth average 12-18 inches.

Kiser Lake has a good population of 7-9 inch crappies that are often concentrated near shoreline cover or brushy areas. If you can find any of the old fish shelters, try jigging a minnow for crappies. Bluegill average 6-8 inches and are a favorite target for fly fishermen armed with poppers. Try casting a popper as you walk the gentle shoreline during the summer months. Cane poles and redworms are still an excellent combination for bluegills at the retreat-like Kiser Lake. Catfish are usually near the dam and along the south shore.

Hot spots: The north shore, which is state park property, is open for quality bank fishing. Weedbed pockets and near the dam are the primary hot spots. The state park has five accessible fishing piers. The park has built structure (brush piles) around the fishing piers, making them excellent places to fish. Try minnows and waxworms from the many fishing piers for the bluegills. The west side of the lake is best known for largemouth action; later in the summer some of these fish migrate to the southeast portion of the lake among the lily pads. Drag a black and silver spinner bait through the lily pads. Fluorescent colors also work well here.

Underwater structure: Two artificial reefs and Christmas trees have been placed in the lake. The lake has dense aquatic vegetation which gets heavier throughout the season.

Boat launching: The boat concession stand next to the state park office rents 14-foot aluminum boats. There are two state park ramps, one near the office and the other at the campground. Other ramps are around the lake. Small sailboats are popular at Kiser Lake. Most other boat traffic is rowboats and canoes.

Ice fishing: It's fair for panfish. Kiser is underused as an ice fishing destination.

Insider tips: The Kiser family willed the lands to the state and stipulated that no motors would ever be used on the quiet lake. The peaceful state park has hiking trails, camping, fishing piers, natural areas, a 600-foot beach and a small concession stand. Scuba diving is permitted as long as you mark your diving area and dive with a buddy. There are two state-operated concession stands on the lake.

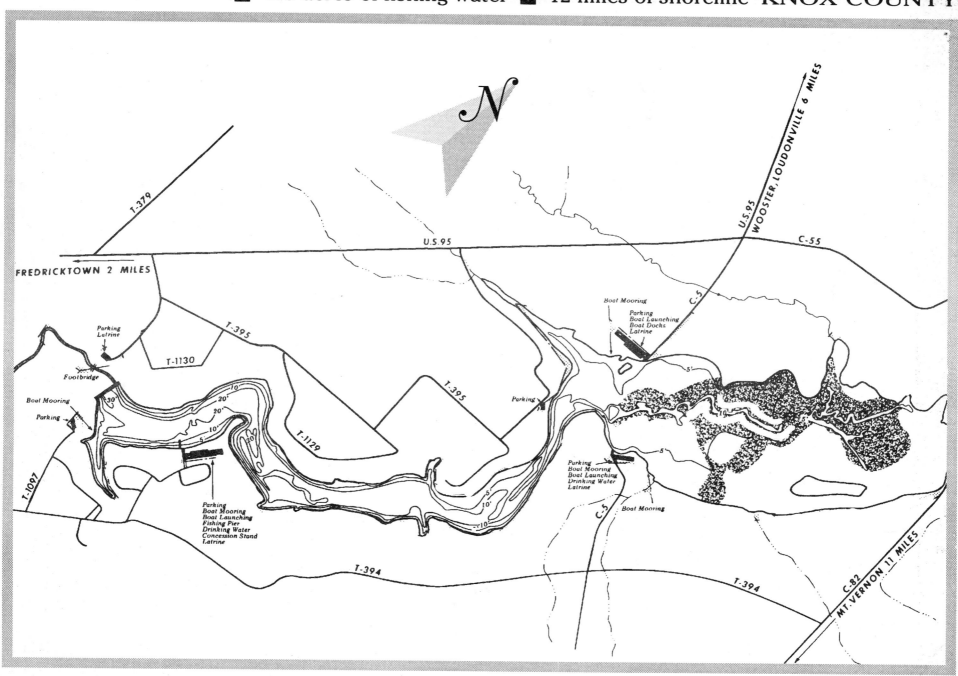

Location: In Knox County 1.5 miles northeast of Fredericktown via SR 95.

Wildlife district office: (614) 644-3925.

Fishing opportunities: Largemouth bass, crappies, bluegills, perch, catfish and muskie.

Water conditions: Clear.

Bottom composition: Soft, mud, organics.

Horsepower restrictions: 10 hp and electric motors.

Special restrictions: Bass must be 18 inches or longer to keep them.

Boat rentals.

Stocking: Catfish, muskies in the early 1980s.

Outlook:
Largemouth bass - excellent
Black crappies - improving rapidly
Bluegill - good
Channel catfish - excellent

Knox became a Division of Wildlife "bass study" lake in 1984. Because of the intense management, it is probably the best big largemouth lake in the state. This is a dynamite lake to fish, even if you don't have a boat. Knox Lake is definitely a 10 on my scale—almost any time of the year. The lake has a huge population of gizzard shad, which helps to accelerate the growth of largemouth. Many anglers also use shad-like lures and presentations. Best of all, Knox Lake is a quiet, interesting and peaceful place to fish.

The dam on Knox Lake was completed in 1954.

How to catch 'em: About half of the west lobe of the lake is flooded timber with a deep, narrow stream channel winding through it. This area is shallow and has lots of standing trees. This is one of the best early spring bass fishing locations in the state. As the water warms in this rich area, follow them to deeper water, sometimes all the way to the dam at the opposite end of the lake. Spinnerbaits, plastic worms and crankbaits are effect a big part of the year. White, black and chartreuse colors are popular recommendations by the semi-pro bass anglers who fish the lake heavily. These avid bass anglers work the woody shoreline cover and vegetated areas. The lake has a huge population of largemouth that run 10-18 inches.

Catfish anglers should fish at night and stick with standard baits, including ripe beef and chicken liver, gobs of worms or crayfish. Increasing numbers of bluegills (6-8 inches) are caught using worms around devices and any cover. Occasionally a medium-sized muskie is wrestled to the surface. Avid muskie anglers may want to concentrate their efforts on Alum Lake, near Columbus, where 40-plus pound fish are being taken from the initial early 1990s stocking. Black crappies are making a big comeback in the lake. Local experts say the lake is becoming a very good black crappie site.

Hot spots: The west half of the lake has been heavily managed and underwater structure placed. For bank fishing, head for the north shore boat ramp area. Structure is close to shore. Mid-summer, fish the dam end, at the fishing pier and along both shorelines extending east and west.

A few pike and smallmouth can be caught in the tailwaters. Fishing along the gabion baskets installed along the tailwater's shoreline is excellent. Several pools and riffles were created in the late 1960s.

Underwater structure: Sportsmen's clubs and the division have begun to place different types of structure in the lake and left overhanging trees along the shoreline. Both bass and crappies have benefited from the management activity. In the east end, about one-fourth of the trees have been felled along the shoreline to provide additional cover.

Boat launching: Two marinas with boat rentals and launching ramps operate on the mostly narrow lake. If you fish the east end of Knox in the spring, bring extra shear pins.

Ice fishing: Mostly panfish are taken during the hard-water months. Most of the action is in the central east end of the lake and most anglers use larval baits, tear drops and small minnows.

Insider tips: This is a premiere largemouth bass lake, with six- to eight- pounders taken with some regularity. Be careful of the stumps in the east end. Bring lots of shad lures.

Kokosing Lake

KNOX COUNTY ■ 154 acres of fishing water

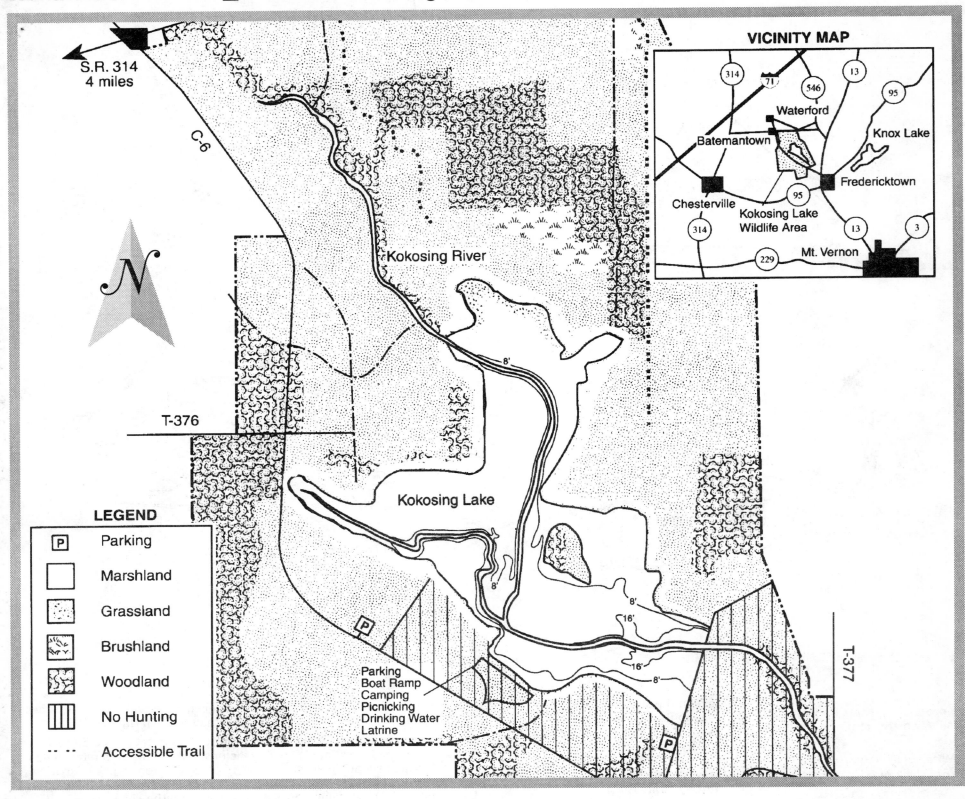

VICINITY MAP

LEGEND

P	Parking
	Marshland
	Grassland
	Brushland
	Woodland
	No Hunting
- - -	Accessible Trail

Parking
Boat Ramp
Camping
Picnicking
Drinking Water
Latrine

Kokosing River

Kokosing Lake

S.R. 314
4 miles

C-6

T-376

T-377

N

Location: In Knox County, 1.5 miles northwest of Fredericktown and five miles northeast of Chesterville. The lake can be reached by traveling two miles northwest of Fredericktown on Waterford Road (CR 6). 45 miles to Delaware. It's 25 miles to Mansfield.

Wildlife district office: (614) 644-3925.

Fishing opportunities: Largemouth bass, channel catfish, bluegill and crappies.

Water conditions: Colored.
Bottom composition: Mud, stumpy.
Horsepower restriction: 6 hp.
Camping: Managed by the U.S. Army Corps of Engineers.
Depth: Up to 15 feet at the dam.

Outlook:
Largemouth bass - fair to good
Crappies - fair
Rock bass - fair
Bluegill - fair

The Kokosing Wildlife Area is 1,113 acres of managed by the Division of Wildlife for fishing, hunting and passive use. The dam, small campground and day-use facilities are in the southwest corner of the tract north of County Road 6 and are managed by the Corps of Engineers. There is a five-acre island in the south end of the lake. A 1.5-acre pond lies in the northeast corner of the area, along with four acres of marsh. The area is carefully managed using crop rotations, mowing and food source plantings.

The site was constructed by the U.S. Army Corps of Engineers for flood control and recreation in 1971. The land has been hunted since 1969.

How to catch 'em: The lake has

lots of flooded trees and a diverse habitat. Because of the relatively small size of the lake, anglers can usually zero in on the branching creek channel and fish-loving depths near the face of the dam. The headwaters can be good for suckers and rock bass. A fair population of 7-8 inch crappies are best taken along the brushy shoreline or around fallen trees in the early season.

Some report decent spring fishing for bass against the island on the northwest side. Anglers also cast any type of spinners and fish along the gentle dropoff along the south side of the wooded island. A few 20-inch bass are taken annually from quiet Kokosing Lake. Fish the shoreline cover in the spring and along the dropoffs along the old creek channel during the summer.

Hot spot: The headwaters of the lake can be a good place for smallmouth bass.

Underwater structure: Flooded timber has been placed; there are no man-made devices in the lake.

Boat launching: A single ramp serves the small lake off County Road 6. Near the launch are a picnic area, drinking water, camping and rest rooms.

Insider tips: The fishing is fair to average on the small lake, but the hunting is reported to be very good. The major game are fox squirrel, cottontail rabbit, woodchuck, bobwhite quail and ring-necked pheasant. Waterfowl is abundant during migration. Kokosing is not a prime fishing destination, but it is near some medium-sized cities and located in a quiet managed wildlife area. Bring your binoculars, a picnic, and enjoy some fishing and poking around the nature area.

Ladue Reservoir

■ 150 acres of fishing water ■ 20.4 miles of shoreline GEAUGA COUNTY

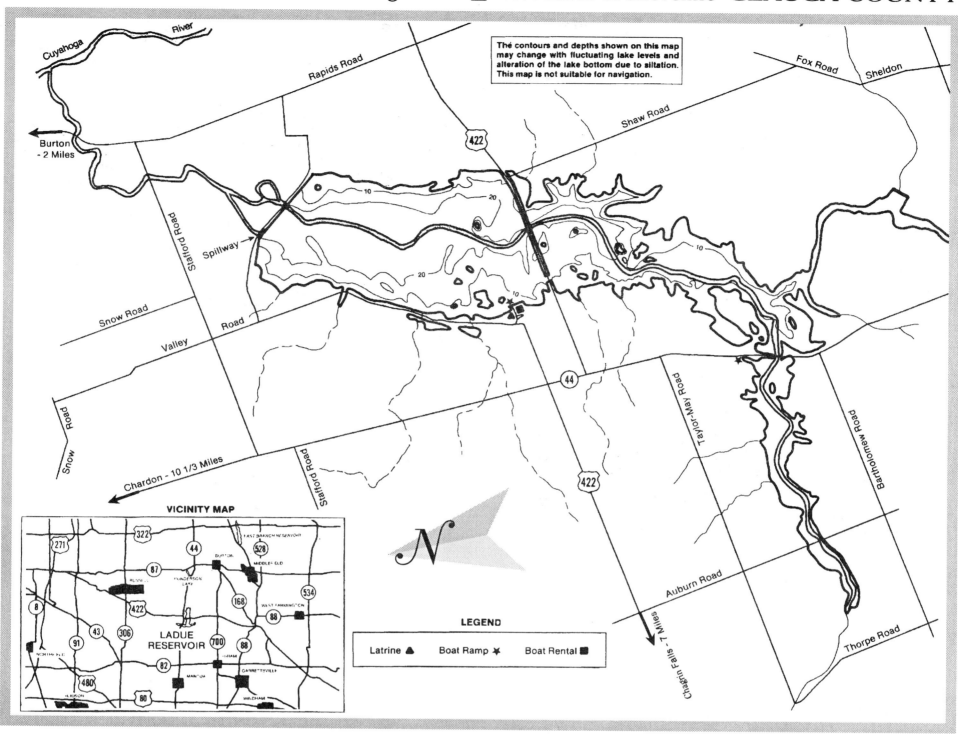

The contours and depths shown on this map may change with fluctuating lake levels and alteration of the lake bottom due to siltation. This map is not suitable for navigation.

VICINITY MAP

LEGEND

Latrine ▲ Boat Ramp ✷ Boat Rental ■

Location: In Geauga County, 30 miles east of Cleveland at the intersection of U.S. Route 442 and SR 44. SR 44 lies along the west side of the reservoir and U.S. Route 422 crosses the reservoir. It's 50 miles from Canton and 40 miles from Youngstown.

Wildlife district office: (216) 644-2293.

Fishing opportunities: Largemouth bass, walleye, crappie, channel catfish, bluegill and yellow perch.

Water condition: Medium clear.

Bottom composition: Clay and sediment.

Fishing is by boat only.

No shoreline fishing.

Permit required (small fee).

Horsepower restriction: Electric motors only.

Stocking: Walleye.

State record: Channel catfish, 38 pounds in 1992.

Outlook:
Largemouth bass - Very good
Walleye - good
Yellow perch - poor
Channel catfish - good
Crappies - improving, seasonal

Access to the reservoir is by permit only. Permits are available at the boat house, on Valley Road east of Washington Street, one-half mile east of SR 44. A small portion of the lake is restricted. The boat house is open April - October.

Ladue Reservoir was built in 1963 on a tributary of the Cuyahoga River to provide an additional water supply to Akron. The Division of Wildlife began managing the fish population in 1983. The area is in a region of glacial deposits characterized by many kames and small relict glacial lake and ponds. The lakes has good contour, with many humps and scattered weedbeds of milfoil and curly pondweed.

How to catch 'em: Late April and early May is a prime time for top-notch crappie fishing. Walleye hang off the many islands with still fishing jig and minnow or nightcrawlers.

There are good numbers of 15 inch and larger walleye. You can try trolling (with your electric motor). First-time visitors to the lake should concentrate on largemouth bass in May. Target the shallow weedy areas using small crankbaits and light-colored big-blade spinners. Largemouth bass run from eight to 22 inches and are found in good numbers. In the spring and early summer, the south end of the lake can yield some excellent largemouth catches.

Channel catfish are taken at night using scented or cut baits. Backwaters and stream tributaries can be good places to try, as can still fishing the channel. For bluegills, find the brush and go deeper as the waters warms. Good luck on perch. A few small yellow perch can be pulled from weedy areas and off dropoffs.

Hot spots: They include around the islands for walleye and north of the bridge for panfish and ice fishing. Some bluegill anglers like the humps and dropoffs near the east end of the bridge.

Underwater structure: Although there are no manmade structures, there are plenty of rocky points, contours, humps and scattered weedbeds.

Boat launching: Two ramps are on the west side of the lake, both off SR 44. A boat rental is at the ramp nearest the big bridge.

Ice fishing: There is little activity, and anglers are restricted to the northern half of the lake (north of U.S. Route 422). Walleye and crappies through the ice can be productive. Jigging spoons tipped with a minnow and outfitted with stinger hook(s) worked off the bottom is the best technique for Ladue walleye.

Insider tips: The largemouth bass population is improving and catches are excellent in the spring. Look for rapidly improving walleye fishing, due to heavy stocking and good habitat.

Lake Erie

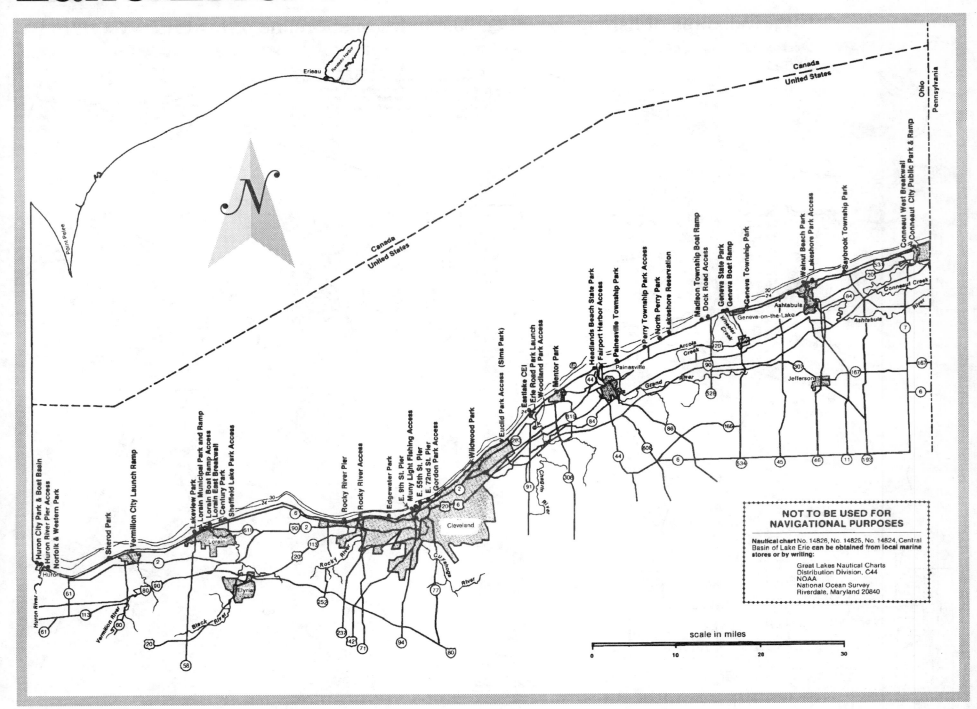

NOT TO BE USED FOR NAVIGATIONAL PURPOSES

Nautical chart No. 14826, No. 14825, No. 14824, Central Basin of Lake Erie can be obtained from local marine stores or by writing:

Great Lakes Nautical Charts
Distribution Division, C44
NOAA
National Ocean Survey
Riverdale, Maryland 20840

scale in miles

Location: Northern Ohio.

Wildlife district offices: Central basin (419) 424-5000, (216) 644-2293.

Fishing opportunities: Walleye, yellow perch, smallmouth bass, white bass, trout (steelhead and browns), some salmon (coho, chinook and pink) and freshwater drum.

Water conditions: Clear.

Bottom composition: Gravel, shale bedrock covered by mud and sand.

Horsepower restrictions: None.

Average depth: 56 feet.

All types of marine services along the coast.

Outlook:
Walleye - excellent
Trout - good
White bass - very good
Smallmouth bass very good
Largemouth bass - fair
Panfish - good to very good

You can't write an Ohio fishing book without mentioning Lake Erie. You also can't give it justice in the space we have. Sorry. Therefore, I want to merely give anglers a starting

point from which to find additional information and maps. From the telephone numbers above you can order a variety of Lake Erie publications including boating rules, status of the Lake Erie fisheries, fishing regulations, maps, how to avoid Lake Erie nets, information on fishing-related businesses, charts and charter boats, and much more. For a complete list of Ohio fishing publications write: Ohio Dept. of Natural Resources, Fountain Square, Columbus, Ohio 43224.

Lake Erie offers some of the most productive fish spawning grounds in the Great Lakes, especially the popular western section that includes more than 100 miles of shoreline and terrific islands just a few miles offshore. First-time anglers to Lake Erie would be wise to try this section bounded by Michigan waters to Huron, Ohio. From charter boats to fishing offshore and atop breakwalls, this area can be productive for all types of fishing.

Walleye: Lake Erie is the "walleye capital of the world." The best fishing is usually one to three miles offshore, over reefs and near islands, from June to September. Some walleye are taken up to 20 miles offshore, especially from Fairport to

Ashtabula. Fish from these waters tend to average larger than in the western section. Shallow waters near shore should be fished by drifting or casting weighted spinners with worms or trolling deep-diving lures. For the best results, troll deep-diving lures by flat line, downriggers or planer boards. Finding the depth of the fish determines your trolling method.

Smallmouth bass: Some breakwalls and harbors, especially around Kelley's Island, Bass Island and Ashtabula and Conneaut harbors, are excellent places to cast jigs, spinners or crankbaits. Try drifting live bait, live minnows, worms or crayfish.

Yellow perch: The best tasting perch come from Lake Erie where they are abundant year-round from piers, shorelines or boats. Most Lake Erie anglers fish minnows on spreaders for perch along a variety of locations including the Cleveland lakefront, dozens of piers, Cedar Point, the island, near the shoreline and up to two miles offshore. Perch fishing is particularly good near major rivermouths.

White bass: These schooling fish, once located, are easy to catch on small spinners and jigs minnows.

They can be taken up to four miles offshore, along warmwater discharges, over shoals and reefs and around the islands in May and June.

Trout: From steelhead to browns and coho, Lake Erie's trout and salmon fishing is best from September through April. You can take a charter or try locations that include the Cleveland lakefront, Rocky River, Euclid Creek, Chagrin River, Grand Rapids, near Geneva State Park and many other areas. Try casting or trolling spinners when the water temperature exceeds 40 degrees. In colder conditions, tie dime-sized spawn bags or small jigs tipped with maggots. Try other live baits, too.

Of course, lots of other species like largemouth bass, freshwater drum, channel catfish, chinook and pink salmon, crappies and even bluegills are in the clear lake.

Insider tip: Fortunately, the huge lake has had much written about it and there are many resources available for the avid angler. Visit your bookstore or library or write the wildlife division for tons of information on the lake.

Lake La Su An Wildlife Area

■ 14 Lakes ■ 82 acres of fishing water WILLIAMS COUNTY

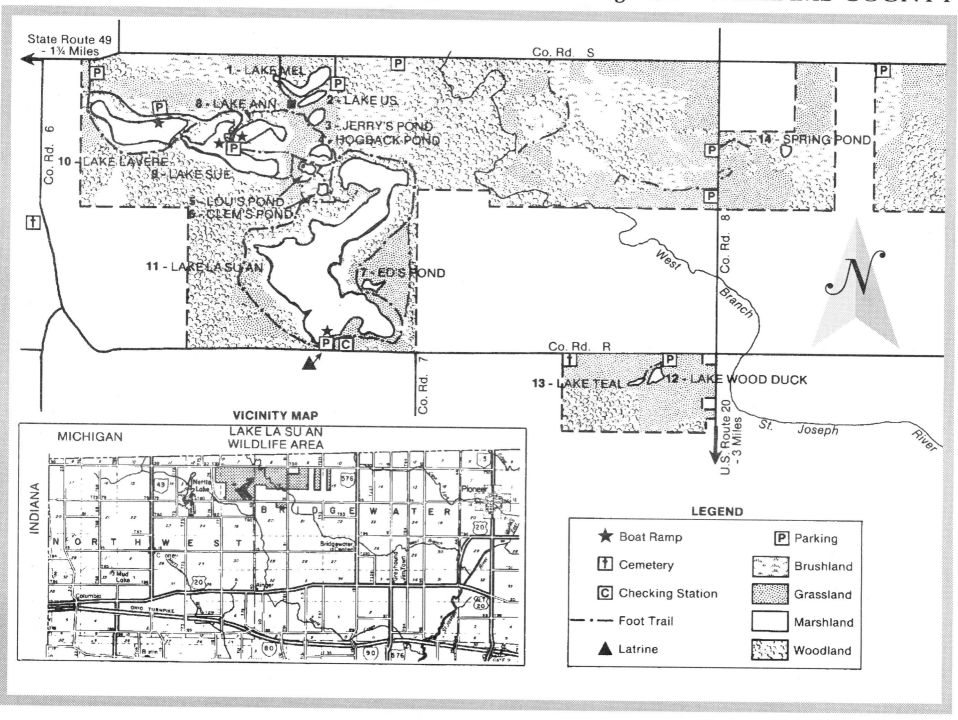

VICINITY MAP

LAKE LA SU AN
WILDLIFE AREA

LEGEND

★ Boat Ramp	P Parking
✝ Cemetery	Brushland
C Checking Station	Grassland
— · — Foot Trail	Marshland
▲ Latrine	Woodland

Location: In the northwest corner of Williams County. Williams County Road R provides access to the area from SR 576. The 14 lakes and ponds can also be reached by Williams County Road 7 from U.S. Route 20. It's 59 miles from Toledo, 41 miles from Defiance and 86 miles from Findlay.

Wildlife district office: (419) 424-5000. Fishing reservations and Lake La Su An information: (419) 636-6189 (voice and TDD-TTY).

Fishing opportunities: Big bluegills and largemouth bass.

Water conditions: Very good.

Bottom composition: natural, mud, soft.

Horsepower restriction: 10 hp limit on Lake La Su An; others lakes electric only.

Managed for "quality" bluegill fishing.

Special restrictions: Registration is required one week in advance to fish the six largest lakes. The permit is free. You are not required to have an Ohio fishing license. Each lake may have different regulations.

Outlook:
Largemouth - excellent
Bluegill - excellent

Lake La Su An Wildlife Area is on the Wabash end moraine, deposited during the Wisconsin glaciations. The area is mostly beech-maple hardwoods and wetlands. The gently sloping wildlife area is managed for hunting and top-quality bluegill fishing. The water areas range in size from one-quarter acre to 82 acres, and several wooded swamps from two to six acres.

The lakes are highly regulated and managed for "quality" bluegill fishing. Anglers must check-in and register to fish. This allows the state to maintain a high density of intermediate-sized largemouth bass, which keep the bluegills big. Many of the bluegills are a hefty six to eight inches in length. All caught fish are inspected and tabulated, allowing fisheries biologists to set harvest quotas and accurately manage the intimate lakes. Once the harvest quota is met, the lakes become catch and release only. The daily bag limits are designed to ensure fair distribution of big bluegills. All lakes are closed to fishing on Tuesdays and Wednesdays. Lakes are also closed certain days following holidays. Call ahead for details.

How to catch 'em: There's no better place in Ohio to fish bluegills. Special regulations, tight control and quality management have made the bigger lakes in this system excellent and pleasant places to fish. Some 11-inch 'gills are taken. Most are in the eight-inch class. The largemouth bass are average-size, but the catch rate is high. Anglers report catching and releasing 20 bass daily. State park officials says the big fish that come out of Lake Alma were usually taken on reds and yellow topwater baits.

Small jigs and grub bodies and worms are the standard baits for bluegills. Minnows may be used as bait. Fly fishermen can have a ball casting tiny poppers from early spring to fall. Routine bass techniques will work here.

The pretty little lakes, with hilly natural shorelines offer plenty of productive bank fishing and quiet scenery.

The nearby West Branch of the St. Joseph River also has good small- and largemouth bass, rock bass, crappies and northern pike.

Boat launching: The four largest lakes have small launching ramps.

Ice fishing: There is a designated season and ice fishing quota. Shanties must be removed each day. Call ahead for details about ice fishing.

Insider tips: The best bluegill fishing in the state! There are four campgrounds within eight miles of the lakes. Call the office for information on camping and motels at (419) 636-6189. Group reservations can be made to fish the productive lakes. If you catch a grass carp, which are placed in the lake to control aquatic vegetation, release it unharmed. This lawnmower-type fish eat their own weigh each day.

Lake Milton

MAHONING COUNTY ■ 1,685 acres of fishing water ■ 21 miles of shoreline

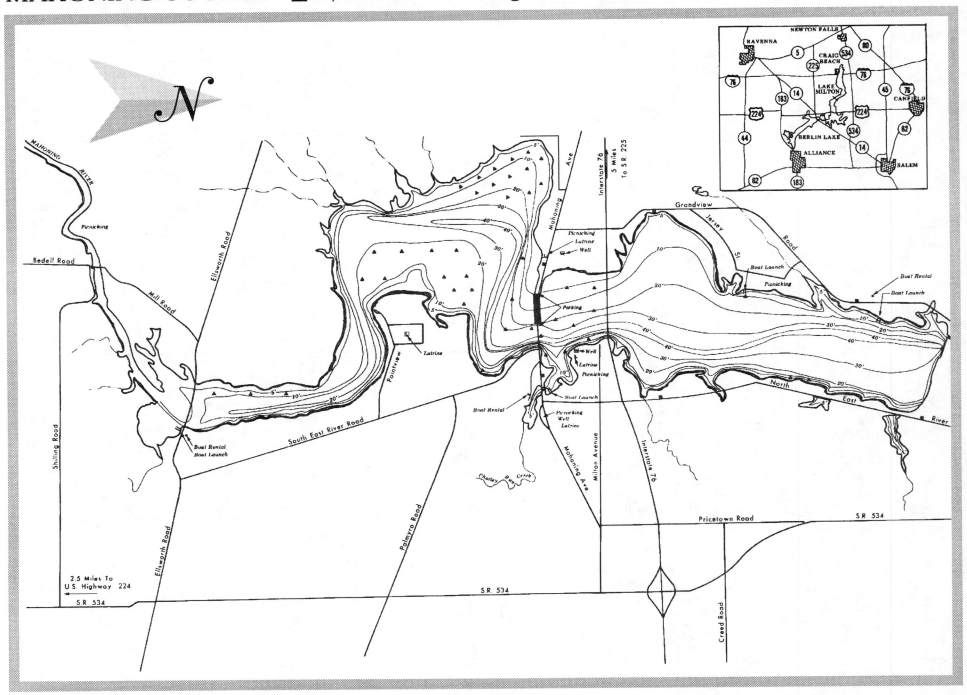

Location: In Mahoning County. Interstate Route 76 bisects the reservoir and SR 534 runs parallel to the lake on the east side. Youngstown is 10 miles east; Akron is 25 miles west.

Wildlife district office: (330) 644-2293. Fishing forecast, Miller's Marina, (216) 654-3081.

Fishing opportunities: Large- and smallmouth bass, walleye, muskie, crappies, bluegill and channel catfish.

Water conditions: Greenish, not muddy.

Bottom composition: Upper end is muddy; sand, gravel and some rock.

Horsepower restrictions: None.

Bait is nearby.

Outlook:
Muskie - good
Crappies - good
Largemouth bass - good
Walleye - good
Bluegills - fair
Channel catfish - good

In the early 1990s the lake was drained, the dam was repaired, and the fish traveled downstream out of the lake. The fishery was totally restarted, stocked with large- and smallmouth bass, walleye, muskie and channel catfish. Crappies and bluegills came in through an upstream reservoir. Both large- and smallmouth bass took well and are in good numbers. Muskie fishing is very good. Sadly, the walleyes have not responded well. An annual stocking of walleye is being considered. Crappie and bluegill fishing is fair to good. At this point, Lake Milton is a bass/muskie fishery.

How to catch 'em: For largemouth bass (average size 15.5 inches), fish the very upper end of the lake in the vegetation using spinnerbaits and plastic worms. Fish your spinners along the edges or drop them into the holes. Smallmouth are best taken on simple jigs at the causeway near the rocks or at the face of the dam, near the rocks.

The best place for muskie is at the upper end of the lake in the original creek channel in August and September. Try speed trolling with large baits. In the mid-1990s, an Ohio angler took the national record for the number of caught and released muskie in Lake Milton. About 160 fish were caught and carefully released by the avid muskie angler. His secret? Large crankbaits and troll fast, up to five or six miles an hour. Troll the baits close behind the boat, too.

Before the lake was drained, a 47-pound muskie (state record for the year) was taken in Lake Milton. The lake has the potential to produce some really big muskies as time goes on. Today, the average muskie is more than 20 pounds.

Crappies average about nine inches, catfish are about 16 inches and bluegills 6.5 inches. Bring your cane pole and can of redworms; the shoreline access is very good. Liver and shrimp will produce very good catches of catfish.

Hot spots: Try the upper creek channel for muskie, near the causeway for smallmouth. Also, find the rocky humps in the lake for smallmouth. Shore fishing from along the causeway is excellent (smallmouth, crappies, channel catfish and sometimes a walleye).

Underwater structure: The upper end is thick with aquatic plants. There are some gravel points and rocky areas. Wooden pallets, Christmas trees, tires, clay tile and big wooden spools were carefully placed in the lake when it was drawn down a few years ago.

Boat launching: The state park has two launches. Miller's Landing is off Mahoning Avenue opposite the park headquarters on the east side of the lake. Robinson's Point, off Jersey Street, is a barrier-free boat launch. Both modern launches are concrete and have parking. The marina is off Northeast River Road and has 75 seasonal slips.

Ice fishing: If walleye reproduction improves, so will the interest in ice fishing on Lake Milton. Some anglers panfish, but the lake is not heavily ice fished at this time.

Insider tips: Once owned by the city of Youngstown (built in 1916), the lake has some houses along the shoreline. Today, the area is mostly a state park that features sprawling day-use areas, short self-guided interpretive trails and excellent, gentle shoreline access. As the lake ages, the fish sizes will increase.

Leesville Lake

■ 1,000 acres of fishing water ■ 27 miles of shoreline MAHONING COUNTY

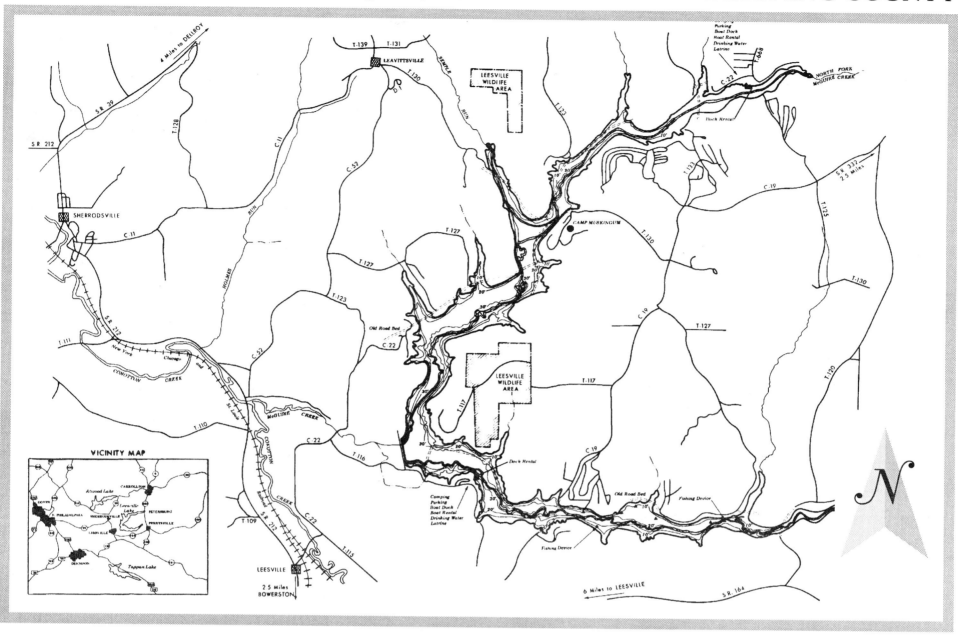

Location: In Carroll County between New Philadelphia and Carrollton. The lake is accessible by SR 39, 212 and 332.

Wildlife district office: (330) 664-2293.

Fishing report: Clow's Marina, (614) 269-5371.

Fishing opportunities: Muskie, northern pike, channel catfish, bullheads, large- and smallmouth bass, crappie, bluegill and yellow perch.

Water conditions: Clear.

Bottom composition: Mud.

Horsepower restrictions: 10 hp.

Stocking: Muskie.

Maximum depth: 47 feet

Campground: 200 sites; call (614) 269-5371.

Boat rental at marinas.

Outlook:
Muskie - excellent
Crappie - excellent
Largemouth bass - excellent

Leesville Lake is the top muskie lake in the state. The average muskie is seven to eight pounds, and 34 inches. But the potential is there for fish to reach 40-45 inches and weight more than 30 pounds. Many of these 30-pounders are reported

annually. The lake is managed for numbers, rather than trophy-size muskie. The Division of Wildlife wants anglers to go to Leesville and catch lots of fish, rather than trolling endlessly for a few difficult to catch trophies. About 2,000 8.5-inch muskies are stocked in the winding lake annually.

The lake, part of the Muskingum Watershed Conservancy, was constructed in 1937 on McGuire Fork Creek for flood control. The dam is owned and operated by the U.S. Army Corp of Engineers. There are about 2,700 acres of land surrounding the lake, some of which can be hunted in season. Campgrounds are at each marina; call (216) 343-6780. The lake is also near the Buckeye Trail, which is open to hikers.

How to catch 'em: Early and late in the season, most anglers take muskie by casting. By mid-season anglers should be trolling. Leesville Lake is in hill country. It is a narrow lake with long narrow arms, clear water and steep shorelines. There is only a small band of vegetation around the productive lake. A technique that is really paying off for muskie is night trolling. These anglers are taking some big fish. According to fish biologists who are in constant contact with muskie club members, the anglers are seemingly taking fish in all areas of the

lake. Apparently there is no pattern; the big predatory fish can show up anywhere. Try trolling from 11 p.m. to 2 a.m. This is a great way to beat the pressure and the heat.

Daytime muskie anglers will want to explore the upper reaches of the lake in the spring. As the water warms, move your efforts closer to the dam.

A fair amount of bass are taken by muskie anglers, often hitting bombers, hellbenders and other large crankbaits. In early summer bass anglers do well along the narrow bands of vegetation casting spinners or flipping plastic worms. Some report that evening topwater fishing for bass can also be productive. Bluegills are in good numbers, but undersized. Easy to catch, the 'gills are evenly distributed throughout the lake and can be taken by children from shore using simple worm and bobber techniques. The average crappie in Leesville is slightly over nine inches and will hit properly presented live minnows or colorful jigs, especially during the spring and early summer. There's no special trick to filling your bucket with catfish. Visit the butcher and buy some old liver, or try commercially prepared doughballs that smells like moldy dog food, gobs of worms or large dead minnows. The best action is at night.

Hot spots: Muskies can be taken all over the lake at night.

Underwater structure: Dropoffs, depth changes and the old creek channel are the primary underwater elements to key on. A handful of manmade fish attractors have been placed in the south end of the lake, but anglers must rely on their sounder or watch other anglers to spot small humps, breaks and points where fish congregate. Like all lakes, keep a eye on fellow anglers and remember where you see them catching fish.

Boat launching: The lake has two full-service marinas and one public launch ramp.

Ice fishing: Very little ice fishing is done on the lake. Ice conditions are often unsafe.

Insider tips: Because of the scenic lake's location, Leesville Lake is rarely too rough to fish. Trophy muskie anglers, those who want to troll for 40-pounders, should try nearby Piedmont Lake or West Branch Reservoir. The MWCD state record sucker came from Leesville. It weighed 9 pounds 4 ounces.

53

Lake Logan

HOCKING COUNTY ■ 400 acres of fishing water ■ 10 miles of shoreline

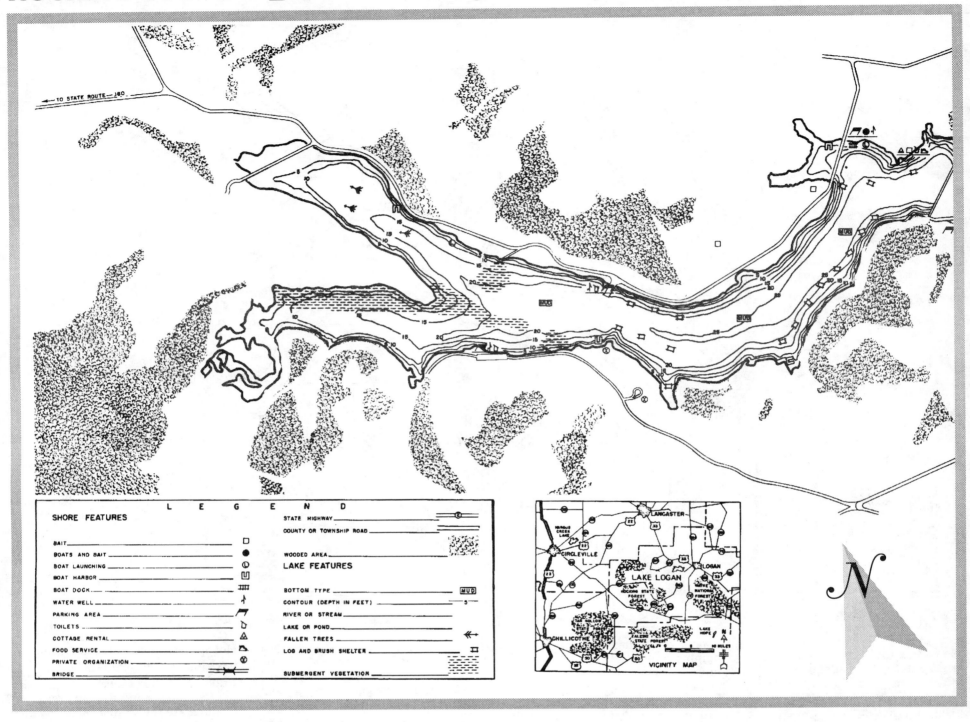

LEGEND

SHORE FEATURES

BAIT	☐
BOATS AND BAIT	●
BOAT LAUNCHING	◑
BOAT HARBOR	⨃
BOAT DOCK	�III
WATER WELL	⅄
PARKING AREA	⊐
TOILETS	⌀
COTTAGE RENTAL	△
FOOD SERVICE	⌂
PRIVATE ORGANIZATION	⊗
BRIDGE	⋈

STATE HIGHWAY	⊝
COUNTY OR TOWNSHIP ROAD	
WOODED AREA	

LAKE FEATURES

BOTTOM TYPE	MUD
CONTOUR (DEPTH IN FEET)	5
RIVER OR STREAM	
LAKE OR POND	
FALLEN TREES	⇇
LOG AND BRUSH SHELTER	⊟
SUBMERGENT VEGETATION	

VICINITY MAP

Location: In Hocking County, off SR 33, two miles west of Logan.

Wildlife district office: (614) 594-2211.

Fishing opportunities: Bluegill, largemouth bass, saugeye, channel and flathead catfish and crappies.

Water conditions: Clears over the summer.

Bottom composition: Firm to marshy and mud.

Horsepower restriction: 10 hp.

Stocking: Saugeye.

Camping: Two private campgrounds are nearby.

Boat rental operated by state park.

Bait and tackle is on the lake.

Outlook:
Bluegill - fair
Largemouth bass - fair
Channel catfish - excellent
Saugeye - good

A world record saugeye was taken out of Lake Logan in March 1993

(the record has been broken a couple of times since). The record fish was 31 inches long and weighed a whopping 12.42 pounds. Also, a former state record largemouth (10 pounds) was recorded in 1970. The lake is an average panfishery with good-sized sections of the lake brushy, making it a fun spot for spring crappie angling. There's lots of bluegills in Lake Logan, but most are pretty small.

How to catch 'em: Bass anglers will want to concentrate on the dam area and the shoreline of the upper end of the lake in the spring. The upper basin is shallow and weedy, with a soft bottom and scattered stumps. Try weedless plastic worms, jig and pigs and spinners. Largemouth have been caught in the 7-22 inch range, meaning there is good representation of several year classes.

Saugeye anglers should spend their time looking for the walleye cousin near the beach in the spring (late March and the beginning of April). These fish are in the beach area during this time of the year because of a yearly spawning response and the preferred substrate. Nearby deep water also keeps them concentrated here for this springtime window of opportunity. Bring an assortment of twister tails, minnows, blade baits and vertical jigs. Try trolling with crankbaits, like surface running Thundersticks. As summer goes on, experiment with plugs that imitate minnows. Lots of 5-10 pound saugeye are taken each year. Channel catfishing is excellent.

Hot spots: For saugeye, vertical jig deep submerged points.

Underwater structure: About 300 Christmas trees have been submerged in the lake over the years. There is pretty good structure in the lake, which is only 25 feet deep in most places. From the dam and spillway back halfway in the lake, the banks are steep. From there the lake bottom levels off to the upper ends of the lake, where it is marshy at Clear Fork and Duck Creek.

Boat launching: Two launches are provided on the lake. The main launch ramp, off Lake Logan Road at the east end of the lake, has two lanes and a courtesy dock. Also at

the east end of the lake is the boat rental which offers packaged snacks and rentals of pontoon boats, rowboats, pedalboats and two-person bass boats with an electric motor. The second launch is a single ramp northwest of the beach.

Ice fishing: Winter fishing is fair, although underfished.

Insider tips: Lake Logan was one of the first lakes in Ohio to be stocked with saugeye. After a slow start, saugeye have done well in the lake. Stocking was resumed in 1990 and is now done annually. A state park on the lake features a beach, hunting, hiking trails, marina and day-use areas but no camping. For more information call the state park at (614) 385-3444. In places, homes and cabins crowd the shoreline.

Lake Loramie

■ 1,500 acres of fishing water ■ 30 miles of shoreline AUGLAIZE & SHELBY COUNTIES

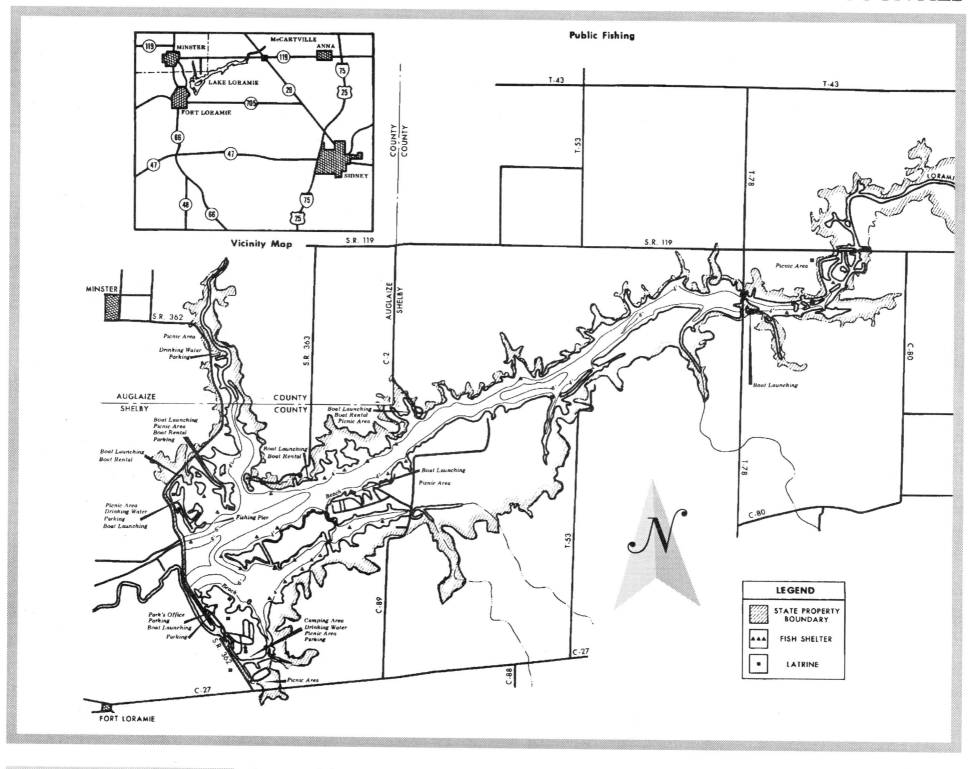

Vicinity Map

Public Fishing

LEGEND

	STATE PROPERTY BOUNDARY
▲▲▲	FISH SHELTER
■	LATRINE

Location: In Auglaize and Shelby counties, two miles east of Fort Loramie on SR 362, and six miles west of Anna on SR 119.

Wildlife district: (513) 372-9261.

Fishing opportunities: Largemouth bass, bluegill, crappies (very good), channel catfish (excellent) and bullheads.

Water conditions: Muddy, little visibility due to agricultural runoff.

Bottom composition: Muddy and shallow.

Horsepower restrictions: Unlimited; speed zones are marked.

Camping: 165 shady sites in the state park; call (513) 295-2011.

Shoreline: Gentle, great for family outings.

Outlook:
Bluegill - good
Catfish - excellent
Bullhead - excellent
Crappie - good

Largemouth bass - fair

Placid Lake Loramie was created when Loramie Creek was impounded in 1844. The narrow lake served as a feeder for the old Miami-Erie Canal. The watershed totals about 70 square miles.

Once a missionary, Peter Loramie came to the area in 1769 ready to preach, but quickly had to trade with the Indians after being cut off from the church. His famous trading post was burned to the ground by an over zealous Gen. George Rogers Clark in 1792. Loramie escaped with the Indians and moved west. In 1794, a fort was built on the site, which finally gave way to the western movement of settlers and the construction of lakes and canals to supply goods and services to the increasing population. Lake Loramie was one of five lakes in the area built to supply the canal with water. In 1917, the state decided to make the area a state park.

A fishing pier and plenty of flat, gentle shoreline make Lake Loramie one of the best lakes in the state to bring children to.

How to catch 'em: The muddy water will cause anglers to work hard, using bright colored lures. Crappie fishing is very good on the lake. Crappies can range from 10-14 inches. Most serious crappie anglers use small live bait, small jigs or spinners and fish the coves, small bays and around any stickups you can find.

The lake habitat is not great for largemouth, yet some fair catches are taken in the spring, when the fish will chase spinners. Run your lure around any pockets or structure.

Although not a sexy prey, huge brown bullheads can be taken easily anywhere in the lake. Twelve-inch-long bullheads are common. Late March is the best time to catch really big bullheads. Use nightcrawlers. While bullhead fishing, you may also catch a few catfish.

Underwater structure: A few brush piles and sunken Christmas trees are loosely scattered around the west half of the lake.

Boat launching: A launching ramp is off SR 362 at Black Island, north of the park office. The Luthman Road launching ramp is at the east end of the lake south of SR 119 on Luthman Road. It has 24 parking spaces and two lanes.

Ice fishing: More for sport than meat, ice anglers can produce fair catches of bluegill, especially at ice out. Few anglers ice fish the lake.

Insider tips: Kids can catch some really large bullheads using gobs of worms and patience. This is a very placid lake, surrounded by a quiet state park that is known for excellent camping and family recreation. The park has a 600-foot beach, 400 picnic tables and hiking trails. Bring your canoe.

Madison Lake

■ 108 acres of fishing water ■ 4 miles of shoreline MADISON COUNTY

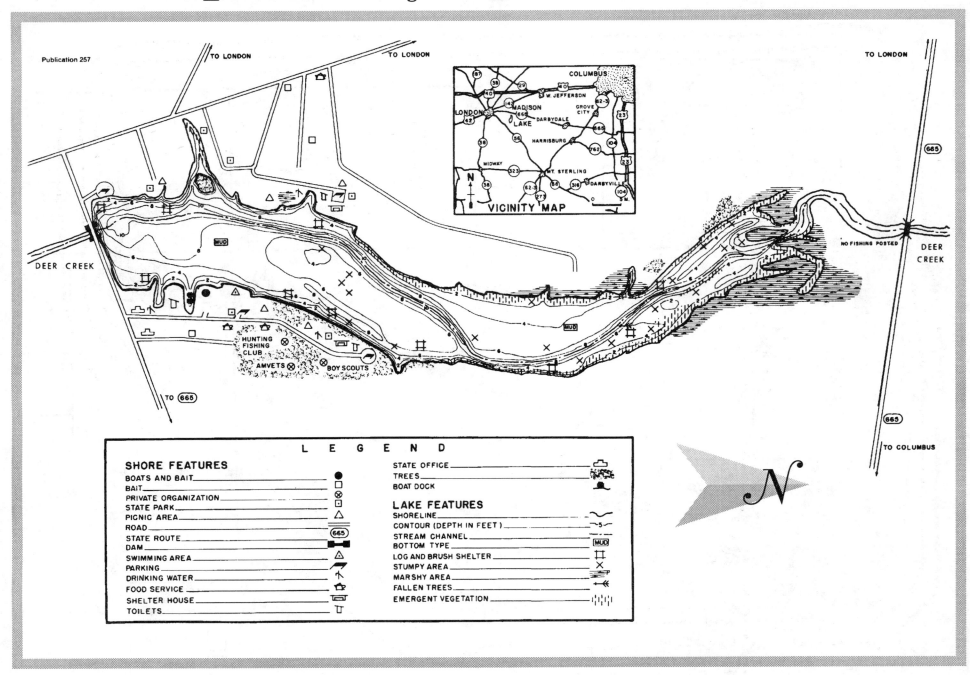

Location: In Madison County, five miles from London. Depart SR 665 at Spring Valley to the lake and state park entrance.

Wildlife district office: (614) 644-3925.

Fishing opportunities: Largemouth bass, channel catfish, bluegill, saugeye and crappies.

Water conditions: Colored.

Bottom composition: Mud, soft, some gravel and rock.

Horsepower restriction: Electric only.

Stocking: Occasional channel catfish; saugeye once.

Bait shop on SR 56.

Outlook:
Largemouth bass - fair
Channel catfish - good
Saugeye - fair
Crappies - good
Bluegill - good

The small day-use state park and lake are quiet. There is no camping and no full time state park staff at the lake, but there is a small wooden fishing platform that is great for kids who live in the area. Most anglers come for largemouth bass and channel cats.

How to catch 'em: Only one planting of saugeye has occurred in the lake, but early indications suggest future plantings could do well in the lake. Madison Lake is not a top-quality fishing destination, but is a relaxing lake to be enjoyed in a small boat filled with kids. The quiet waters will offer some good crappie fishing, especially in the spring.

A fair population of largemouth bass up to 18 inches can be taken in the early season along the channel or shoreline. Local anglers typically cast spinners against the shore with moderate success. In front of the small dam is also a place where fish will congregate early in the summer. Tossing weedless plugs at the shore or dangling a jelly worm when the water is cold are two techniques that might get the attention of a bucketmouth.

Hot spots: Shoreline and brushy areas hold crappies most of the year. Try live bait from the fishing platform at the state park. Large shoreline sections are soft and weedy. Try the rock side of the levee using minnows and night-crawlers. Try walking the shoreline casting spinners and plastic worms.

Underwater structure: There has been some structure added to the lake, but none in recent years.

Boat launching: A single small launch serves the lake on the southeast side along a cove.

Insider tips: Not worth a special trip, Madison Lake is a quiet respite for local anglers or those passing through who would like a quiet afternoon relaxing. The small state park has picnic tables and an unguarded 100-yard-long beach. Seven- to eight-inch channel catfish are stocked about every other year.

Metzger Lake

ALLEN COUNTY ■ 167 acres of fishing water

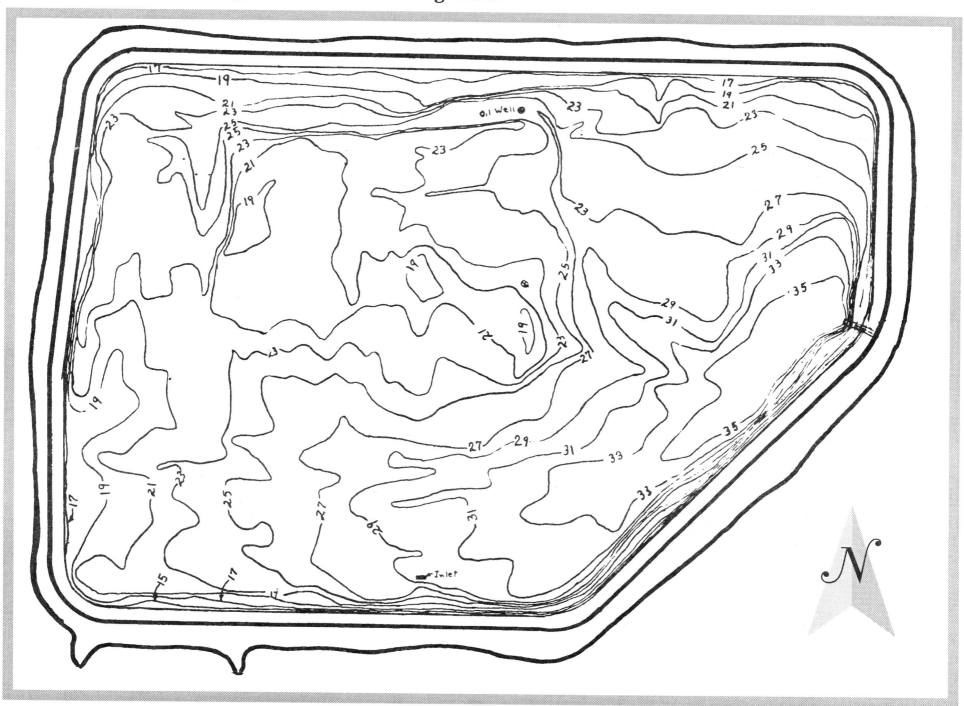

Location: In northwestern Ohio, near Lima and Ferguson Reservoir off SR 81.

Wildlife district office: (419) 424-5000.

Fishing opportunities: White crappies, yellow perch, bluegill, walleye, channel catfish, and small- and largemouth bass.

Water conditions: Clear.

Bottom composition: Mud.

Horsepower restriction: Electric motors.

Maximum depth: 20-25 feet.

Bait and tackle are nearby.

Outlook:
Walleye - good
Yellow perch - fair
Bluegill - good
Channel catfish - good

Metzger is a five-sided upground reservoir. Over the years Metzger has been known for extremely clear water, making the fish bright colored, but a bit difficult to catch.

How to catch 'em: Local anglers like to go after walleye with weight-forward spinners either drifting and casting or trolling. Use a count-down method when casting. A sinking Rapala minnow is also a local favorite. Walleye range in the 16-24 inch size. Because there are little spawning substrate and other factors, there are some large fish in Metzger. This is typical of many upground reservoirs that don't have much spawning.

Panfish are in fair numbers and heavily fished. Perch average 8-10 inches and bluegill are commonly 6-8 inches in length. Spring is the best time for both of these species. Later in the year, catfish up to 22 inches can be readily taken using commercial baits and chicken innards.

Hot spots: Because there is little structure, anglers have a good chance throughout the lake. Bank fishermen do, however, gravitate toward the southeast side, near the footbridge and near any places where the water moves, like inlets.

Underwater structure: The upground reservoir is built like a bathtub. The bottom is flat and there are virtually no humps or structure. This type of reservoir is sometimes called a "tubground" because of its featureless design. According to Wildlife Division biologists, future plans include placing some structure in the body of water. They will probably be submerged Christmas trees, tiles or pallet structures.

Boat launching: Only carry-on boats are allowed. There is no launching ramp—or plans for one—at Metzger Lake.

Ice fishing: Metzger is an older reservoir and receives light ice fishing pressure.

Insider tips: The area around Metzger, suburban Lima, is developing quickly. Ferguson Reservoir is south on SR 81. Try weight-forward spinners for walleyes.

Charles Mill Lake

■ 1,350 acres of fishing water ■ 34 miles of shoreline RICHLAND & ASHLAND COUNTIES

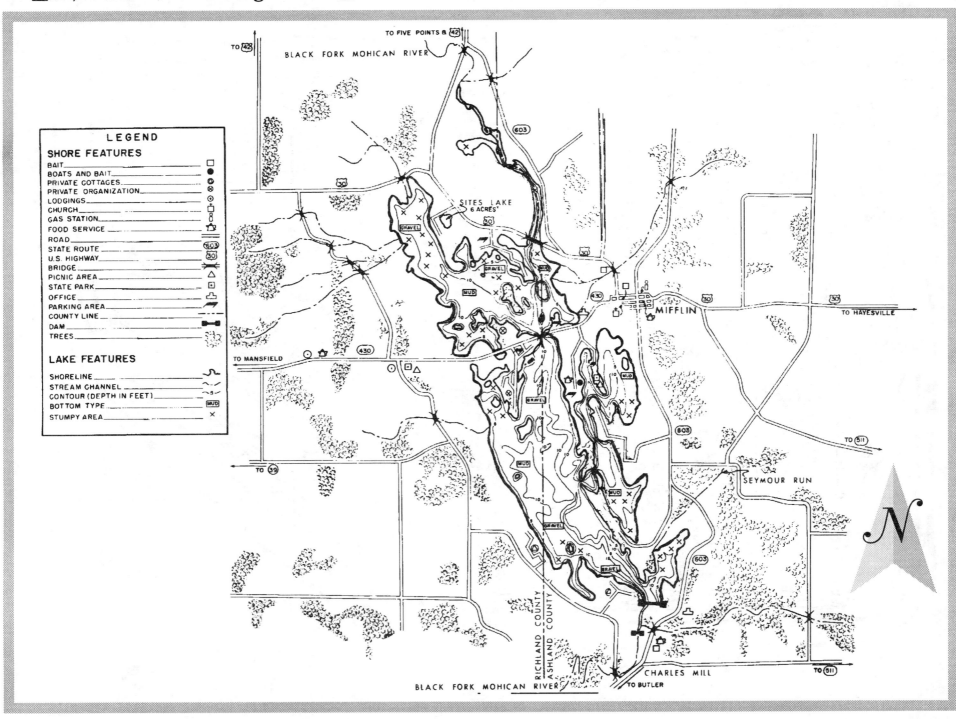

Location: In Richland and Ashland counties. Near Mifflin, SR 430 bisects the lake. It can also be reached from SR 30, I-71 or SR 60. Columbus is 70 miles south.

Wildlife district office: (419) 424-5000.

Fishing opportunities: Channel catfish, flathead catfish, bullheads, largemouth bass, crappies, bluegill and saugeye.

Fishing report: Charles Mill Marina, (419) 368-5951.

Water conditions: Turbid, colored.

Bottom composition: Gravel and mud.

Horsepower restrictions: 10 hp.

Stocking: Saugeye annually.

Maximum depth: 16 feet.

Camping: Charles Mill Parks, (419) 368-6885.

Outlook:
Crappies - good
Largemouth bass - good
Bullhead - good
Saugeye - good
Channel catfish - good

Charles Mill Lake is an on-stream impoundment owned and operated by the Muskingum Watershed Conservancy District. The dam was built in 1935 on the Black Fork Creek for of flood control. The dam is owned and operated by the U.S. Army Corps of Engineers.

How to catch 'em: The lake is shallow and there is a tremendous amount of underwater structure, especially in the north end. Crappies, which average 8-11 inches, relate to brush and shorelines, while good numbers of small 5-6 inch bluegills can be taken on larval baits along shorelines and in deeper water in mid-lake. Silting conditions have made the water shallower around some of the once productive islands in the north part of the lake. Nevertheless, fishing around the islands for largemouth bass can be productive. The colored waters demand bright spinners with big flashing blades. Pork rind trailers are also commonly used on spinners.

Saugeye, which do well in turbid waters, are found in the southern end of the lake and especially in the tailwaters of the dam during the winter and spring. The average saugeye is 12-21 inches, with many individuals larger. Try worm rigs, jigs and yellow twister tails and weight-forward spinners. Look for a good population of 12-24 inch and larger channel and flathead catfish.

Hot spots: Although the entire lake provides good fishing, the four-acre tailwater pool below the dam is a real hot spot. Saugeye anglers do well in these tailwaters using crankbaits, jigs and tails and jigs and minnows. Near the Rt. 430 and Rt. 30 bridges are also good locations to try. The best fishing in the lake is for saugeye, largemouth bass and crappie. Another excellent area of the lake is a bit hard to describe. Look for the narrows about halfway along the east coast of the southern half of the lake. This narrow channel takes you to a small pool, then through another narrow spot to a more open body of water. The pool and this entire area near the developed park offer excellent fishing.

Underwater structure: Complete

with plenty of natural structure, the state has also placed many Christmas trees. Fishing the jagged shoreline around the lake can be productive. There are many fallen trees and brushy tops that offer good hiding and feeding habitat for many species.

Boat launching: Be careful in some of the bays in the north end. There are a lot of stumps in lake, especially in the turbid north end of the lake, past the SR 430 bridge. The marina rents boats and there is a launch near the marina off SR 430. The marina is near Mifflin.

Ice fishing: The lake is not known for ice fishing, but it has possibilities as a crappie lake in the winter.

Insider tips: Hunting is allowed on the adjacent 2,000 acres of MWCD lands. A boater's swimming area is on the northwest end of the lake near the Sites Lake Cottages. The south half of the lake is the most highly used, with developed shoreline areas including a campground, hiking trails, cottages, sailing club and dam.

Mogadore Reservoir

Location: In southwestern Portage County, three miles east of Akron and six miles south of Kent on SR 43, one mile north of U.S. Route 224.

Wildlife district office: (216) 644-2293.

Fishing opportunities: Largemouth bass, bluegill, crappie, redear sunfish, brown bullhead.

Water conditions: Clear.

Bottom composition: Clay and sediment, weedy.

Permit required (small fee).

Horsepower restriction: Electric motors only.

Two small areas are closed to fishing.

Outlook:
Largemouth - good to very good
Bluegills - good
Bullheads - excellent
Redear sunfish - good
Crappies - fair

Mogadore Reservoir was constructed in 1939 and is managed for industrial water supply purposes. The waters are released on an as-needed basis through the Little Cuyahoga River, where it flows through the city of Akron. Waters are used by industries as needed. Mogadore is a great bass and bluegill reservoir. According to Division of Wildlife biologists, some of the best largemouth bass in the state come out of the Mogadore Reservoir each year. The clear, weedy water is a terrific habitat and a delight to fish. Bank access is limited. The lake is heavily fished, but the catches remain good.

How to catch 'em: Although known as one of the state's top largemouth and bluegill lakes, maybe just as much fun is to catch are the abundant big bullheads. Try still fishing with a nightcrawler. If you can keep the bluegills off your hook, you'll catch some really jumbo brown bullheads. Many of the bullheads exceed 12 inches.

An excellent panfish lake, Mogadore has a ton of 'gills that average six to seven inches in length. Bluegill and redear sunfish (average size nine to 12 inches) can be readily taken on worms and larval baits. Some anglers use cane poles to reach into the weedbeds. Crappies (average size is eight inches) haunt the stumpy areas, especially in the spring and summer, and can be brought into the creel on a live minnow and bright jigs.

Most of the largemouth are 12-15 inches, with some exceeding five pounds. Successful anglers cast surface lures and spinners at the shoreline, retrieving at a moderate speed. Keep your lure in the strike zone, working parallel to weedbeds, casting next to tall weeds and across bars. Work your mid-depth lures along ledges and skim the tops and edges of weed clumps. Local experts say shallow dropoffs can also hold largemouth looking for lunch. Try a rubber worm or rattle traps at weedy points. Fly fishermen might want to try deer-hair poppers in the spring and warm summer evenings.

Hot spots: This is a beautiful lake, with lots of pine plantings, near Akron. Find the weed points and places where weeds drop off to flats or bars.

Underwater structure: The thick weedbeds are the structure of note, offering still fishing and topwater action in the spring. Bring your buzz baits.

Boat launching: Three launching ramps, complete with nearby latrines and drinking water, are spread out around the jagged lake. Mostly small fishing boats ply the waters, although some big bass boats sneak around powered only by an electric trolling motor.

Ice fishing: Popular, in fact, the parking lots can be filled on warm winter weekends. This is one of the busiest ice fishing lakes in this part of the state. All of these anglers are after bluegills. Many anglers set their shanties over six-foot-deep water. With the amazingly clear water, you can look down the hole and almost pick the fish you want to catch—hanging a waxworm right in front of its nose.

Insider tips: Huge bullhead, I mean HUGE bullhead—try fishing for them. It's this lake's best kept secret. A rare muskie is taken at the lake.

Monroe Lake

■ 39 acres of fishing water MONROE COUNTY

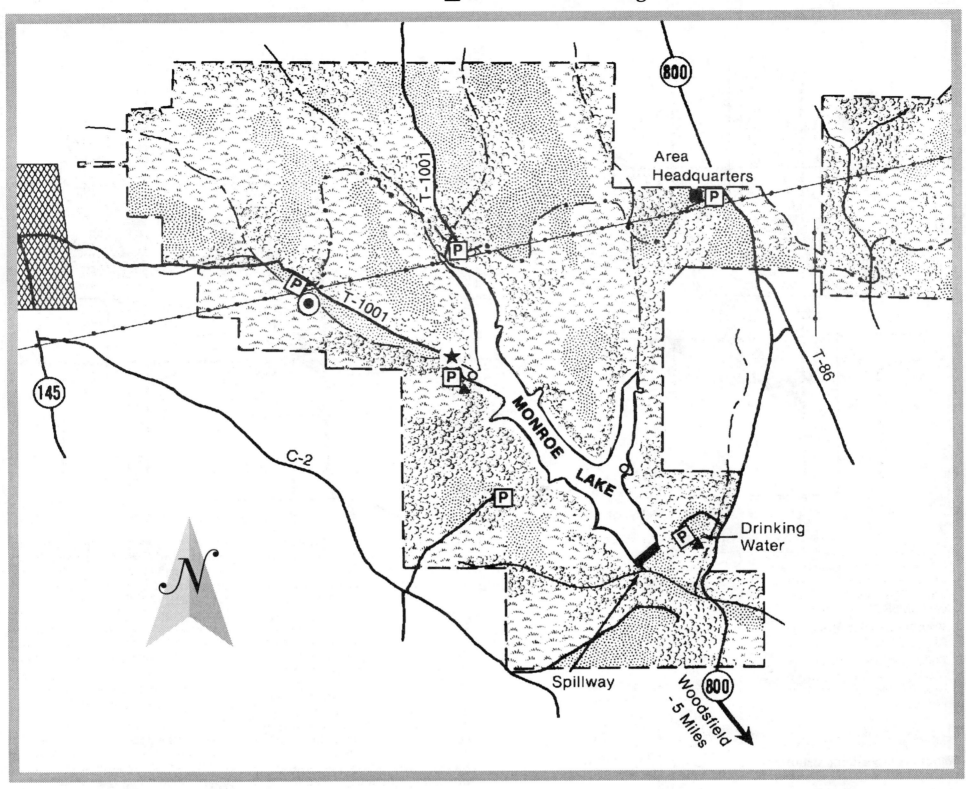

Location: In Monroe County, on both sides of SR 800, five miles north of Woodsfield, 86 miles from Canton, 43 miles from Cambridge and 13 miles from Barnesville.

Wildlife district office: (614) 594-2211.

Fishing opportunities: Largemouth bass, channel catfish, crappie, bluegill, sunfish, brown bullhead and bluegills.

Water conditions: Medium colored to fairly clear.

Bottom composition: Soft, mud.

Horsepower restriction: Electric motors only.

Stocking: Golden trout and channel catfish.

Special regulation: Check the slot limit on bass.

Outlook:
Bluegill, redear - good
Largemouth bass - fair
Channel catfish - excellent
Golden trout - good

The lake is surrounded by a 1,333-acre wildlife area is in a steeply rolling region typical of this unglaciated part of the state. Steep wooded slopes descend to narrow valleys, on which the lake is impounded. The golden trout stocking is basically a put and take fishery. Most of the stocked trout run 10-12 inches. These trout are fished heavily for a month or so, then the lake is only lightly fished afterward.

The lake is basin-like, steep-sided, deep, and cold enough for trout. The deep accessible water allows for some good shoreline fishing for planted trout and other species.

How to catch 'em: The golden trout are known to hit yellow spinners, corn and little balls of Velvetta-brand cheese. Few anglers night

fish with a lantern, but it could be a very good technique on the stocked trout. The lantern brings the fish to the surface, where you then merely jig a simple bait in front of the illuminated fish.

Depending on the season, bass fishing can be fair to good, and they will hit typical presentations of spinners and live baits. The water can be colored, so bright lures are suggested. Bluegills are heavily populated and high quality, with the average size from 6-8.5 inches. Redear sunfish are seen up to nine inches.

Channel catfish are stocked, with many fish in the 10-20 inch range. Both bays, at the north end, are considered great spring through fall spots for good catfish action. Local experts say simple stinkbaits and gobs of nightcrawlers fished on the bottom is still the best technique.

Hot spots: The upper reach of the two arms are good fishing in the spring; move in front of the dam as

the water warms. The small size of the lake allows local and visiting anglers to learn the lake quickly. Mid-lake at the point is always a good bet for full season action.

Underwater structure: More than 200 Christmas trees were submerged in the lake in the late 1980s.

Boat launching: A single ramp for small boats is on the west side of the Y-shaped lake. A small boat mooring site is on the lake.

Ice fishing: Some years the lake gets suitable ice and the fishing is considered good.

Insider tips: A primitive camping area and single latrine are offered at the wildlife area. The area also offers managed hunting for small game, waterfowl and deer.

Mosquito Lake

TRUMBULL COUNTY ■ 7,850 acres of fishing water ■ 40 miles of shoreline

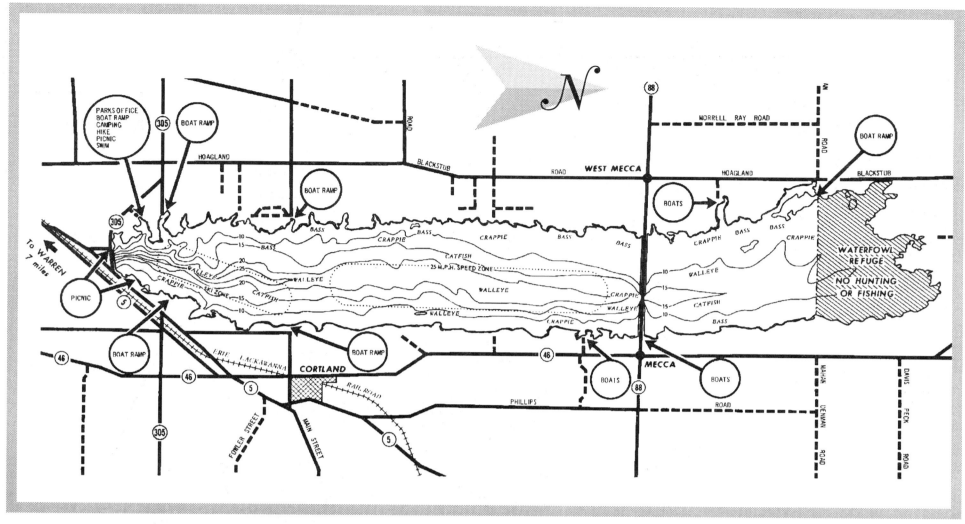

Location: In Trumbell County, 30 minutes from Youngstown and one hour from Cleveland. From SR 45 north of Warren, turn east on SR 305 to the lake.

Wildlife district office: (330) 664-2293.

Fishing opportunities: Walleye, black and white crappies, bluegill, channel catfish and northern pike.

Water conditions: Dark.

Bottom composition: Sandy and muddy.

Horsepower restrictions: None; check speed zones and limits.

Stocking: Walleye annually by the millions.

Camping: 224 sites in the state park; call (219) 637-2856.

Many nearby tackle shops near causeway.

Nearby boat rentals and private marinas.

Special regulations: Check regulations on trot and float lines.

No fishing is allowed in the wildlife area.

Outlook:
Walleye - excellent
Crappies - excellent
Bluegill - excellent
Northern pike - fair

The U.S. Army Corps of Engineers built the rectangular lake by damming Mosquito Creek nine miles upstream from Niles. The primary purposes of the 1944 project were flood control, domestic water sup-

ply and discharge regulation for an industrial water supply and pollution dilution. Recreation and fishing, which is actually a secondary use, is popular.

The lake has an uncontrolled natural spillway. Throughout much of the year water flows south of the reservoir into the Mahoning Valley, but when the lake reaches an elevation of 904 feet above sea level, the flow reverses. Water spills out of the north end into a tributary of the Grand River to eventually reach Lake Erie. The north end of the lake is a designated waterfowl game refuge. The lake can be windswept and rough.

How to catch 'em: Mosquito Lake is one of the best walleye lakes in northeast Ohio (maybe second to Pymatuning, which is jointly owned with Pennsylvania). The lake is also an excellent crappie fishery. Three species are trophy candidates in the lake—include walleye, northern pike (native population, up to 18 pounds) and flathead catfish (up to 40 pounds). Walleye anglers can have a tough time on Mosquito due to dark water and little underwater relief. This is not a northern-style lake with clear water and a rocky or gravel bottom. Further, there are few humps and rock piles in the lake. Early in the season local walleye experts take them out of the vegetation or near wave-washed shores on jigs and minnows. Midseason, anglers take suspended marble eyes at mid-lake. Remember, walleye move, so should you as the water warms. The average size of walleye kept by anglers is 15 inches.

Mosquito is an average largemouth

bass lake, with most of the fish taken in deeper water over the old stream channel in the north. Cast spinners and crankbaits around the stumps. Try casting past the stump. When just past the stump hesitate momentarily and allow the bait to settle, then continue to retrieve at a moderate pace. Another local favorite cited in the Division of Wildlife map is to use a sliding bobber on a casting line. A stop knot is tied so that the bait will be at the desired depth and the bobber free to slide down to a small lead sinker. Below this is a short section of leader bearing a 1/0 hook baited with a large minnow.

Serious crappie (average size is 10 inches) anglers fish early in the season along the causeway. Here schools of crappie can congregate in submerged brush or along dropoffs. When fishing from a boat, anchor as soon as you've caught the first one; you are likely on a school typically in 10-20 foot deep water. For bluegills, which are usually in the 6-9 inch range, try redworms and maggots or rubber spiders in the bays along the causeway. White bass anglers can toss small spoons, white bucktail, white spinners or white flies. Yellow perch are evenly distributed, but you will find most of them in the deepest waters, early. Catfish will respond to commercial baits, big dead minnows, smelly shrimp and chicken innards.

Hot spots: Pike fishing can be great, but you've got to probe the shallows early with spoons and spinners. The lake has good natural reproduction of predators. Bring your heavy fly rod and streamers for some real

fun in the spring on aggressive pike. Walleye and flathead catfish anglers should concentrate their efforts in the area south of the causeway. The area north of the causeway is better for crappie. Check the weedbeds at the south end of the lake, along the coves and points. These areas are excellent for early season walleye.

Underwater structure: Because of the lake's shallowness, little manmade structure has been introduced.

Boat launching: There are at least eight launching ramps evenly scattered around the large lake. Some charge a user fee. The state park operates two ramps. The largest, which is in the park, has six lanes and parking for several hundred cars; the other park ramp is at the west end of Main Street in Cortland in the southeast corner of the lake. Boating and fishing are banned in the wildlife area.

Ice fishing: The lake is popular for walleye and crappies. For walleye, fish on the bottom using a bright jigging spoon tipped with a minnow and a stinger hook. Flutter the light-colored spoon on the bottom and move often.

Insider tips: Mosquito Lake State Park has a 224-site campground, 600-foot swimming beach, picnic areas, two miles of hiking trails and a six-lane launching ramp. Boaters should remember that the lake is large and shallow, and can get rough quickly. The rural lake is surrounded by public lands; there are no cottages or private docks.

Nettle Lake

■ 94 acres of fishing water ■ 3.5 miles of shoreline WILLIAMS COUNTY

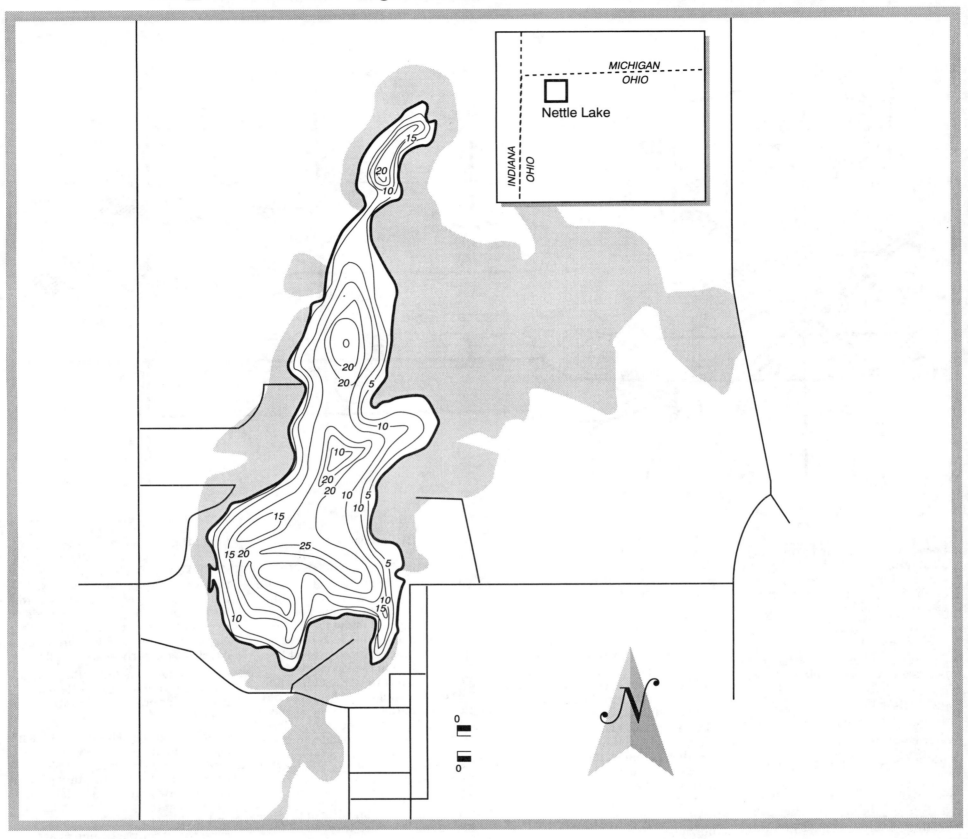

Location: In Williams County, northwest Ohio. One mile east of Route 49 on Q50 Road.

Wildlife district office: (419) 424-5000.

Fishing opportunity: Largemouth bass, black and white crappie, bluegill and channel catfish.

Water conditions: Medium to dark.

Bottom composition: Mud.

Horsepower restrictions: None.

Camping: On the lake.

Outlook:
Largemouth bass - good
Crappie - excellent
Bluegill - good
Channel catfish - good

Nettle Lake is a natural glacial pot-
hole-like lake with lots of cover. The lake has significant weeds and lily pads. Most of the shoreline is privately owned. There are more lily pads on Nettle Lake than any other lake in the district. The scenery is great—gently floating lily pads and scatterings of cattails.

How to catch 'em: Nettle Lake is a decent place to catch panfish and largemouth bass. Locals say skimming topwater lures over and near the lily pads is a great way to spend an evening. During the day, other anglers try flipping plastic worms and crawling rubber frogs over the pads and between the rooted vegetation. Most of the bass are in the 12-23 inch range.

Good populations of easy-to-catch white and black crappies are in the 6-13 inch size. Evenly distributed, crappie anglers suggest waxworms

and redworms as the preferred baits at Nettle Lake. Bluegills are a bit small, often only six to seven inches, but they are fun during the spring. A good population of 14-24 inch channel catfish can be taken throughout lake. Many experienced catfishermen probe the east bank with cut and stinkbaits. A few yellow perch are taken in the deep spots.

Hot spots: For bass, fish any lily pad cover you can find. Cast spinner baits from a canoe for fast action most of the season. The north end of the busy lake has some deep spots, humps and gentle drops. Shoreline access is limited. The entire shoreline is developed and public access is limited for fishing and boat launching.

Underwater structure: No man-made structure has been placed in

the lake; however, there is good natural cover including rooted and floating vegetation and bottom humps. Docks also provide good fish cover and places to cast at with spinners.

Boat launching: There is no public boat access, but you can go to a marina and pay a reasonable launching fee at two private ramps.

Ice fishing: Very little ice fishing occurs on the heavily populated lake.

Insider tips: Once in a while, a walleye is caught, a remnant of a stocking effort several years ago. Bring your canoe and topwater lures for a warm summer evening catching bass.

New London Reservoir

HURON COUNTY ■ 220 acres of fishing water ■ 2.6 miles of shoreline

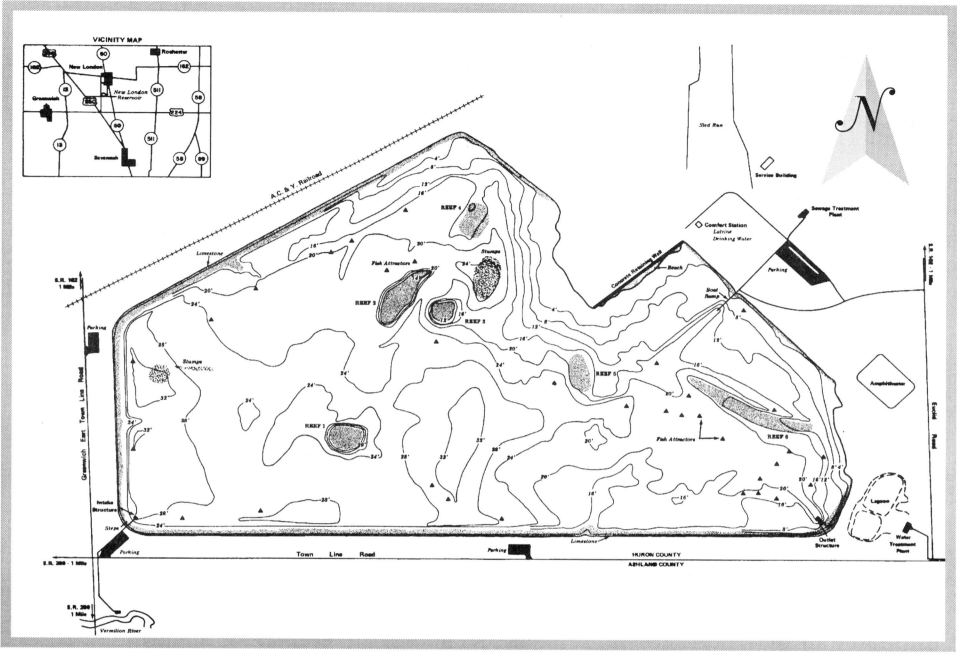

Location: In Huron County, one mile east of U.S. Rt. 250 on Town Line Road, next to the Vermillion River.

Wildlife district office: (419) 424-5000.

Fishing opportunities: Walleye, yellow perch, rock bass, channel catfish, bluegill, sunfish, bullheads, suckers, white crappies and large- and smallmouth bass.

Water conditions: Clear.

Bottom composition: Mud, soft.

Horsepower restrictions: Electric only.

Maximum depth: 35 feet.

Average depth: 22 feet.

Outlook:
Walleye - good
Yellow perch - fair
Rock bass - excellent
Channel catfish - good
Bluegill - fair
White crappie - fair
Large- and smallmouth bass - good

New London Reservoir is an upground reservoir with steep rip rap banks and very good natural reproduction of most species. The reservoir was built in 1975 into the side of a hill by engineers and biolo-gists that were sensitive to the needs of various underwater structure and spawning areas. During excavation a number of fish concentrating and attractor devices were built or left in the reservoir.

How to catch 'em: Although not a trophy lake, New London offers some fine fishing, even during the heat of the summer.

During the spring local anglers run deep-diving lures along the reefs at the deep end of the lake. Try jig-type baits over these deep areas for smallmouth, bluegills and crappies. Good numbers of 10-18 inch small-mouth are also present on all the stone-surface reefs, while bluegill tend to hang near the mid-lake boulder piles, particularly in the shallower water. Bluegills will bite properly presented redworms—larval baits on small weighted hooks.

Walleye averaging 16-24 inches are evenly distributed around the lake, and usually taken on minnows, various spinners and worm combinations. In the spring look for walleye along the shoreline in shallower water; by summer drift fish the deep water over structure. Their cousins, yellow perch, are often found near rock piles and they will charge minnows and worms also. Largemouth bass are often shoreline-based in upground reservoirs and shallow water. Bring your usual box of artificial lures, rubber worms and live bait rigs. Try fishing over the ramps.

Hot spots: The natural-like northern shoreline can be a terrific area in the spring to cast for bass. New London, with its diverse habitat, offers anglers a chance to try many patterns including fishing cover areas, shallows, humps and rock piles, along shoreline feeding areas and in deep water.

Crappies, as always, relate to cover or attractor devices where small jigging spoons and simple minnow rigs will garner their attention throughout most of the year.

Underwater structure: Built in the mid-1970s, the bottom of the reservoir has various features including 33 stone piles up to six feet tall and 50 feet long, five reef areas and humps. Good stands of aquatic vegetation are along the north edge of the reservoir. The north end has natural shallowing complete with cattails and other aquatic edge flora.

Also over the years, Christmas trees have been submerged to further enhance fish resting, feeding and hiding habitats. Engineers also left a number of six-foot-tall stumps that lie in 25-30 feet of water, and a fence row in the north end of the reservoir. In addition, three construction ramps and riprap areas were left to enhance spawning and feeding for various species of fish.

Boat launching: The city of New London operates the reservoir's only launching ramp on the northeast corner. The lake and ramp are best for small craft.

Ice fishing: Some ice fishing for crappies is done on the lake. Most anglers use simple larval baits and tiny spoons or teardrops tipped with mousies. Concentrate on the two stump fields and boulder piles. Some good-sized walleye have been taken through the ice on simple jigs and minnows fished on the bottom. Clear water makes ice fishing challenging.

Insider tips: A small swimming beach, latrines, amphitheater, drinking water and sledding hills are scattered around the side of the reservoir. The reservoir has two parking lots, one on the south and the other on the west side. New London offers many underwater structures to explore.

Nimusila Reservoir

■ 811 acres of fishing water ■ 16 miles of shoreline SUMMIT COUNTY

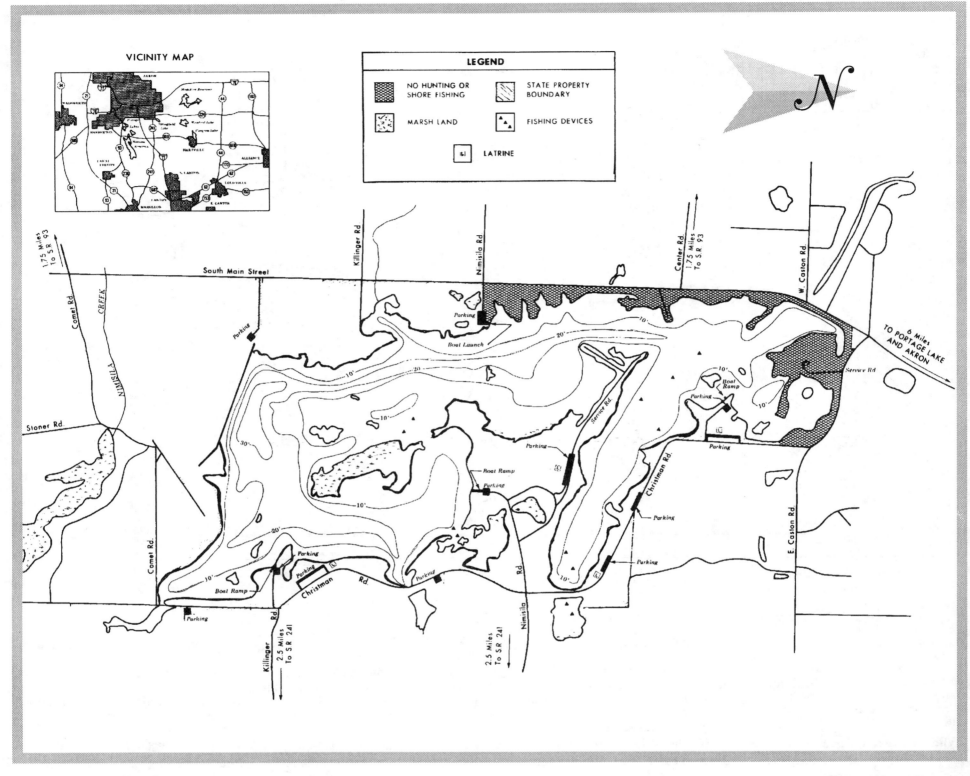

VICINITY MAP

LEGEND

NO HUNTING OR SHORE FISHING

STATE PROPERTY BOUNDARY

MARSH LAND

FISHING DEVICES

LATRINE

Location: In Summit County, two miles south of SR 619, two miles east of SR 93 and 2.5 miles west of SR 241.

Wildlife district office: (330) 644-2293.

Fishing opportunities: Largemouth bass, bluegill, crappies and channel catfish.

Fishing forecast: Sports Warehouse, (216) 644-6722.

Water conditions: Medium clear.

Bottom composition: Mud.

Horsepower restriction: Electric motors only.

Stocking: Saugeye.

Camping at the state park.

Bait at the south end of the lake (Eddy's Bait).

Outlook:
Saugeye - very good
Largemouth bass - excellent

Crappies - good
Catfish - good

You will find many sailboaters on the placid lake during the summer cruising the mid-lake and cove mouths. The quiet reservoir is a pleasant and quality fishing destination. The only complaint about the lake is usually from the bass anglers, who say that they can't catch the bass because of all the saugeye getting on their hook. This is a terrific lake to bring a 12-foot boat and a cooler full of sandwiches to. It's not wind-swept, and the island and bays are easy to navigate. The pretty little reservoir was built in 1936 as a water supply.

How to catch 'em: Nimisila Reservoir is one of the best largemouth bass lakes in this part of the state. It is an outstanding lake for big bass and quality environs. Biologists love to tell about their electro-shocking surveys, often rolling six-pound bucketmouths in the narrow coves of Nimisila. Bring

a box full of crankbaits and various colored pig and jigs. In the early spring, bass anglers should also cast medium running lures and retrieve them slowly. Lots of anglers also enjoy summer evening fishing using topwater lures that are sometimes viciously attacked by the largemouth.

Minnow and jigs around the many small structures produce good catches of panfish in the spring and early summer. Some northern pike are taken in the marshy areas along the east during the short early spring season. Night angling for catfish is very good during the summer months. Try dead minnows, nightcrawlers and commercial stink baits.

Hot spots: The best are shallow coves for bass and weedbeds.

Underwater structure: Much of the shallows are heavily vegetated. Some of the cattail islands can hold early season bass. Many Christmas trees are scattered throughout the

lake annually to provide panfish habitat.

Boat launching: Four ramps serve the lake. Sixteen-foot and under boats will have no trouble getting into the water at the small ramps. Some anglers paddle the lake in canoes or rowboats.

Ice fishing: Anglers come in good numbers for panfish. Most ice fishermen scatter over the mid-lake, on top of cover, and jig or suspend waxworms and other larval baits. The Portage Lakes are better known for winter fishing.

Insider tips: The Portage Lakes are about five miles away. The shoreline is almost totally wooded, but there are plenty of places to fish. Waterfowl is hunted by drawing each fall. The lake is windless and gentle, and a great largemouth fishery.

Norwalk Reservoirs

HURON COUNTY ■ 159 acres of fishing water ■ Five miles of shoreline

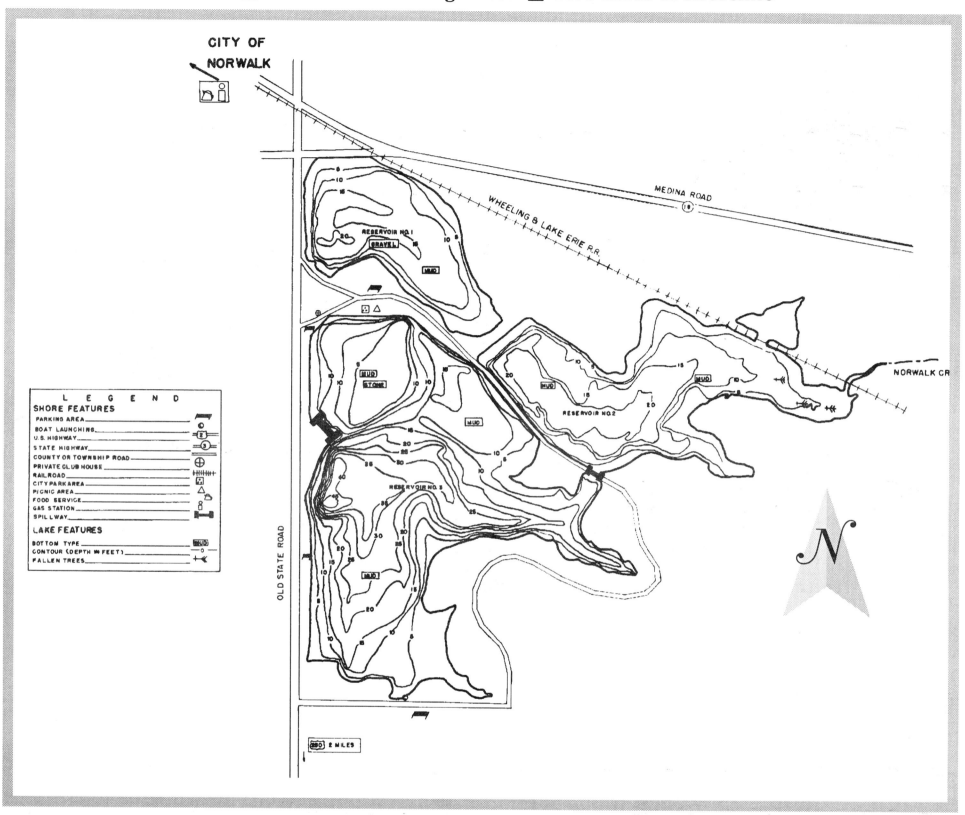

Location: In Huron County, southeast of Norwalk at the corner of Medina (SR 18) and Old State Road. Two miles from Route 250.

Fish opportunities: Largemouth bass, northern pike, bluegill and crappies.

Water condition: Quite clear.

Bottom composition: Stone and soft mud, good variety; aquatic vegetation.

Horsepower restriction: Electric motors only.

Stocking: Reservoir No. 2 - catfish; Reservoir No. 3 - walleye and saugeye annually.

Special restrictions: Closed at night.

The three neighboring reservoirs, which are a water supply for the city of Norwalk, are built into natural land forms and offer narrow bays, contours and lots of great bank fishing. The No. 1 reservoir is not stocked and is a poor fishing reservoir with limited access. The south end of Reservoir No. 3 can be filled with heavy vegetation, especially later in the summer. This irregular-shaped reservoir has a good reproducing population of largemouth bass and northern pike, which is unique. Normally pike (and bass in many waters) are a put-and-taken, stocked fish. There are significant numbers of northern pike in this reservoir. The property is city owned.

How to catch 'em: Along the large dikes (west side), which are comprised of rip rap and boulders, are some steep dropoffs and good patterns. Bass lurk in the underwater vegetation and especially at the point in the southeast corner on Reservoir No. 3. Largemouth fishing is good much of the year due to deep water and good hiding areas. Pike fishermen should plan a spring visit to work the shorelines and edges of heavy weedbeds. Most pike anglers like to cast spoons; some use live bait later in the year.

Most anglers stand on the rip rap on the west shore of the big reservoir and cast spinners into the deeper water, retrieving at various speeds. Pike and largemouth bass are taken this way.

Hot spots: The total shoreline of Reservoirs 2 and 3 are accessible and offer good angling opportunities. No. 3 is about 80 acres.

Underwater structure: Fish attractors, made from wooden pallets, have been randomly scattered around the shore of the bigger reservoirs. Bluegill and crappies hang in these pallets year-round. Dangling live bait in this area works well. Look for some brush and fallen trees along the shore, next to dropoffs.

Boat launching: Hand launching small boats is allowed.

Ice fishing: Reservoir No. 3 is one of the best places in the state for pike through the ice. Anglers generally use a tip-up or hand jig shinny spoon tipped with a lively minnow.

Insider tips: Bring your fine wire leaders and casting spoons to try for pike in the spring and early summer. Also bring your picnic lunch when you visit. The area is well-landscaped with lots of pine trees that offer shade and protection from the winds. Shoreline fishing is excellent around the two main reservoirs. The entire family can enjoy fishing here.

65

O'Shaughnessy Reservoir

■ 1,000 acres of fishing water ■ 17 miles of shoreline DELAWARE COUNTY

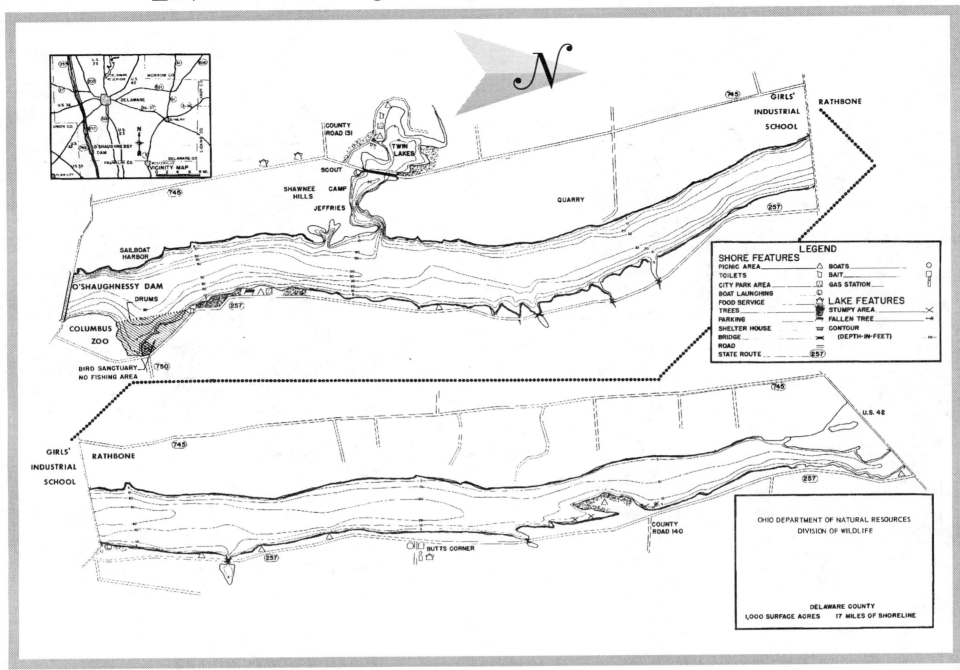

Location: Adjacent to the Columbus Zoo, between SR 257 and SR 745. Lands adjacent to the lake are owned by the city of Columbus and private owners.

Wildlife district office: (614) 644-3925.

Fishing opportunities: Crappies, saugeye (very good) and northern pike.

Water condition: Medium clarity.

Bottom composition: Limestone and mud.

Bait and tackle: In Rathbone and between Route 42 and Home Road on the east side of the lake.

Outlook:
Largemouth bass - excellent
Crappie - fair
Bluegill - good
Saugeye - good

Stocked: Saugeye.

Long and narrow, O'Shaughnessy is a very good saugeye lake. The lake is limestone-based with many areas having a rock bottom. The lake is convenient to fish. Nearby are city parks, food service, gasoline stations and good bait and tackle shops.

How to catch 'em: Stay in the flats. Many saugeye stack up and are taken below the dam near the zoo. Jigging and twister tails are the best methods in front of the dam.

Twin Lake, which connects to O'Shaughnessy, is an excellent bass fishery (saugeye, too) and the site of many bass tournaments. Once an old quarry at the entrance to the Twin Lake cove, plenty of bass and saugeye are found in the flats just north of the channel. The fish will also suspend off the dropoff there.

Twelve-inch crappies are routine.

Good numbers of medium-sized (5-6 pounds) channel catfish are taken using stink baits. Some pike are taken south of the town of Prospect near the low-head dam. This is one of the few areas in central Ohio that hold northern pike and the fishing pressure for them is high. Spring pike anglers use spoons and some fishermen take up the challenge with at least eight weight rods and heavy tippets. Minnow imitations jerked through the shallows can produce awesome strikes and flashing teeth. Most of the pike are hammer handle-size, but a few 12-15 pound northerns are taken—and hopefully released.

Underwater structure: At the end of County Road 140 is the largest stumpy area in the lake. Look for fallen trees in this area, that has a shoreline access area and picnic spot.

Boat launching: One large and modern access is on the east side of the lake, and other gravel ramps are scattered around the skinny lake. Unlimited horsepower boats are allowed on the lake.

Insider tips: Concentrate on the flats and adjoining dropoff at the mouth to Twin Lakes. For saugeye and bass also try north of the bridge at Home Road on the east side of the lake along a big rock flat and main creek channel. When the fish are active, work the flats. Don't forget spring pike action!

Oakthorpe Lake

FAIRFIELD COUNTY ■ 40 acres of fishing water

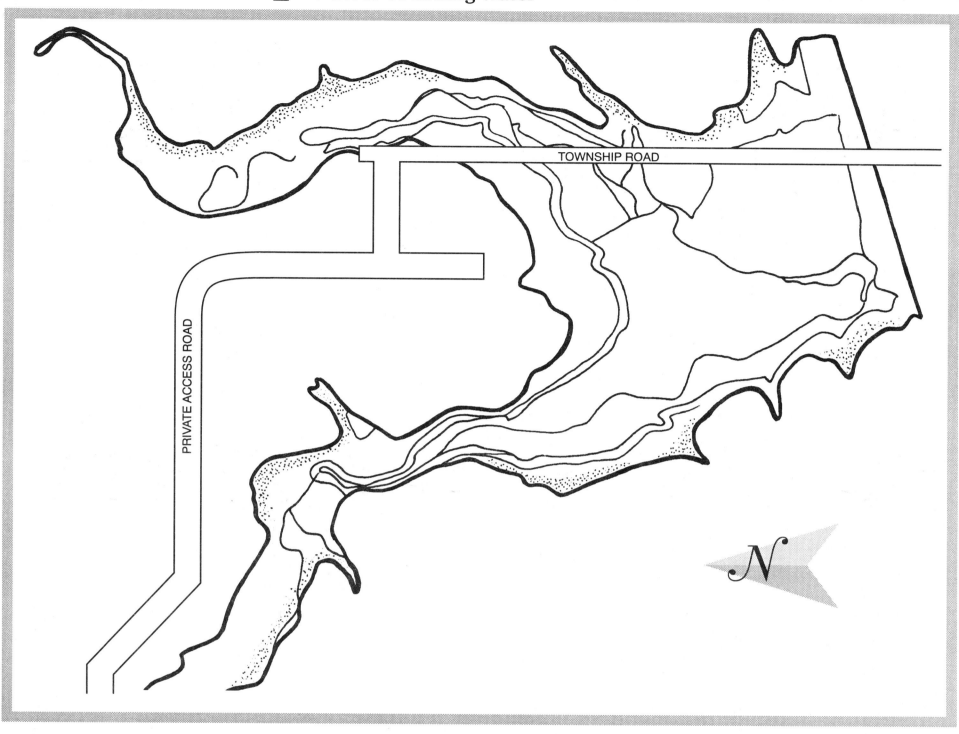

TOWNSHIP ROAD

PRIVATE ACCESS ROAD

N

Location: In Fairfield County.

District wildlife office: (614) 644-3925.

Fishing opportunities: Largemouth bass, redear sunfish, crappies and roughfish.

Water conditions: Medium.

Bottom composition: Mud, soft.

Horsepower restrictions: Electric motor only.

Average depth: 15 feet.

Check bass regulations.

Outlook:
Largemouth bass - excellent
Redear sunfish - good
Crappie - good
Carp - good

The small lake is surrounded by meadows, except on the north end where woods touch the shoreline. Also at the north end is a peninsula that is wooded. This is the only lake in the region that has redear sunfish. Typically redear sunfish are found in the more southern parts of the state. Many of these colorful and frisky fish are in the 7-8 inch range.

How to catch 'em: The east end, near the dam, has quite a bit of vegetation where spinner baits can bring up bass and some panfish. Oakthorpe is an above average bass lake. According to biologists, anglers use everything on the lake for largemouths including multi-colored plastic worms, white spinners, flipping in the pads, small crankbaits, jigs and pigs, and topwater lures in the evening. Bring a batch of weedless baits for the areas of the lake with vegetation.

Electro-fishing surveys indicate that some huge carp are in the lake. In fact, 25-pounders, which are like reeling in a log, have been taken. Young anglers from the area are known to catch some whopper carp.

Hot spots: The wooded shoreline on the north end of the lake holds excellent populations of largemouth bass that can range from 14-22 inches. Also, anglers should key on the deep dropoffs on the western side of the lake.

Underwater structure: Some fishing devices were installed in the 1970s, none in more recent times. The size of the lake allows anglers to survey and fish it in an afternoon.

Boat launching: The gravel ramp is for small boats only.

Ice fishing: Some local anglers venture out on the lake during the winter.

Insider tips: This is a lightly fished, excellent largemouth lake. Don't tell your friends.

Oxbow Lake

■ 36 acres of fishing water ■ 1.5 miles of shoreline DEFIANCE COUNTY

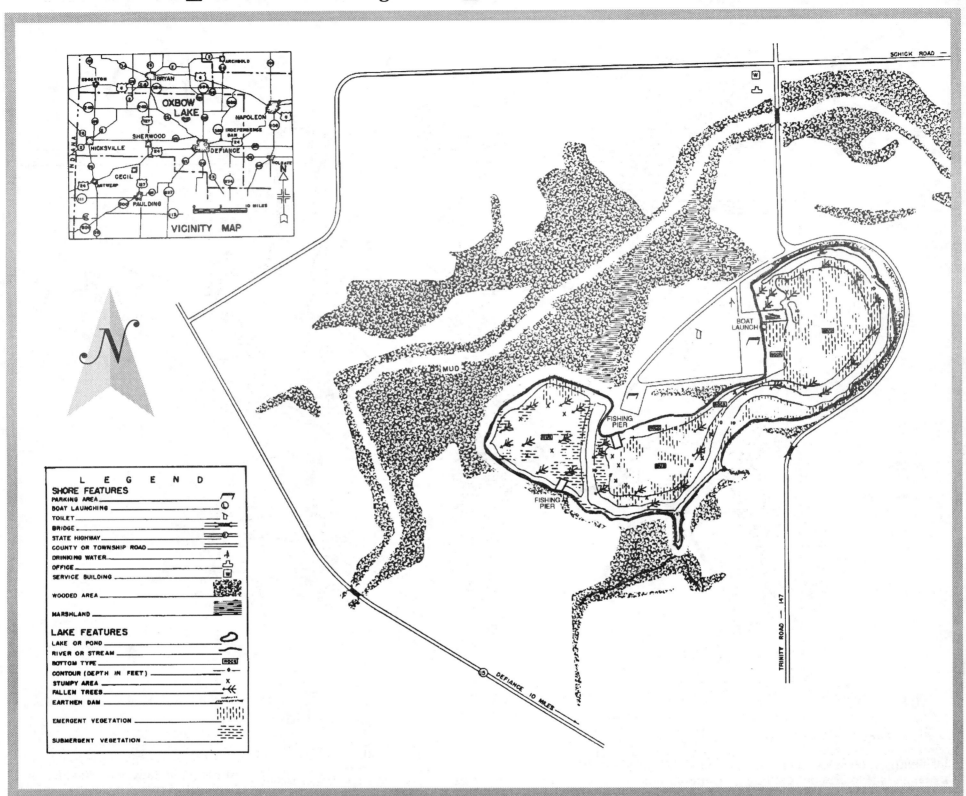

VICINITY MAP

N

```
L E G E N D
SHORE FEATURES
PARKING AREA
BOAT LAUNCHING
TOILET
BRIDGE
STATE HIGHWAY
COUNTY OR TOWNSHIP ROAD
DRINKING WATER
OFFICE
SERVICE BUILDING
WOODED AREA
MARSHLAND
LAKE FEATURES
LAKE OR POND
RIVER OR STREAM
BOTTOM TYPE
CONTOUR (DEPTH IN FEET)
STUMPY AREA
FALLEN TREES
EARTHEN DAM
EMERGENT VEGETATION
SUBMERGENT VEGETATION
```

Location: In Defiance County, 10 miles northwest of Defiance off SR 15 at Schick Road.

Wildlife district office: (419) 424-5000.

Fishing opportunities: Largemouth bass, green sunfish, bullhead and bluegill.

Water conditions: Very clear at normal levels.

Bottom composition: Mud; mud and sediment over stone.

Stocking: Largemouth bass and bluegill.

Special regulations: Check largemouth minimum length limit, currently 18 inches.

Outlook:
Largemouth bass - very good
Bluegill - fair and improving
The Wildlife Division has placed

some fishing structures around the state-owned lake, which has two accessible fishing piers, a new launching ramp and a courtesy dock on the north side. The lake was reclaimed in the mid-1990s, which means it was drained, cleaned and structure moved. The lake has a lot of fish-holding stumps and vegetation remaining. All of the stunted fish (mostly bluegills) were removed and an aggressive management and stocking effort has been underway since. The lake is managed exclusively for largemouth bass and bluegills, with the objective to develop the lake as a jumbo bluegill producer.

The high size limit on largemouth bass keeps the predators pressure on the bluegills to prevent stunting. Many small lakes, if not managed this way, quickly go out of balance and produce only a stunted bluegill. When that happens, it will quickly

hurt the bass population. If a small lake develops a high density of small bluegill, they often end up eating all the bass eggs during spawning time. The end result is fewer and fewer bass—and a completely poor fishery.

The small lake, which, by the way, is a real oxbow, is surrounded by woods and an intimate place to seek good-sized largemouth and bluegills. Because of its size and increasing quality, the lake is a pleasant place to bring children. Productive bank fishing is easy around the entire lake.

How to catch 'em: Casting small spinners, Little Cleo's, jigs and grub bodies all work well at the improving little lake. Also try some redworms and minnows.

Boat launching: A small launching ramp and courtesy dock are on the north lobe of the oxbow-shaped lake. Access is off of Schick Road.

Ice fishing: Oxbow Lake is a fair to good ice fishing site, only 15 minutes from Defiance. Some bass are taken through the ice, but it is primarily a bluegill lake in the winter. Bring your live bait, wax worms and tiny hooks and bright teardrop-sized jigs. One local expert says he simply spuds his hole next to the guy with the most fish on the ice. Other anglers say that right in front of the main parking lot is as good a spot as any to try.

Insider tips: Bank fishing for bass and bluegill is excellent at the tree-lined and quiet lake. Some really big bluegills can be taken here.

Paint Creek Lake

HIGHLAND & ROSS COUNTIES ■ 1,190 acres of fishing water ■ 30 miles of shoreline

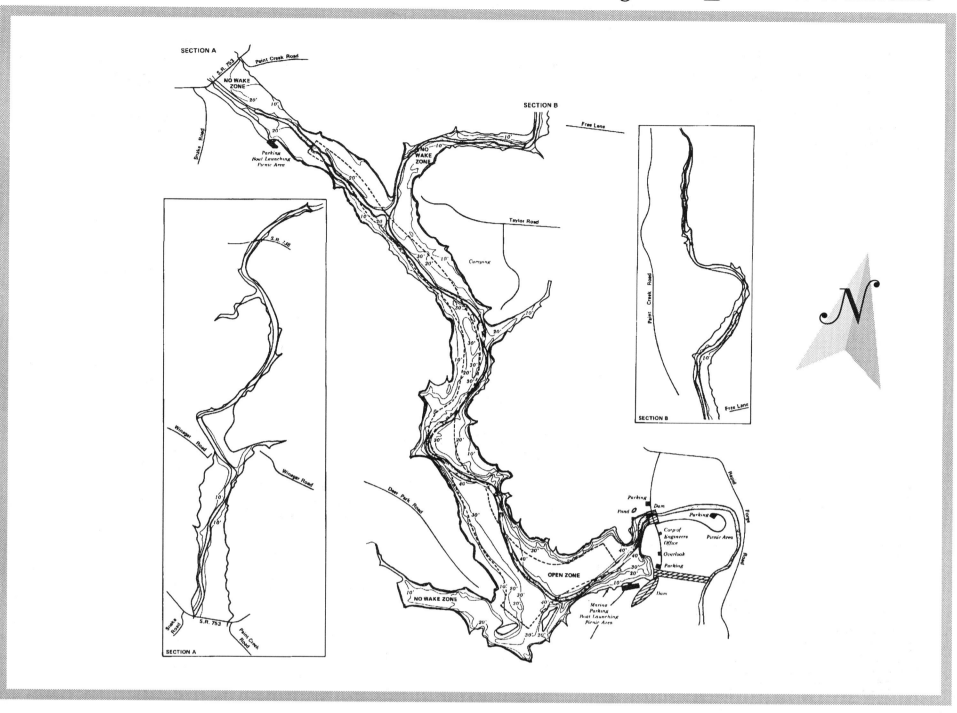

Location: In Highland and Ross counties, 50 miles from Cincinnati and 60 miles from Dayton. It is also 10 miles east of Hillsboro, one mile north of U.S. 50 on Rapid Forge Road, and five miles south of Greenfield on SR 753.

Wildlife district: (513) 372-9261.

Fishing opportunities: Largemouth bass, crappie, spotted bass, catfish, saugeye and bluegill.

Water conditions: Medium clarity.

Bottom composition: Variable, from fine silt in the upper reaches to rock.

Horsepower restrictions: None.

Camping: 199 sites in the state park; call (513) 981-7061.

World's record: Former world record saugeye, seven pounds (1988).

Boat rental: 100-slip marina, fuel.

Shoreline: Very steep in places, 30-foot drops from limestone cliffs on the east side.

Dam: 118 feet high. **Depth:** Maximum at dam is 50 feet.

Bait shops are in the area.

Outlook:
Channel, flathead catfish - very good
Crappie - good
Largemouth bass - good
Saugeye - very good

The Paint Creek region lies at the edge of the Appalachian Plateau. This escarpment makes the boundary between the hilly eastern section of the state and the flatter western portions. This entire region of rolling hills is rich with Ohio shale, which overlays limestone of the river valleys and outcrops on ridges.

Paint Creek is the longest creek in the country. A variety of habitats makes the large reservoir an attractive destination for anglers, tournaments and the well-known Carppiethon, which annually offers more than $333,000 in prizes. Crappies can be huge and bluegills are under fished.

The lake is stocked with saugeye, tiger muskie and pike. There is excellent natural reproduction of white and black crappie, bluegill, smallmouth, spotted bass, rock bass and channel catfish. The U.S. Army Corp of Engineers has a lake map. Call (513) 365-1470.

Saugeye have been planted in significant numbers since the mid-1990s. Most of the fish are 10-16 inches; some are up to 26 inches in length.

How to catch em: Many good-sized saugeye are taken below the dam in the tailwaters from November to February during high flows. Fish like the oxygenated water and aquatic life in the tailwaters. In the lake, try drifting any point or dropoff. In the lake itself, you'll find good numbers of crappie, catfish and saugeye.

Crappies can reach 15 inches and are found in very good numbers in flooded timber during the spring and early summer. Many local anglers claim the best time of the year for crappie is when the waters begin to cool, October - December. Crappie experts suggest jigging in the tops of fallen trees during any time of the year. Largemouth bass can be up to four pounds and are usually found in rocky areas, especially in the fall.

Spotted bass frequent the shoreline, around big limestone rocks, logs and stumps. Cast spinners and crank baits around the objects, working the down current side. Artificial worms can also be worked in a tapping retrieve past any structure. For bluegill, bring your boat and a big can of redworms and small gold hooks.

Underwater structure: Rock to silt, the many small covers and fallen timber offer excellent habitats to explore. Flooded timber and the creek channel are fish holding elements.

Boat launching: The Rattlesnake arm (off Cope Road on the west side of the lake) and Taylor Road boat ramps are both near good fishing areas.

Ice fishing: Very little, mostly due to poor ice conditions.

Insider tips: Try for saugeye under the dam. The state park has a modern campground, eight miles of hiking trails, 350-foot beach and day-use amenities. One local bait and tackle shop strongly suggests crayfish as a good all-purpose summertime bait.

Piedmont Lake

GUERNSEY, HARRISON & BELMONT COUNTIES ■ 2,270 acres of fishing water ■ 38 miles of shoreline

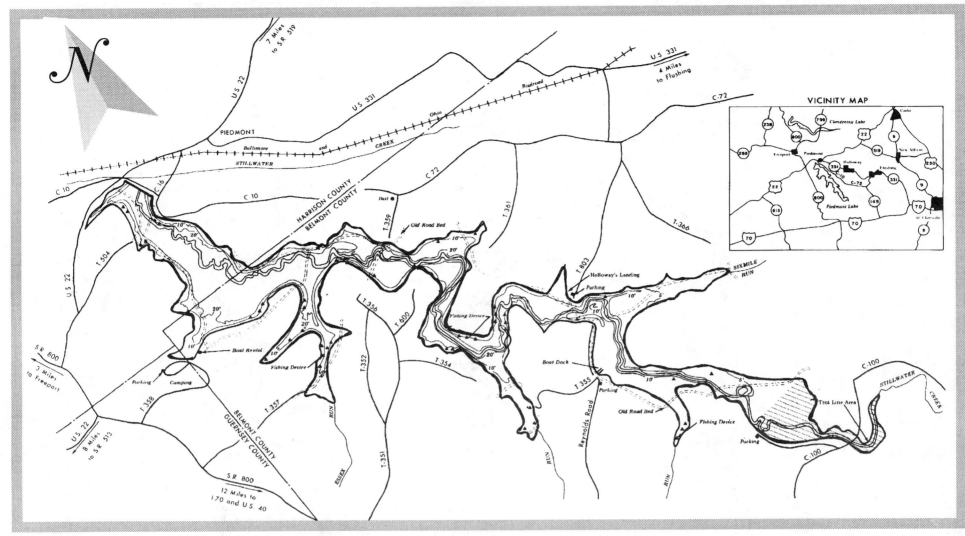

Location: Most of the lake is in Belmont County, near Piedmont. It's accessible by I-70 and SR 800 and 22. The lake is midway between Cambridge and Cadiz.

Wildlife district office: (614) 594-2211.

Fishing opportunities: Muskie, channel and flathead catfish, bullhead, large- and smallmouth bass, crappie, bluegill, yellow perch, walleye and saugeye.

Water conditions: Medium to clear.

Bottom composition: Mud, some firm areas.

Maximum depth: 38 feet.

Horsepower restriction: 10 hp.

Stocking: Muskie and saugeye.

Camping: 80 sites at Piedmont Marina, (614) 658-3735.

Boating supplies at marina.

Outlook:
Bluegill - good
Bass - excellent
Channel catfish - excellent
Walleye - excellent
Saugeye - excellent
Muskie - excellent

Piedmont Lake is long and narrow and occupies a valley between rows of rolling wooded hills. The lake has quiet long bays, medium-dense aquatic vegetation and clean water. In most areas, the shoreline is steep, but there is bank fishing access along the park property and day-use areas. Because of the 10-horsepow-er limit and somewhat limited boat access, Piedmont Lake is an excellent fishing experience. Recreational boating is limited and there are no waterskiers or power-boats.

This productive lake offers a very real possibility of catching a 40-pound muskie. Surveys also indicate that excellent year classes of muskie are growing well and are in good numbers—so the future is also bright. Piedmont Lake is owned by the Muskingum Watershed Conservancy District and the park includes hunting areas, marina, launches, 80-site campground, lunch counter, docks and motel units. The conservancy owns about 4,400 acres of land around the lake. The lake is considered to be the most scenic of the conservancy holdings.

How to catch 'em: Except for Lake Erie, Piedmont Lake is the best fishing lake in the state. The lake has trophy-class muskie fishing, outstanding large- and smallmouth fishing (it's unusual to have both in an inland lake), and excellent saugeye and panfishing. Smart muskie hunters can catch fish during the day, but night fishing has become popular and productive. The very best night fishing of these toothful denizens is during the heat of the summer (July and August) in the deeper waters near the dam. Try shad-like lures for the big muskie.

A few 14-pound walleye have been sampled by biologists and good numbers of saugeye can also be taken at Piedmont. Use standard walleye techniques, i.e., find the structure and jig a minnow after May. In the early season they will chase crankbaits and minnow imitations. Try nightcrawler rigs, too.

Smallmouth are taken from mid-lake to the dam, especially in April. Most anglers use live nightcrawlers and spinner baits around the rocky shoreline and shale points. If you can identify long sloping points, many smallmouth will relate to them, especially if they are near deeper water. A few smallmouth bass (and muskie) are taken trolling deep points and breaks using deep-diving, shad-like lures or spinners. Largemouth bass are most often taken from mid-lake to the upper or shallower end. Early season is the most successful time when grape-colored worms, spinners and night-crawlers can bring in good catches. As the water warms, move to night fishing along the shore or deep structure.

Crappie fishermen will have excellent success around felled trees and brush. Fish the underwater tree-tops with minnows or jigs with small tails. If you can't catch a summer catfish at Piedmont, you're in big trouble. Bring your livers and stinkbaits or try a trotline in the designated area in the upper end of the lake.

Hot spots: The many narrow bays are excellent largemouth hot spots. The best smallmouth fishing is reported to be near the dam. In fact, many smallmouth anglers say they catch quite a few muskie on jigs meant for smallmouth.

Crappies anglers should try the Six Mill Run and Stillwater Creek forks at the upper end of the lake.

Underwater structure: Various fishing devices have been placed in the lake including 32 tons of clay tile that were placed to develop five reef structures. Also, 225 shoreline trees were felled as fish attractors and about 1,200 Christmas trees have been submerged. Most of the Christmas trees were placed in 7-15 feet of water.

Boat launching: Two modern launches are on the lake; one at the marina and the other off SR Rt. 800 (Reynolds Road). Sleeping aboard watercraft is permitted in designated areas only. On summer weekends, plan to be at the marina by dawn to get a parking place. The marina has a food concession and marine supplies.

Ice fishing: Piedmont typically has poor, unsafe ice. Therefore ice fishing is not popular.

Insiders tips: This is probably the best overall fishing lake in the state. Plenty of local information is available at area bait and tackle shops and at the marina. Bring your muskie plugs and a stout rod. A 42 pound muskie was sampled by netting during a recent survey. This is a rare inland lake that supports such a good large- and smallmouth fishery.

Pleasant Hill Reservoir

■ 850 acres of fishing water ■ 13.4 miles of shoreline RICHLAND & ASHLAND COUNTIES

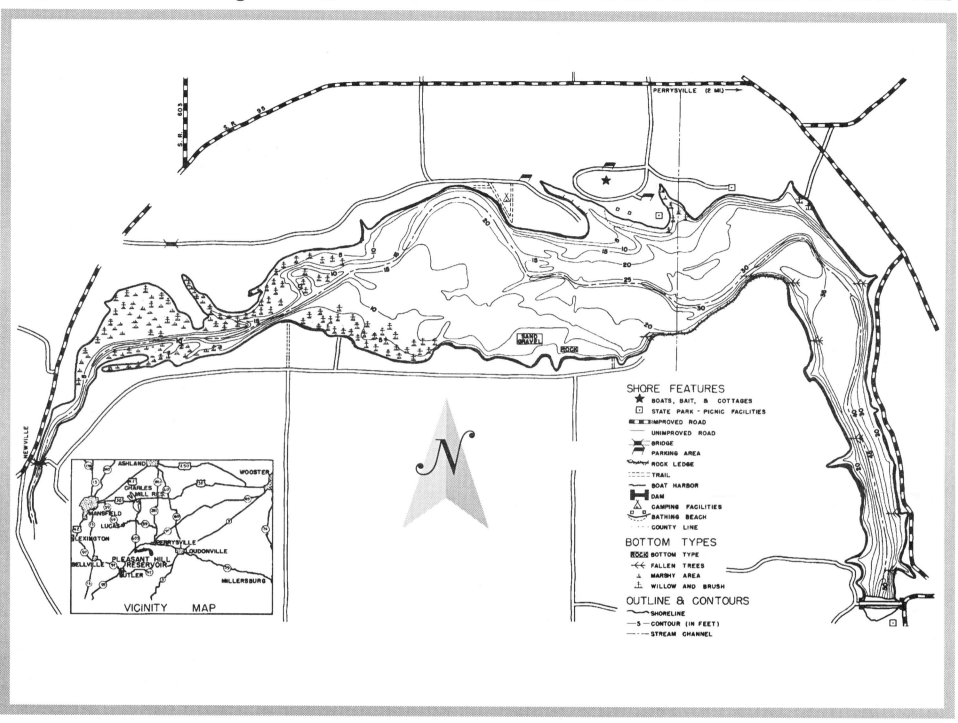

SHORE FEATURES
★ BOATS, BAIT, & COTTAGES
▣ STATE PARK - PICNIC FACILITIES
▭ IMPROVED ROAD
─── UNIMPROVED ROAD
✕ BRIDGE
PARKING AREA
ROCK LEDGE
····· TRAIL
BOAT HARBOR
H DAM
△ CAMPING FACILITIES
BATHING BEACH
······ COUNTY LINE

BOTTOM TYPES
ROCK BOTTOM TYPE
✕✕ FALLEN TREES
⊥ MARSHY AREA
⊥ WILLOW AND BRUSH

OUTLINE & CONTOURS
─── SHORELINE
─5─ CONTOUR (IN FEET)
--- STREAM CHANNEL

VICINITY MAP

Location: In Richland and Ashland counties. It's east of Mansfield, two miles west of Perrysville off SR 95

Wildlife district office: (419) 424-5000.

Fishing opportunities: Saugeye, black and white crappies, large- and smallmouth bass, bluegill, channel catfish, white bass, muskie and bullhead.

Water conditions: Clear.

Bottom composition: Rock on the west, gravel and sand, and mud on the west end.

Horsepower restrictions: None.

Stocking: Annually, saugeye and others.

Outlook:
Saugeye - excellent
Crappies - good
Large- and smallmouth bass - very good
Bluegill - fair
White bass - good
Channel catfish - good
Muskie - fair

Bullhead - fair

Large sections of the shoreline, particularly on the western side, have tall cliffs and large boulders along the water's edge. There is no shoreline fishing from these areas, but from a boat anglers can work around the boulders and rugged shoreline and do well on smallmouth bass. Pleasant Hill is a high-use lake, often very busy with powerboats and other recreational activity.

How to catch 'em: Look for smallmouth along the cliffs and saugeye in the mid-lake, especially where east of it says sand/gravel on the above map. Spring and early summer (fall is good for saugeye also) are generally the best times to fish the reservoir. Saugeye run from 12-26 inches and are often found in the sandy beach areas in 10-15 feet of water. Many local anglers claim night fishing for saugeye is very productive using dark-colored lures. In the winter, try the trailwaters.

Smallmouth are best taken in May using small jigs with rubber worms and tails. Some of the agile small-

mouth can run up to 18 inches and are often found in the lower lake from the lodge to the dam. Try fishing the embayments with grape worms and long grub bodies over hard bottoms. Largemouth run 12-23 inches and are abundant in the upper part of the lake.

Bluegills can run six to eight inches, but there are lots of smaller fish too. White bass are found in good numbers and can reach 14-15 inches. Try shad like crankbaits, do-jigs, small spinners and live minnows on the schooling white bass. Both black and white crappies are found in good numbers throughout the lake. Most of the crappies are found in brushy areas, relating to any structure and can average 7-14 inches. Local experts say the best crappie fishing is just before a front moves in.

Hot spots: The point at the mouth of the bay where the boat launch is located is an excellent place for saugeye. Most of the fish are taken in 15-20 feet of water, right at the end of the underwater point. Anglers drift, troll and jig against a

tight line. Good boat handling is important to cover this stretch. Another good saugeye spot is at the point where the lake turns south. Drift with jigs over the 30-foot-deep water, along the shoreline and into the radius of the curve.

Underwater structure: Natural structure.

Boat launching: The concessionaire at the boat launch (off SR 95) sells bait and tackle. The launch is busy with water skiers and recreational boaters. Be careful handling your boat in the west end; it can be stumpy.

Ice fishing: Bluegills are the primary target for ice fishermen. Local experts suggest areas in front of the boat launch and over the stream channel.

Insider tips: Try timing your fishing trips on the weekdays when the lake is quiet. The few, but large, muskies that are in the lake have migrated from Clear Fork, more than 20 miles away.

Portage Lakes

SUMMIT COUNTY ■ 37.84 acres of fishing water ■ 1,681 miles of shoreline

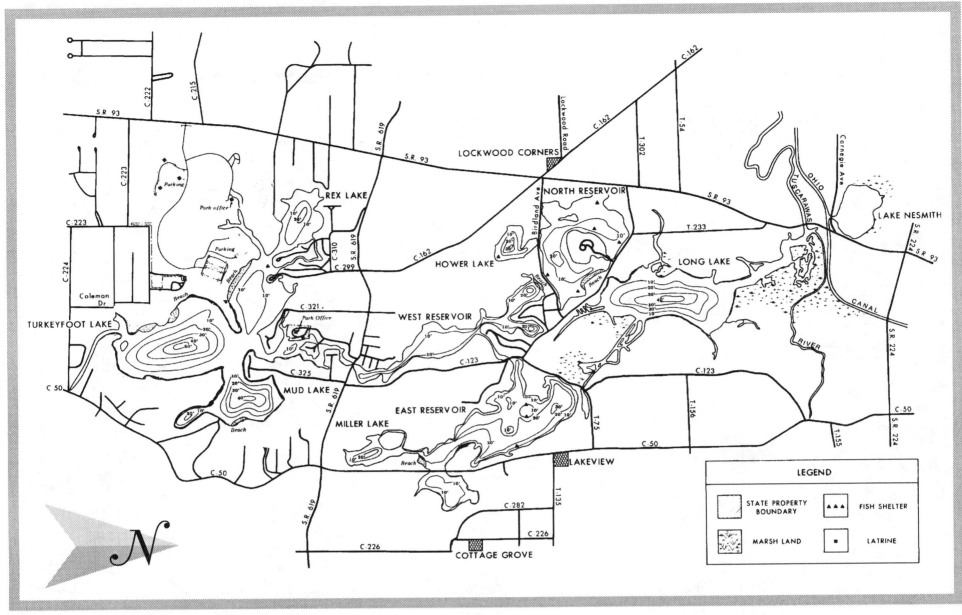

Location: In Summit County, south of SR 93. SR 619 bisects the lakes, which is near Cottage Grove and Lockwood Corners.

Wildlife district office: (330) 644-2293.

Fishing opportunities: Largemouth bass, crappie, bluegill, bullhead, eastern chain pickerel, redear sunfish, catfish and some muskie and other rough fish.

Water conditions: Medium clear to muddy.

Bottom composition: Sand, silt, muck.

Horsepower restrictions: None on most lakes.

Stocking: Saugeye, all lakes.

Boat rental.

Camping: 74 rustic sites in the Portage Lake State Park. Call (330) 644-2220.

The string of lakes that comprise the Portage Lake system are both manmade and natural. In 1825 these lakes, located south of Akron, were created as part of the network of water supply reservoirs that were to supply the canal system. By 1913 the canal was abandoned. However,

during this period the rubber industry was expanding and waters were diverted for industrial use and development along the canal and in Summit County. The lakes are heavily populated, with houses squeezed along every inch of shoreline.

There are five main lakes on three topographical levels. Long Lake (225 acres), the lowest lake, was formed by flooding a swamp area. North Reservoir (219 acres), at the middle, was formed by a dike flooding a flat area of land and a small pothole lake known as Hower Lake. At the highest level, and impounding the largest acreage of water— 1,207 acres—are three separate reservoirs: East (380 acres), West (162 acres) and Turkeyfoot (665 acres). Turkeyfoot Lake is connected to West Reservoir by a channel. West Reservoir overflows into North Reservoir and is connected to East Reservoir by a channel. East Reservoir has a control structure from which water is released into a channel which flows to Long Lake. The lakes average from 10-16 feet in depth. These lakes are known for very good bass and panfishing. Many bass tournaments are held on the lakes. North and Long lakes are the quieter of the group. There is heavy recreational boating on Turkeyfoot Lake, and all of the lakes. Expect a wait at the launches in the summer).

How to catch 'em: Although known mostly as a largemouth and panfish series of lakes, Portage Lakes is a rapidly improving saugeye fishery. First time anglers might consider heading to Long Lake and fishing for largemouth bass. Then go to Turkeyfoot or North and fish for saugeye that average 22 inches. Saugeye will spend much more time in shallow and weedy water than walleye. Stay in the shallower waters in Turkeyfoot and North in the early summer. Early season saugeye are taken on jig and minnow; later try your crankbaits.

Tournament bass anglers report catching quite a few saugeye when they are cranking for bass. A good population of 12-inch bass are in Turkeyfoot and Long lakes. Years ago muskie were stocked in the lake, and every now and then one is caught, but it's rare. Crappies are active in April, May and June, and catfishing is very good in the summer using stink baits. Six- to eight-inch bluegills are in most of the lakes.

Hot spots: Where West Reservoir comes closest to North Reservoir, there is a pipe connecting the two. At this pipe a current is created, and some big saugeye have been taken just off this mild current. Try fishing this bit of moving water after dark with a jig and minnow. North Reservoir has some good shoreline

access. A handicapped accessible pier is also in this area. Start fishing early to avoid the heavy recreational activity and don't forget to fish around the many docks with spinners and crankbaits in the evening.

Underwater structure: Christmas trees are placed in the lake on an annual basis. The lakes have some depth, up to 40 feet. Work ledges and any gentle drops.

Boat launching: There are several launches around the lake. One of the best is a four-lane launch in the state park where plenty of parking and other amenities are located. Nearby Nimisila Reservoir is electric motors only. Another launch is in Old Park Picnic Area off SR 619.

Ice fishing: Each of the lakes is popular with ice fishermen.

Insider tips: Occasionally you will see gar sunning themselves in the lake—a few are caught. The Division of Wildlife District regional headquarters is located in the Portage Lakes. The Portage Lakes State Park has five picnic areas, five miles of hiking trails and camping. In 1961 the state record chain pickerel came from Long Lake. It was six pounds and 26 inches long. There are total of 13 lakes (many small) in this area.

Punderson Lake

■ 101 acres of fishing water   ■ 2.6 miles of shoreline   GEAUGA COUNTY

Location: In Geauga County, west of SR 44 and south of SR 87 in the vicinity of Burton, Newbury and South Newbury, 13 miles south of Chardon.

Wildlife district office: (330) 644-2293.

Fishing opportunities: Largemouth bass, bluegills, crappies, golden trout and yellow perch.

Water conditions: Clear and deep.

Bottom composition: Decayed vegetation, muck.

Depth: Up to 75 feet.

Horsepower restriction: Electric motors only.

Stocking: Golden trout every spring and fall.

Boat rental: At the launch ramp - north end.

Camping: 201 sites in the state park; call (216) 564-2279.

Punderson is a quiet lake with a tree-lined shore and state park that lines the entire western length. Before it was state-owned, the lake was under private management and an admission was charged. Punderson Lake is the largest natural lake in the state and is a remnant of the last ice age more than 10,000 years ago. As the glacier moved northward, it gouged out basins and left behind huge blocks of ice that melted into lakes.

The stocked golden trout are actually a color phase of rainbow trout. Over the years, hatchery managers have selectively bred for the yellowish-orange trout. Today, the bright-colored fish is planted in many Ohio lakes and they are easy to catch.

How to catch 'em: The golden trout averages eight to 10 inches and are stocked from the marina at the north end of the lake. They are the main draw and can be taken on just about any bait. These fish are not known for their smarts, and are pretty much fished out by early summer. Panfishing is considered very good. Bluegills suspend near limited fishing devices and can be taken on red meal and waxworms, or artificals like rubber-legged crickets and flies. Crappies at Punderson prefer small minnows and spinners tipped with a bit of pork rind or redworm.

Punderson is also a good largemouth bass lake, but limited structure makes finding the fish more difficult. Shorelines in the spring can be good with crayfish-colored lures. Later in the season, try all the tricks including live bait (minnows and crawlers), slow-sinking divers and jigs with tails or pork.

Hot spots: The golden trout don't move too far from where they are stocked. Fish near the marina using waxworms, corn, cheese, mousies, salmon eggs or flies. There is plenty of shoreline access and a fishing pier is in front of the state park lodge on the southwest side of the lake.

Underwater structure: Although three deep holes are evenly distributed, the bottom is void of much structure. A few devices can be picked up on your fishfinder, or watch the locals who usually know where some underwater structure is located. Aquatic plants grow around the entire lake edge down to a depth of 15 feet.

Boat launching: The still lake is a good place to belly-boat and easy to maneuver with a small electric-powered craft.

Ice fishing: Because golden trout are stocked in the fall, the ice fishery is very good.

Insider tips: The state park has 14 miles of hiking trails, a camp store and marina, 26 cabins and a 31-room lodge. Bring a can of corn and try your luck on the heavily stocked golden trout in the spring. Emerald Lake, a small natural pothole, is north of the main lake and can be fished. Access is by foot. Some nice day-use areas are on bluffs above the lake.

Pymatuning Lake

ASHTABULA COUNTY ■ 14,650 acres of fishing water ■ 77 miles of shoreline

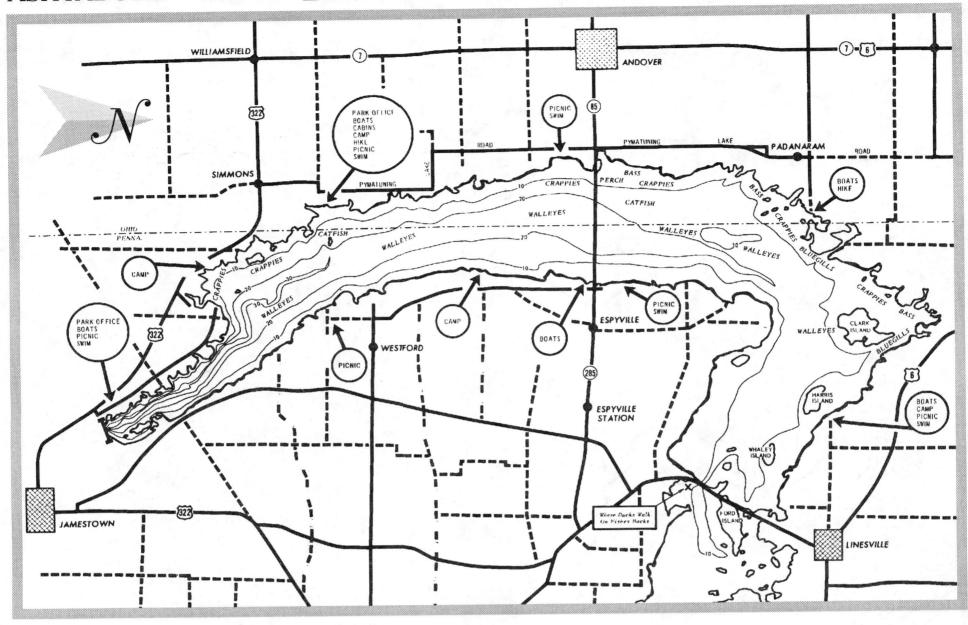

Location: In Ashtabula County, 40 miles north of Youngstown and 60 miles east of Cleveland on the Pennsylvania border. From either I-90 or I-80, depart on U.S. 6, which bisects the lake.

Fishing opportunities: Walleye, perch, crappies, muskie, white bass and large- and smallmouth bass.

Wildlife district office: (330) 664-2293.

Fishing forecast: Gateway Bait & Tackle, (216) 293-7227.

Water conditions: Medium clear.

Bottom composition: Gravel and sand.

Horsepower restrictions: 10 hp limit.

Stocking: Walleye and muskie (stocked by Pennsylvania).

Camping: State parks in both states, private campgrounds.

Special regulations: Check muskie and bass rules.

Outlook:

Walleye - good
Crappies fair to good
Bluegills - excellent
Muskie - poor
Smallmouth bass - fair

Pymatuning means "a crooked man's dwelling place" and "good walleye fishing." It is the biggest inland lake in northeastern Ohio and can get rough when the winds whip up. Jurisdiction is shared with the commonwealth of Pennsylvania. A license from either state is good on the entire lake if you are fishing from a boat or on the ice. If you are on the shoreline, you must have a license from the state you are standing in. Sixty percent of the anglers that come to Pymatuning fish for walleye, the rest are after crappies and panfish.

How to catch 'em: Pre-spawn and spawn (March and early April) walleye are almost always at the long gravel and sandy points. Use a jig and minnow. Later in the spring, most anglers drag nightcrawlers in deeper water up to 15 feet. By mid-summer, the walleye suspend and are difficult to catch. If you drift over suspended fish with a jig or hang a crawler, some can be taken, but the action is slow. Good numbers of walleye exceed 15 inches, and firm 10-pounders are common. More than 50,000 walleye are caught annually from the sprawling, but quiet lake. To catch one of these fish, remember to fish low and slow, troll or drift and bump the bottom.

A big Crappiethon tournament points out the popularity and quality of the fishery. Many of the fish are 10 to 12 inches (a few up to 14 inches!) and the very best fishing is the spawning period from mid-April through May. During this fast-action season, try a small jig or bobber and minnow near stumps. Bluegills are big, seven to nine inches, and can be taken from shallow bays on worms. Fly fishermen should think about casting a grub-tipped fly for bluegills.

At Pymatuning, when anglers aren't fishing for walleye, they are fishing for crappies—and the bass fishery goes severely underfished. Bass fishing is good to very good, although few anglers bother with it on the huge lake. Both species are present in the lake. Good bass areas include the stumpy area north of the causeway near Clark Island and along the western shoreline. Bring your entire tackle collection. Try plugs, spinners, live baits, crawlers, bottom rigs or spoons.

Muskie fishing is only fair, but if you hook up, you won't forget the fight and power of this major-league game fish. Good muskie fishing can occur in stumpy areas and near any flats. Around two small islands at the south side of the lake are good places to troll for the hard-to-catch denizens. You gotta cover a lot of water to catch muskie.

Hot spots: Check the bays for big crappies in May. The stump fields are great places to panfish. Bank fishermen might want to try the area at Fishing Point, near the Ohio state park cabins on NR 30. Along the breakwall at the beach is also a popular spot.

Underwater structure: From the causeway south, there are humps, bars and points. From the causeway north, you'll find some sand, silt and muck. There are plenty of submerged stumps in this area. Many of the stumps, depending on the water level, are just below the surface. Go slow.

Boat launching: On the Ohio side there are five all-weather concrete ramps. There are at least that many on the Pennsylvania side. There are four large marinas that rent boats, beach stores, two state campgrounds, private campgrounds and cabins rentals on both sides of the lake.

Ice fishing: Pymatuning is heavily ice fished for both walleye and crappie.

Insider tips: Pymatuning is a fisher's lake (a few sailboats also operate on the lake). This wide-open lake can get rough fast. Pymatuning is a destination lake and family vacation spot. Bring the family; there's lots to do in the area aside from fishing. The Ohio state park has 373 camping sites (call 216-293-6030), 62 cabins, five picnic areas, a beach, hiking and naturalist's programs.

Rocky Fork Lake

■ 2,080 acres of fishing water ■ 30 miles of shoreline HIGHLAND COUNTY

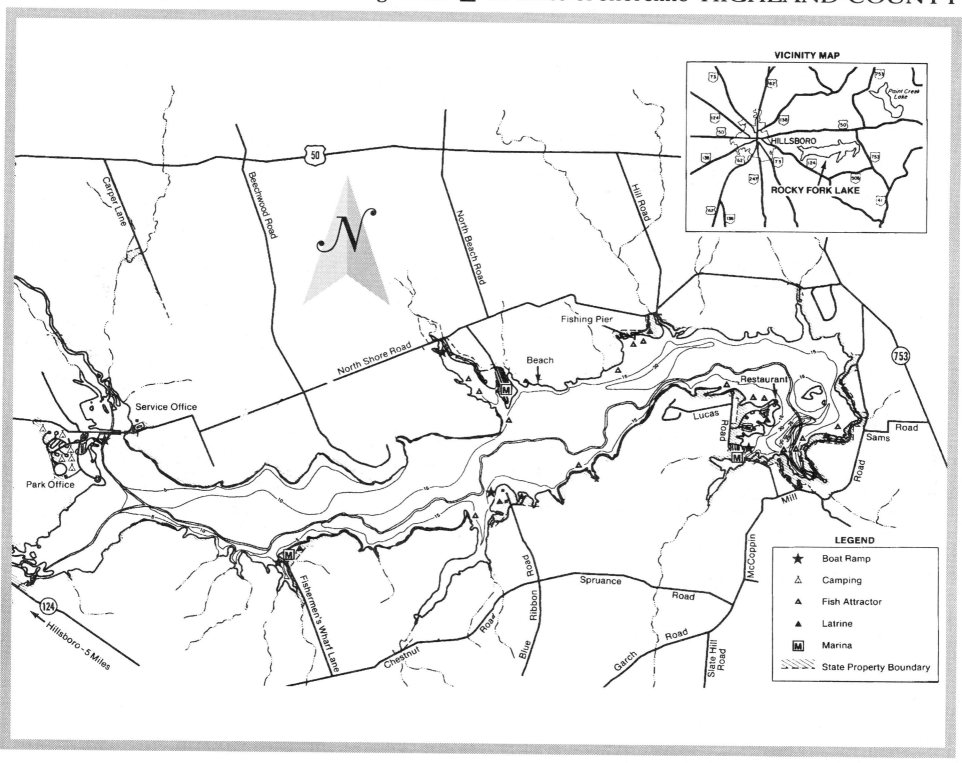

Location: In Highland County, 55 miles east of Cincinnati, five miles east of Hillsboro, 30 miles west of Chillicothe. The lake is accessible from U.S. Route 50 and SRs 124, 506 and 753.

Wildlife district office: (513) 372-9261.

Fishing opportunities: Crappies, bluegills, flathead and channel catfish, largemouth bass and muskie.

Water quality: Good.

Bottom composition: Mostly fine particle silt, and sand. Some rock.

Stocking: Walleye and muskie annually.

Horsepower restrictions: None. Mooring and boat rental are available at the state marina.

Camping: 225 sites at the state park, call (513) 393-4284.

Bait: At the modern lake marina and nearby tackle shops.

Shoreline: Half is private property.

Outlook:
Channel catfish - good
Crappie - good
Largemouth bass - fair
Muskellunge - good
Walleye - good

Crappies are the main fare at long and narrow Rock Fork Lake. Some large muskies and a few big walleyes are also taken from the lake.

The lake is nestled among a patchwork of farmlands and deciduous woodlots, and surrounded by private campgrounds, bait and tackle shops, party stores, RV storage and marinas. The state park campgrounds is filled by Friday during much of the summer.

How to catch 'em: As muskie fishing goes, a good number of the denizens are taken during June, July and August. Muskie enthusiasts should troll big plugs along points and dropoffs and pray for a strike. The big fish require wire leaders and plenty of patience. Try trolling near the marina and across from the beach. One local muskie angler swears by dark-colored plugs and a slower than normal trolling speed. He also says criss-crossing over areas where water depths change brings additional strikes. If you love muskie fishing, don't forget to try Cowan Lake.

Largemouth bass can be taken working diving and surface lures and rubber worms around brush, stick-ups and stumps. The point off Blue Ribbon Road is one hot spot. Shoreline anglers can do well on crappies if they fish the brush and structure. Rocky Fork Lake walleyes are most often taken off the bottom using a nightcrawler rig or jigs and minnows. Tight line drifting across the old channel across from the fishing pier at the end of Hill Road can be productive. Local experts also say that anglers should try working around the small island in front of the state park restaurant.

Catfish anglers should try scented doughballs, or beef or chicken livers, along the east shore and in the upper end of the lake. Staff says night fishing can be good during the entire summer.

Boat launching: The lake has five launching ramps and the East Shore Marina and Restaurant that offers docking, ramp and food service. The South Beach and Fisherman's Wharf launch, both on the south side of the lake, are popular with anglers. The North Beach Ramp, south off of North Shore Road, has a fuel pump and rentals.

Insider tips: 40-pound flathead catfish are taken every year during the middle of the summer. About 100,000 walleye and 4,000 10-12 inch muskies are planted each year. Rock Fork is 10 minutes from Paint Creek. The Rocky Fork State Park has a full-service campground, four miles of hiking trails and a nearby scenic mill. Many pontoon boats operate on the lake.

Rose Lake

HOCKING COUNTY ■ 17 acres of fishing water

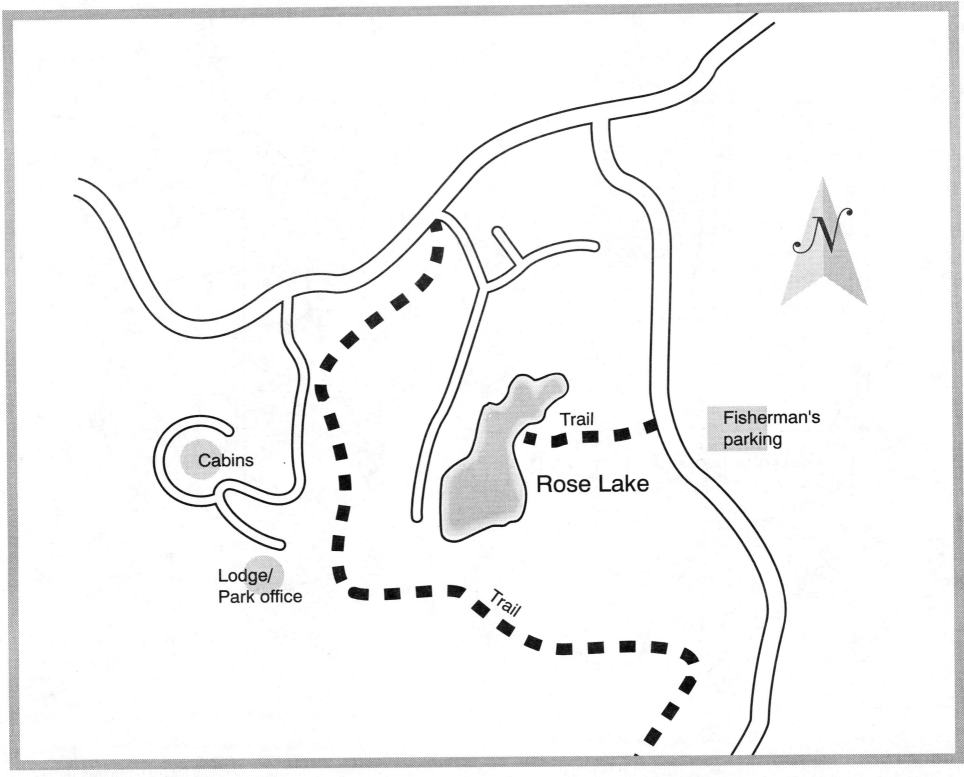

Location: In the Hocking Hills State Park, near Old Man's Cave. Take U.S. 33 to SR 664 and follow it south about 12 miles to the lake and rugged state park.

Wildlife district office: (614) 594-2211.

Fishing opportunities: Bluegills, largemouth bass, channel catfish and golden trout.

Water conditions: Clear.

Bottom composition: Firm.

Horsepower restriction: Electric only.

Stocking: Catfish and trout (annually).

Camping: Cabins and hundreds of sites, (614) 385-6841.

Outlook:
Bluegill - good
Largemouth bass - good
Channel catfish - excellent
Golden trout - excellent

The lake is near Old Man's Cave and the main campground in the beautiful Hocking Hills State Park. The remote spring-fed lake is a walk-to-only lake. You may carry in a small johnboat or canoe and use an electric motor. The lake sits in a tight valley among steep ridges, gorges and cliffs. Therefore on two sides of the lake are very steep hills, making shoreline access all but impossible. Both pines and hardwoods cover the hills offering anglers one of the most picturesque fishing experiences in the state. The intimate lake is also the water supply for the popular state park.

Hocking Hills is the most scenic place in Ohio. Each of the six state park units in the region has unique natural features including rushing waterfalls, deep gorges and huge caves set in beautiful woodlands. The surrounding cliffs and layered sandstone have been inhabited for thousands of years.

How to catch 'em: Non-reproductive trout are planted in the lake each spring. From this time until early summer trout fishing is very good—and sometimes crowded on the scenic little lake in the early season. Most trout anglers go after the hatchery-raised fish with small bladed spinners, corn on a bare hook or flies. The earlier in the year that you try for trout the better. As soon as the cool spring-fed lake begins to warm the trout might be either fished out or driven to the bottom.

Largemouth bass are tough to fool in this clear water. A park ranger said he has seen fly fishermen use wet streamers with some success on bass in the early season. Try for 6-8 inch bluegills in May and June, and good-sized catfish throughout the summer season. A delicate presentation, light line and evening fishing is the best pattern on this beautiful lake.

Hot spots: There are two accesses to the lake, one from the main campground and the other is Fishermen's Parking, which is about a one-half mile walk through a pine grove to the lake.

Underwater structure: Rose Lake is mostly featureless. A few small humps and old pockets of vegetation are where many fish suspend.

Boat launching: Hand-launch canoes and small johnboats from the walking path.

Ice fishing: Very little ice fishing is done on the lake.

Insider tips: This may be one of the most quiet, scenic and peaceful lakes in the Buckeye state. At one end of the lake is a beaver community—they are busy damming and building and are often seen by hikers and anglers. Plan on one of the most scenic and difficult fishing experiences in Ohio. Be ready to tour the area, including Old Man's Cave, Cedar Falls, Conkles Hollow, Rock House and Canwell Caves.

Ross Lake

■ 125 acres of fishing water ROSS COUNTY

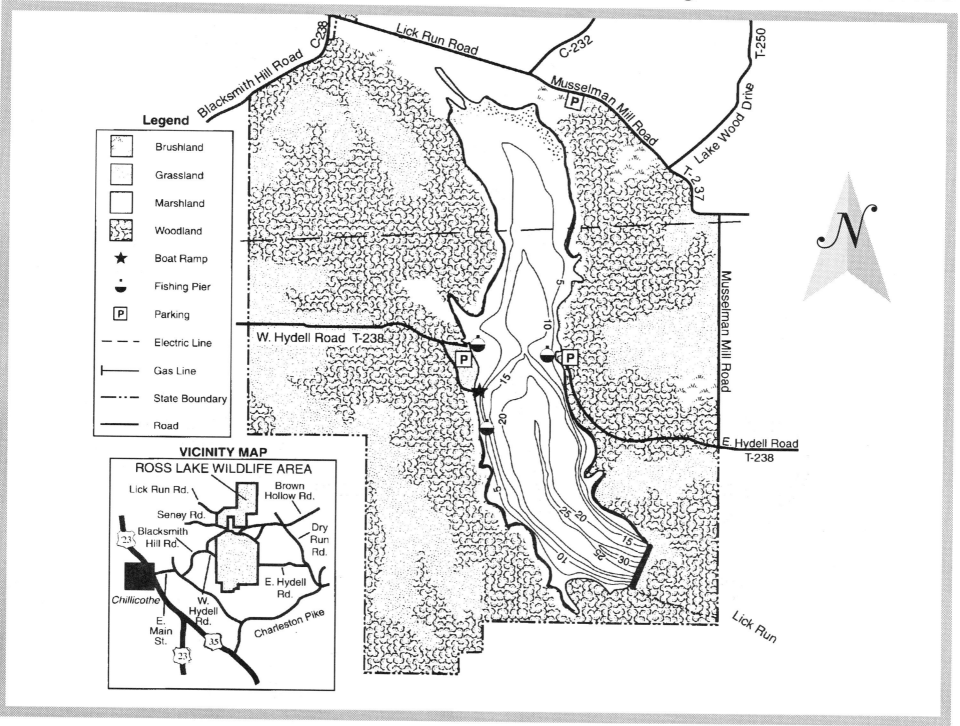

Location: In Ross County, two miles east of Chillicothe. Access is from U.S. Route 35 via the East Main St. exit and Blacksmith Hill Road (C-238.) Ross Lake is 48 miles from Columbus and 53 miles from Portsmouth.

Wildlife district office: (614) 594-2211.

Fishing opportunities: Bluegill, largemouth bass, channel catfish and some crappie.

Water conditions: Medium.

Bottom composition: Mud, firm in sections.

Horsepower restriction: Electric motor only.

Special regulations: Check bass length restriction.

Stocking: Channel catfish.

Outlook:
Bluegill, redear - fair to good seasonally
Largemouth bass - excellent
Channel catfish - excellent
Crappie - fair

Historically, Ross Lake has been a very good bass lake. There are good numbers of fish, with some individual largemouth up to 7-9 pounds. Year classes are well represented and the fishery is consistent. The lake is comparatively shallow and runs along the Lick Run valley between steep slopes and flat-topped hills which are covered by brushlands, old fields and mature woodlands. About half of the woodlands are hickory and oak, along with beech and sugar maple.

How to catch 'em: Bring your weedless baits to Ross Lake and find the old Hydell roadbed. Bluegill fishing is only fair, with 90 percent of the individuals being five to seven inches long, which is an overpopulation problem. Redear are moderately populated with six-to 10-inch fish the average size.

Good catches of early spring crappies are reported, with plenty of ten-inch fish being taken. Bass fishing is excellent and peaks in April and May, but can be very good into the warmer months and again in the fall. Try the stumpy upper half of the lake in the spring and move deeper after May. Local experts say night fishing with surface lures can also be good at this time of the year. Catfish up to 32 inches have been sampled. Cats are found evenly distributed throughout the lake.

Hot spots: In the spring (late April to late May) try the upper basin above the old roadbed (Hydell Road). During this time, the upper end of the lake becomes turbid due to rough fish and bass spawning. Along the west and southwest shoreline below the earthen fishing pier is also good. There are some shallows around some willows that hold fish. Also in the spring, try the dam. In the summer anglers will want to focus on the Hydell roadbed and at the fishing peninsulas where the road used to run across the lake. About midway between these facing peninsulas, over the old roadbed is an old culvert and other structure that hold good numbers of fish. This is a place where 30-40 bass can be caught in a day. Use weedless baits and classic worms.

Underwater structure: The upper part of the lake is weedy. This excess vegetation has kept the bluegill fishing down over the last decade. The division has felled shoreline trees, and more than 1,000 Christmas trees have been strategically submerged in recent years.

Boat launching: A two-lane ramp is at the end of Hydell Road (T-238) on the west side of the lake. The lanes are separated by a courtesy dock. A shoreline fishing area and dock for anglers with disabilities is in this area.

Ice fishing: Fair to good ice fishing takes place on the lake as weather permits.

Insider tips: Bring the kids—small bluegill are easy to catch and in huge (out of balance) numbers. Grass carp have been stocked in the lake to help with the dense vegetation problem. If you catch a grass carp, release it. A hand-surfaced fishing pier on the east side of the lake is accessible by fishermen with disabilities. A northerly wind can make the small lake choppy.

Lake Rupert (Wellston Wildlife Area)

VINTON COUNTY ■ 325 acres of fishing water

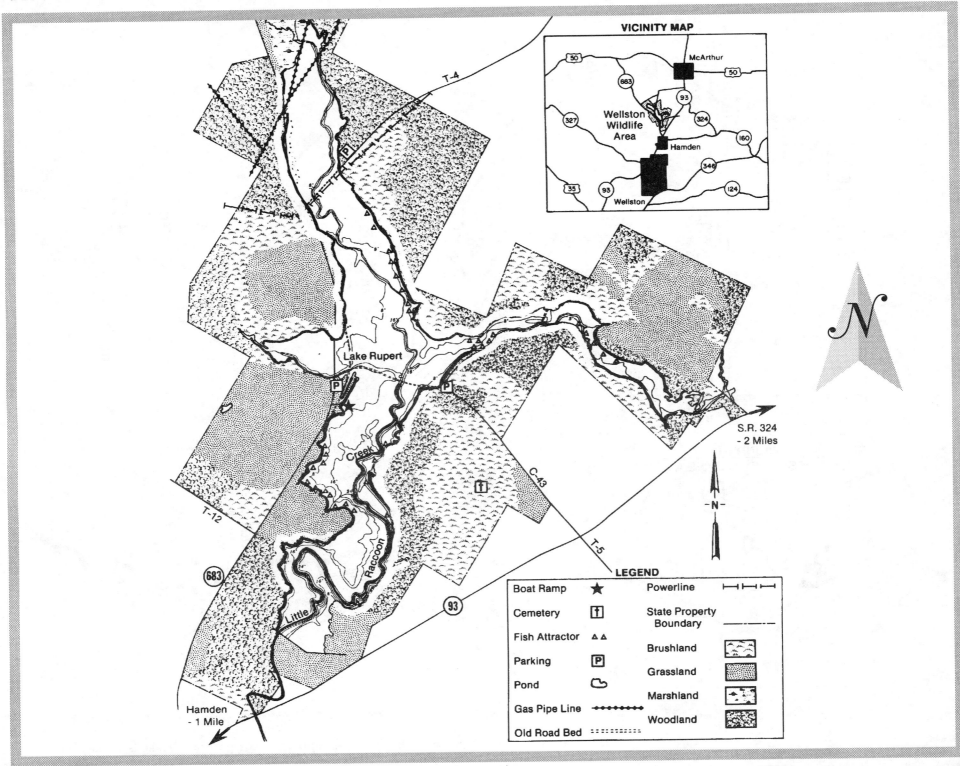

VICINITY MAP

LEGEND

Boat Ramp	★	Powerline	
Cemetery	✝	State Property Boundary	
Fish Attractor	▲▲		
Parking	P	Brushland	
Pond		Grassland	
Gas Pipe Line		Marshland	
Old Road Bed		Woodland	

Location: In Vinton County, one mile north of Hamden along SR 683, one-half mile north of the intersection with SR 93. It's 32 miles to Athens, 75 miles to Columbus and 30 miles to Chillicothe.

Wildlife district office: (614) 682-7524.

Fishing opportunities: Largemouth bass, northern pike, walleye, saugeye, some perch, bluegills and channel catfish.

Water conditions: Colored to medium clear.

Bottom composition: Soft, mud.

Horsepower restriction: 10 hp.

Stocking: Saugeye.

Outlook:
Bluegill, redear - good
Largemouth bass - excellent
Channel catfish - good-excellent
Walleye - excellent
Saugeye - excellent

The lake is formed by a big valley that's been dammed up. The deepest water is at the dam.

How to catch 'em: Slow trolling with spinners and nightcrawler rigs for walleye and saugeye is popular from the dam back to the narrow bay. Try drifting the east shoreline with a spinner, minnow or live nightcrawler, or working deep diving minnow imitation lures for walleye and saugeye. Bluegills can also be taken here and along the old roadbeds during spawning time. For big bullhead, head to the upper end of the lake and try small crayfish or shrimp on the bottom.

Largemouth bass fishing takes off in early March as the water in the coves starts to warm up. The fish often feed in these springtime shallows if they are near deep water where they can make a quick escape if spooked. Live nightcrawlers, according to local experts, are the top bait in the early spring. Later, during April and May, keep trying live nightcrawlers or cast spinners.

After the spawn (mid-May), look along sloping points using diving and rattling lures. After the water warms in mid-June, stick close to the shore and fish at dawn and dusk, or in deep water working any dropoff with diving minnows or crankbaits. Some bass anglers also bounce lures along the old creek channel during the heat of the summer.

Pike fishing is only fair, but worth your time in the spring when the fish move into 50-degree water. Cast spoons in the shallow north end of the lake, and as the water warms, use large live minnows to tease the big 'gators.

Hot spots: The Little Raccoon streambed in the middle of the lake is known for good walleye and saugeye. From the dam back up to the center of the lake are walleye and saugeye zones. The narrow bay that runs east and west from the middle of the lake is a terrific place for bass from spring until early summer. The north end, which is thick with lily pads, is a good place to seek pike, catfish and bass in the early season. The feeder stream in this area also gives up good numbers of channel cats, especially when the water is up or rising.

Underwater structure: About 450 Christmas trees have been submerged in the lake.

Boat launching: A newer ramp, with lighted parking, is at mid-lake on the west shore.

Ice fishing: Ice fishing is popular. The most popular location for ice fishing is near the intersection of T-4 and 683, on the west side of the narrow lake.

Insider tips: No swimming is allowed the pretty lake. The 1,298-acre wildlife area is managed for upland game and other species. Wellston Wildlife Area can be busy, but it's a pleasant nature area and great escape for a day or two.

Rush Lake

■ 300 acres of fishing water ■ 9.3 miles of shoreline FAIRFIELD AND PERRY COUNTIES

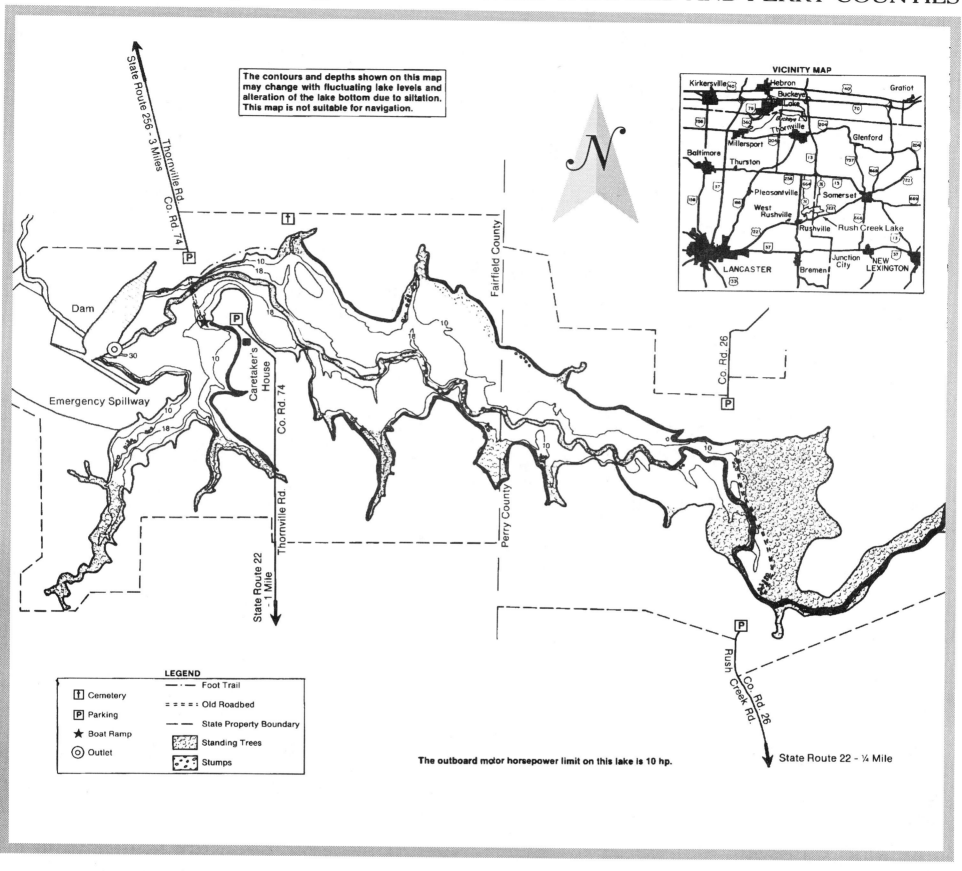

The contours and depths shown on this map may change with fluctuating lake levels and alteration of the lake bottom due to siltation. This map is not suitable for navigation.

The outboard motor horsepower limit on this lake is 10 hp.

LEGEND

✝ Cemetery	— · — Foot Trail
P Parking	= = = = Old Roadbed
★ Boat Ramp	— — — State Property Boundary
⊙ Outlet	Standing Trees
	Stumps

VICINITY MAP

Location: In Fairfield and Perry counties, approximately 13 miles northeast of Lancaster and six miles southwest of Somerset, with access on CR 26 and CR 74 off SR 22.

Wildlife district office: (614) 481-6300.

Fishing opportunities: Largemouth bass, channel catfish, bluegill and crappies.

Water condition: Very good, clear.

Bottom composition: Gravel and rock, considerable weed structure.

Horsepower restriction: 10 hp.

Depth: Up to 18 feet.

Outlook:
Largemouth bass - very good
Bluegill - fair, improving
Crappie - fair

Rush Creek Lake is much like Buckeye Lake (which, acre for acre, may have more fish than any other in Ohio). Construction on Rush Creek began in 1981, and was filled to pool limit in 1984. You can walk and fish from around the entire lake shore. The physical structure, embayments and vegetated coves make for an even distribution of fish and good natural habitats.

How to catch 'em: First-time anglers to the lake should begin from the north shore parking lot and work the shoreline east. In the spring and early summer, newcomers to the lake might also probe the

shorelines from either CR 26 access point. You can also fish these areas pretty well from the bank. A favorite largemouth spot is near the north parking lot off CR 26. Fish the dropoff that gives way to the creek channel. The mouths of the narrow bays along the south shore are also reported to be excellent places to buzz spinner bait in the mid-season.

Hot spots: Lots of catfish are taken from the channel that carves through the backwater. Excellent bottom fishing can be done in all parts of the lake if you anchor over the creek channel. Drifting along the creek channel is always a good pattern. Catfish anglers recommend fishing live bait as deep as possible.

Underwater structure: The shallower east end of the long lake has

some brush and cover over bluegill spawning beds. These are excellent areas to try during the spring and early summer.

Boat launching: There are four vehicle access points. The small boat launch is off CR 74, to the south, near the caretaker's house, one mile off SR 22.

Ice fishing: As the panfish increase in size, ice fishing is gaining popularity. Anglers typically fan out from the access on north and south CR 74.

Insider tips: Fish the east end of the lake in the spring. Local experts say topwater fishing for largemouth can be very good.

OHIO

Salt Fork Lake

GUERNSEY COUNTY ■ 2,952 acres of fishing water ■ 74 miles of shoreline

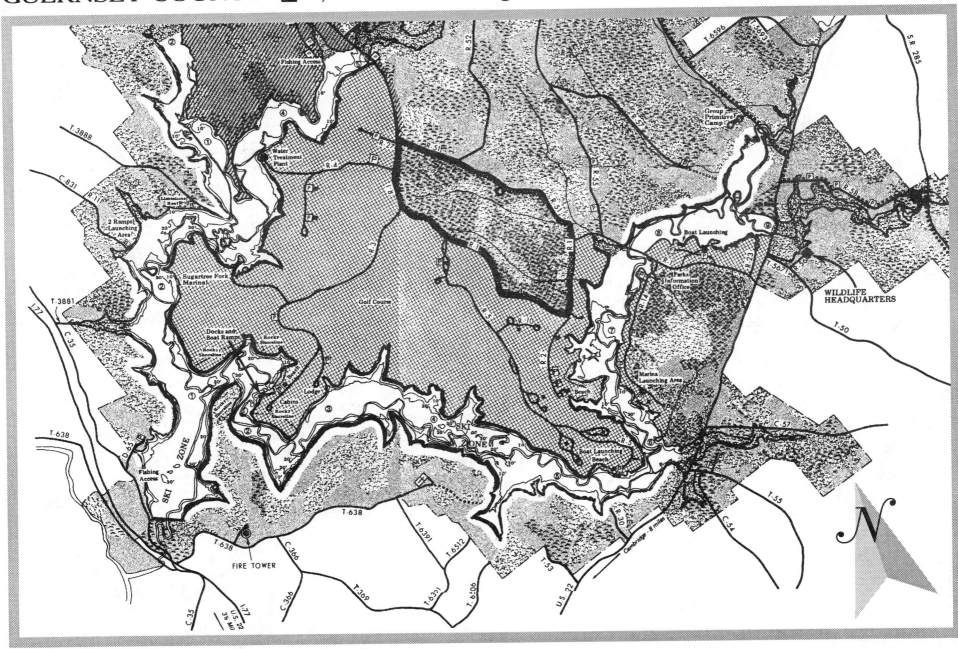

Location: In Guernsey County, in southeastern Ohio, seven miles east of Cambridge on U.S. Route 22. The lake is 88 miles from Columbus, 69 miles from Marietta and 60 miles from Steubenville.

Wildlife district office: (614) 594-2211.

Fishing opportunities: Bluegill, redear sunfish, crappie, large- and some smallmouth bass, channel catfish, flathead catfish, walleye and muskie.

Water conditions: Upper areas muddy after rain; generally clear.

Bottom composition: Mud, flooded timber.

Horsepower restrictions: None.

Stocking: Muskie and walleye annually, occasionally channel catfish.

Camping: 212 camping sites and 54 cabins are operated by the state park; call (800) 282-7275.

Boat rental at marinas.

Special regulation: Size limit on largemouth bass.

Average depth: 12-14 feet, up to 35 feet at the dam.

Outlook:
Bluegill, redear - good

Large- and smallmouth bass - excellent
Channel catfish - excellent
Walleye - good
Muskie - excellent

The lake is in hilly southeastern Ohio, along steep to rolling terrain that is scattered with small streams and teeming with wildlife. The elevations vary from 790 to 1,065 feet in the oak and hickory hills. The lake occupies bottomland and was constructed in 1967. Trees and shrubs were left standing in many embayments and an artificial reef was constructed on the north branch to provide fish cover.

How to catch 'em: You must troll a lot to pick up muskies. Generally, muskie anglers troll large crankbaits, spinners and plugs. Avid muskie anglers report that various colors work, and that the trick is to have your baits in the water when the predatory denizens go on the bite. Troll the south shore near the dam and the north shore between the state park lodge and the swimming beach. Try trolling the lure close to the boat or off boards.

Largemouth bass are in high numbers and exhibit a good range of year classes. Bass anglers use the entire arsenal on the lake including plastic worms, spinner baits and crank baits. Bass fishing is at its peak in April, May and early June, when the fish rise to shallow waters. In summer, bass are more likely to be found in deeper waters near dropoffs and deep weedbeds, in the old stream channel, old roadbeds, or other natural humps on the bottom. The smallmouth fishery continues to offer quality catches during spring and fall. Walleyes are represented by several year classes, with some individuals weighing up to 14 pounds. Jig a minnow or twister tail for walleyes over any gravel, rock or sandy bottom.

Both white and black crappies, white being more abundant, are found in and around underwater cover. Bluegill are of average size, ranging 5-7 inches and are in moderate abundance. Redear sunfish are increasing in numbers. Channel cats range from 12-15 pounds.

Hot spots: In the spring, try the shallow embayments that have lots of timber, stumps and structure for largemouth bass. The lower end of the lake, toward the dam, is the muskie zone. This area is especially good during July and August; the rest of the game fishery is best April to June.

Underwater structure: Fish management crews have been active over the years placing Christmas trees throughout the year. If found, these trees are excellent for spring crappie fishing.

Boat launching: Six paved ramps suitable for trailered boats are scattered around the lake. There are also a number of primitive areas where you could launch a cartop boat or canoe. The largest ramp is at Salt Fork Marina. Modern two-lane launches are a also at Sugartree Fork Marina, the campground beach, in the cabin are of the state park and behind the office. The state park has 470 docks; 364 more are at Salt Fork Marina. Both marinas have rentals, fuel and so on.

Ice fishing: Depending on the weather, of course, ice fishing can be popular.

Insider tips: Once warm weather hits, the lake is busy with recreational boating, water skiing and personal watercraft. The wildlife area is open to public hunting and there are a variety of land uses around the lake. During netting surveys, 20-40 pound muskies are collected daily. A 65-foot tour boat cruises the lake. The large state park has a lodge, golf course, hunting and hiking trails.

Seneca Lake

■ 3,550 acres of fishing water   ■ 48 miles of shoreline   GUERNSEY & NOBLE COUNTIES

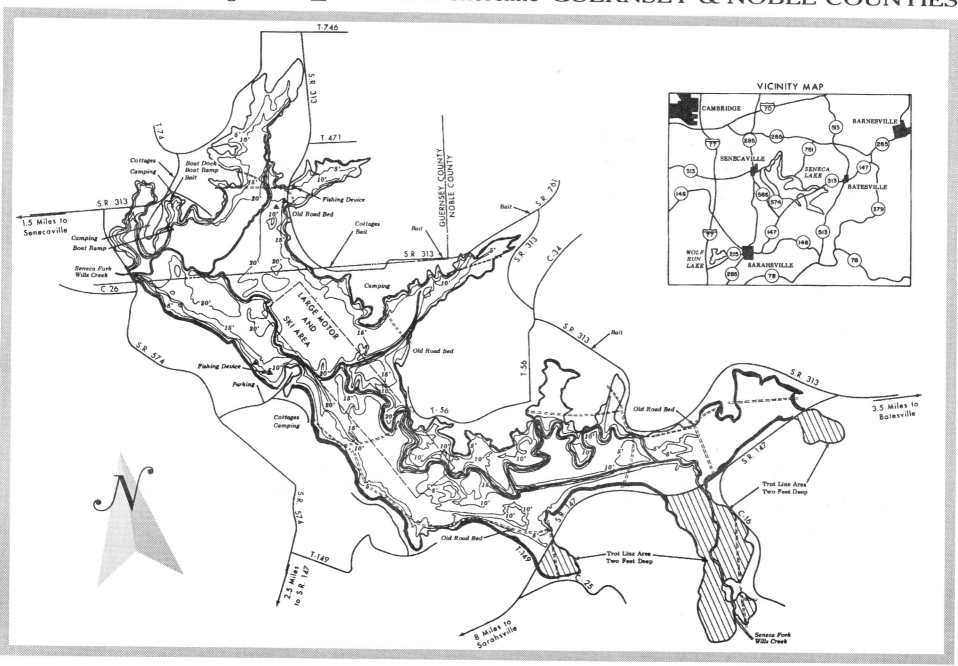

Location: In Guernsey and Noble counties, two miles east of Senecaville on SR 313, 12 miles southeast of Cambridge via I-77 and SR 313.

Wildlife district office: (614) 594-2211.

Fishing opportunities: Largemouth bass, bluegill, crappie, flathead and channel catfish, yellow perch, walleye and muskie.

Fishing forecast: Senecaville Fish Hatchery, (614) 685-5541.

Water conditions: Medium clear.

Bottom composition: Varied; firm, mud, vegetation.

Stocking: Striped bass, walleye.

Horsepower restriction: 180 hp.

Maximum depth: 31 feet.

Boat rental.

Special regulation: Check for minimum length on bass.

Camping: 576 sites in two locations; call (216) 343-6647.

Outlook:
Bluegill - good
Largemouth bass - excellent
Channel catfish - excellent
Walleye - good, improving
Striped bass - good
Crappies - fair

The dam was built across the valley of Seneca Fork of Wills Creek by the Army Corps of Engineers in 1938 for flood control and recreation. The lake, which is the third largest in the state, was opened for fishing in 1940. The lake is closely managed and the emphasis is on trophy bass. Seneca Lake is cyclical in its crappie production (as are most lakes). This is a main reason hundreds of Christmas trees are annually placed in the lake.

The lake is part of the Muskingum Watershed Conservancy District.

How to catch 'em: Bass fishing at Seneca is excellent. The season begins during the early warming days of March in the shallow coves close to deep water. Annual electroshocking surveys produce many six-pound largemouth. The big fish will take simple nightcrawlers in the early season. When the water warms to 60 degrees, the shallow bays should be scoured with rubber worms and spinners. Topwater fans can find good fishing along the shoreline and around structure during summer mornings and evenings. Many bass anglers also flip worms in weeds and around docks. During the day in the summer, local experts work long sloping points with deep-divers or bottom-bouncing lures. For bass action, also find old roadbeds, any dropoffs and the creek channel.

Walleye populations are improving in the lake, with some 30-inch fish recorded by biologists. A good base of young fish will make the lake a top fishery over the coming years. For best results drift or troll spinners tipped with a live nightcrawler or minnow. In deeper water use diving minnow imitations. Recreational boating traffic on the lake is heavy and hard on walleye fishermen. Serious walleye anglers should try mid-week or early morning and evening venues. Panfishing is very good. There is a heavy population of six- to eight-inch bluegills throughout the lake. Simple worm rigs work well. There is trotline area for catfishing in the upper end of the lake. Rod and reel anglers can take good catches of cats on prepared baits, shrimp and smelly liver.

Hot spots: The upper part of the lake from the dam back about one-third the length of the lake is the best sport fishing zone (especially during the spring). Cadillac Bay, filled with lily pads, is productive in the spring and early summer. A few muskie are taken at the dam and in Cadillac Bay each year.

Underwater structure: About once every five years Christmas trees are submerged at prime fishing locations in seven - 15 feet of water. A variety of nature drops and points can be found on the map or by watching other anglers. Use your fish finder to spot patterns.

Boat launching: The launch ramp is near the roadside park off SR 313. A full service marina offers boat rentals, marina supplies, docking and a nearby restaurant. Call (614) 685-5831 for details.

Ice fishing: Depending on the ice conditions, anglers can venture onto the lake for good panfishing and some walleye taken off the bottom.

Insider tips: Sleeping aboard watercraft is permitted in designated areas only. The lake is managed to produce broodstock to make hybrid stripers for planting around the state. The MWCD park operates a beach, nature center, cabin rentals, hiking, campgrounds and marina. The lake has a boater's swim area.

Shreve Lake

WAYNE COUNTY ■ 58 acres of fishing water

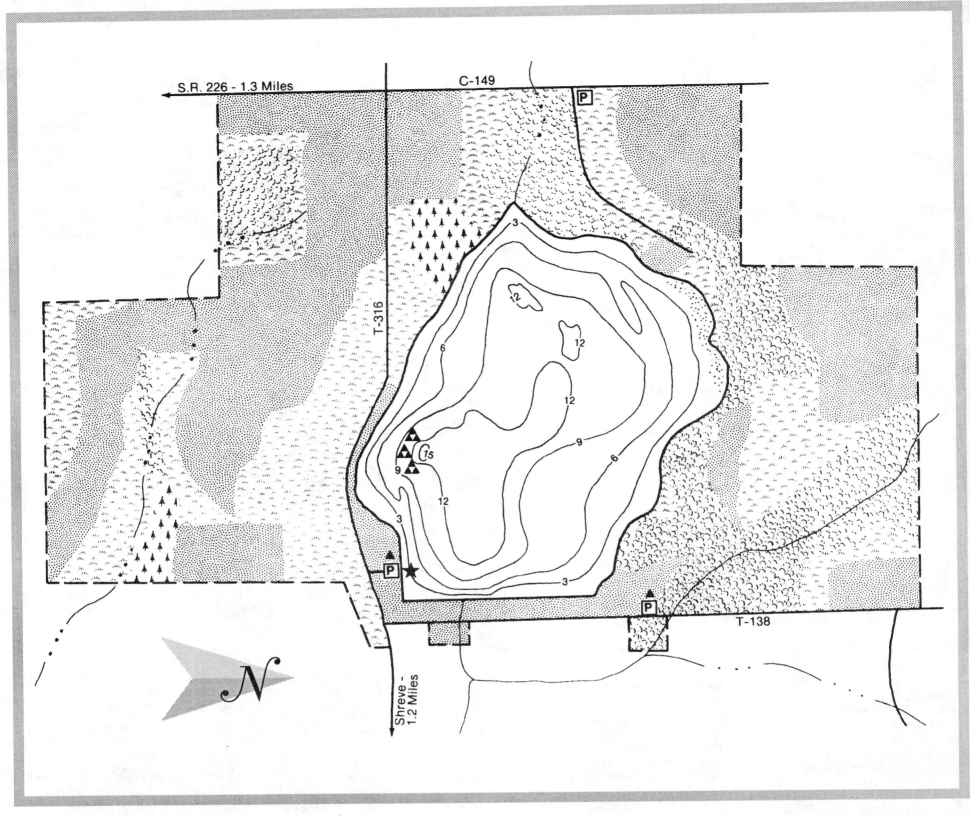

Location: In Wayne County, 12 miles from Loudonville, 18 miles from Wooster and 20 miles from Millersburg. It's about 1.2 miles west of Shreve, north of SR 226. County Road 140 is on the western boundary.

Wildlife district office: (330) 644-2293.

Fishing opportunities: Channel catfish, largemouth bass, sunfish, some pike and rough fish.

Water conditions: Murky and colored, farm runoff.

Bottom composition: Mud.

Horsepower restriction: Electric motors only.

Depth: Shallow.

The main reason you visit Shreve Lake, which is in the 228-acre Shreve Lake Wildlife Area in northeastern

Ohio, is for peace and quiet. As the district fish biologist said, "it's a great place to do paperwork." I agree. Better yet, bring your family for an afternoon of fishing the small lake and wandering about the wildlife area. The steeply rolling topography is well drained and evidence of glacial sandstone is present.

The wildlife area was purchased with federal money in 1958. The natural marsh was enlarged by the construction of an earthen dam and the diversion of a small stream from the north into the lake. The dam was completed in 1961 and the lake was filled in 1962.

How to catch 'em: Panfishing and bass fishing are good—not excellent, but good. The lake is weedy and user friendly. In a boat, you could fish every spot on the lake in two hours. The small lake can be fished with simple live bait rigs, or

toss artificals and enjoy the solitude. The lake is so small, the fish can't get away from you.

If you are serious about catching fish (and not relaxing), try visiting in the spring and early summer for largemouth bass. Spinner and crankbaits can excite the fish at this time of the year. A few fallen trees, stumps, mild dropoffs and weedbeds also contain both panfish and largemouths.

Try tiny hooks armed with redworms, leeches or crickets for medium-sized bluegill. Crappies are evenly distributed and often relate to submerged stumps and brushy areas in the spring, and deeper water during the summer. Bright jigs, worm rigs and lively minnows can bring in a few scrappy crappies. Fly fishermen should try casting poppers, rubber spiders and other terrestrials.

Hot spot: Fishing is good from the handicapped accessible pier.

Underwater structure: A handful of fish attractors have been placed in the lake.

Boat launching: The single concrete ramp is on the northeast end of the oval lake, just off T-138.

Ice fishing: Also quiet in the winter, only a handful of anglers ice fish Shreve.

Insider tips: Bring your own bait and supplies. There are no marinas or nearby supplies on this very small, relaxing lake. Anglers who hunt should check out the area. Small game and deer hunting is considered good. While fishing the lake, watch for raccoon and muskrats, and birds overhead.

Lake Snowden

■ 131 acres of fishing water ■ 7.1 miles of shoreline ATHENS COUNTY

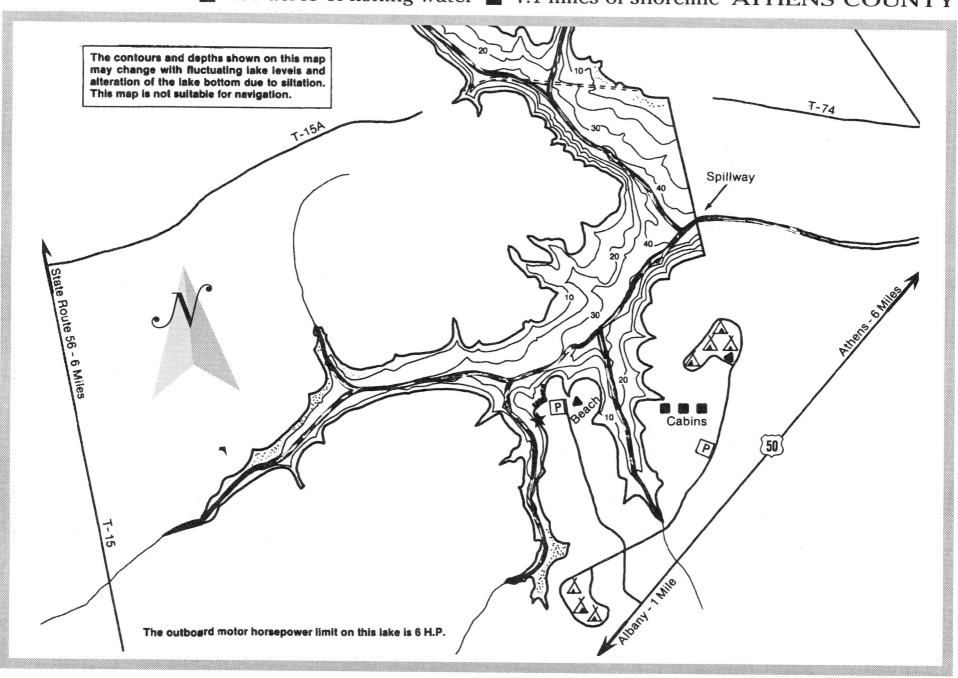

The contours and depths shown on this map may change with fluctuating lake levels and alteration of the lake bottom due to siltation. This map is not suitable for navigation.

The outboard motor horsepower limit on this lake is 6 H.P.

Location: In Athens County, six miles southwest of Athens and one mile northwest of Albany, with access from U.S. Route 50. The lake is 80 miles from Columbus, 145 miles from Cincinnati, 190 miles from Cleveland.

Wildlife district office: (614) 594-2211.

Fishing opportunities: Largemouth bass, crappie, northern pike, channel catfish and bluegill.

Water conditions: Medium clear, colored seasonally.

Bottom composition: Mostly mud, some gravel.

Horsepower restriction: 10 hp.

Stocking: Channel catfish.

Depth: Up to 40 feet.

Camping: 95 sites, some cabins; call (614) 698-6373.

Special regulations: Check slot limit.

Outlook:
Bluegill, redear - good
Largemouth bass - excellent
Channel catfish - excellent

Lake Snowden was filled in 1972 and has since received as much bass management as any lake in Ohio. The first studies began in the early 1980s and were continuously evaluated for a six-year period. Based on these concentrated studies, the lake has responded very well to Division of Wildlife management efforts.

The lake is also an excellent channel catfish fishery. Because of the ability of managers to regulate the bass size, bluegill fishing has also proven to be excellent. Good habitat, including rooted aquatic vegetation, submerged trees, overhanging brush and a varied shoreline makes the good an overall good fishery.

How to catch 'em: Catfish are densely populated and sizes generally range from 11-17 inches. However, 10-pounders are taken with some regularity. Catfish are stocked on alternate years and the population is destined to remain strong. Try for them along extending points, the dam area and shoreline points. The best fishing is when the water is 60 to 90 degrees. Bring a bag of stink bait or doughballs.

Most of the bluegill (average size 6-8 inches) congregate around deep-water structure, especially when the water is 55 degrees or colder.

These denizens are best teased with fat waxworms, redworms or other small baits fished on a small hook. During the warming months, local anglers say many bluegills can be caught near the surface, especially when they are moving from their spawning beds in the late spring. Bring your fly rod and popper or other terrestrials. Sunfish average 6-9 inches and mix with the bluegill.

The many bass tournaments conducted on the lake are a testament to the quality of the fish. Largemouth start hitting lures in March as the water warms and don't slow down much until freeze-up. Most early season bass are caught over deep water structure on jig and twister tails or pork rind-jig combinations. You can also run deep-diving crankbaits for much of the year. When the water temperature reaches about 70 degrees, the fish start moving and bait casting rigs can best fling spinners, buzz baits and surface lures.

Tournament anglers often use plastic worms around weeds and repeated casting of medium divers around any ledges or humps. The mouths of small bays and coves are popular places to drift and cast at the shore. Some tournament anglers contend

that black and silver, crayfish and chartreuse are the best colors.

Hot spots: Try a dark-colored jig and pig along the vegetation lines during the summer at night for bass.

Underwater structure: In the back of some of the finger-like coves, some trees are down offering brushy structure that holds panfish and other species. The lake has a good balance of aquatic vegetation. Weedbeds are distinct and fishing in and around the pockets can be productive.

Boat launching: The launch, along a gravel bay, can be difficult to get in and out of. The traction is poor. The launch is off Route 50 near the swimming beach, six miles from Albany.

Insider tips: Several catfish and bass tournaments occur on the lake. One stocking of saugeye was undertaken in 1994. The division is hoping to have annual saugeye stocking started soon. The park has camping, concessions, a swimming beach, bathhouse, docks and day-use areas.

Spencer Lake

MEDINA COUNTY ■ 78 acres of fishing water

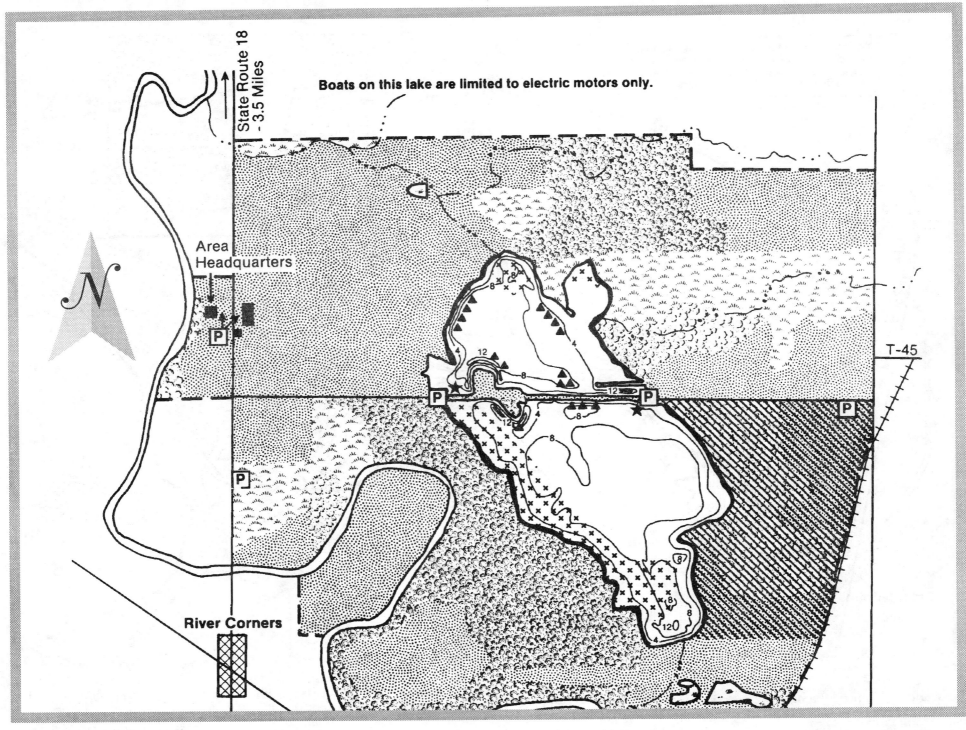

Boats on this lake are limited to electric motors only.

Location: In Medina County, two miles east of the village of Spencer, north of SR 162. SR 162 and Medina County Roads 27 and 58 provide good access.

Wildlife district office: (330) 644-2293.

Fishing opportunities: Channel catfish, largemouth bass, crappies, grass carp and bluegills.

Fishing forecast: River Corners General Store, (216) 648-2858.

Water conditions: Medium clear to medium green.

Bottom composition: Mud.

Horsepower restriction: Electric motors only.

Stocking: Channel catfish.

Outlook:
Largemouth bass - good
Bluegills - excellent
White crappies - good
Channel catfish - excellent
Brown bullhead - good

Quiet Spencer is mainly a bass/bluegill/catfish lake. The small lake was flooded in the early 1960s. The lake is unusual in that it is constructed on a "saddle," or watershed divide, and has a dam on both ends of the lake. A storm in 1969 washed out the north dam. It was rebuilt in 1970 and the lake was enlarged to its present size of 78 acres. The lake is part of the Spencer Lake Wildlife Area, a 618-acre natural area. Waterfowl hunting is popular here.

The lake was drawn down in 1985 to facilitate a fishery rehabilitation project. Three locations along the causeway were recontoured and deepened to 12 feet. This area is now an excellent shoreline fishing area. The lake was refilled and restocked with largemouth bass, bluegills and catfish in 1986. The lake is popular with Cleveland-area anglers and gets a lot of fishing pressure.

How to catch 'em: The catfishing is so good at the lake, Wildlife Division biologists are studying the lake to see why. They hope to learn why the catfish population is so well established, indications of certain preferred breeding habitats, natural reproduction rates and so on. The catfish are big, too. Most anglers use simple catfishing techniques, including cutbait, cow liver and nightcrawlers fished on the bottom at night in the summer.

The average channel catfish is about 18 inches. Many bullheads are a foot long—and tasty. Some nine to 10-inches crappies are taken in the spring and early summer on leeches, maggots and crickets. Bring your fly rod and cast poppers and bugs with leg, for fast action in the early season.

Try for spring largemouth bass along the stumpy west shore or at the face of the causeway. Most bass anglers cast spinner baits of every types and color. One local expert says he topwater fishes for bass and does well using Spook- and surface rattle-type lures. Flipping worms in the weedbed can produce bass, and small live baits will bring in the bluegill, which average six to eight inches.

Hot spots: The unassuming lake has superior shoreline access. About 85 percent of the shoreline is accessible and fishable. Two fishing piers that are accessible by people with disabilities are also on the rectangular lake.

Underwater structure: The clear water promotes considerable aquatic plant growth. Scattered weedbeds are always a good bet for panfish and largemouth bass. A field unit is stationed at the lake and a lot of structure has been placed over the years.

Boat launching: Two concrete launching ramps are on the east and west side of lake.

Ice fishing: On sunny winter weekends, the lake can be busy with anglers panfishing.

Insider tips: The lake is surrounded by lush and rolling agricultural lands. Bring your own bait. The lake can be crowded. Yogi Berra made a remark that fits Spencer, "Nobody comes here anymore because it's so popular."

Stonelick Lake

■ 171 acres of fishing water   ■ 10 miles of shoreline CLEMONT COUNTY

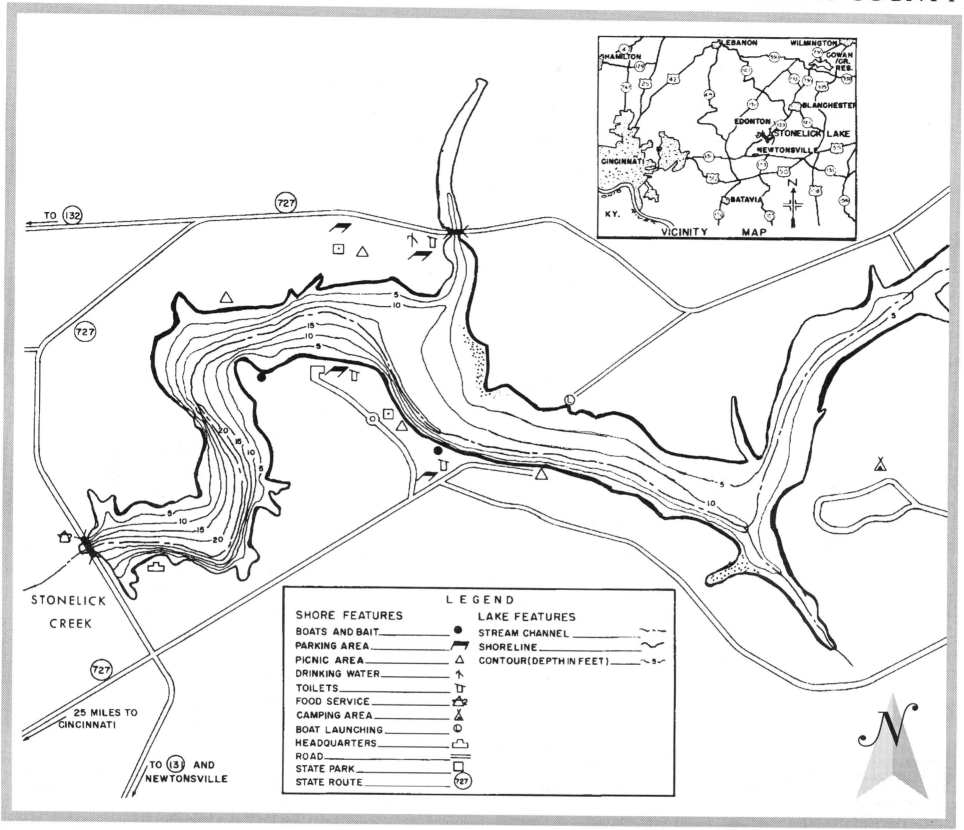

LEGEND

SHORE FEATURES
BOATS AND BAIT ●
PARKING AREA
PICNIC AREA △
DRINKING WATER
TOILETS
FOOD SERVICE
CAMPING AREA
BOAT LAUNCHING
HEADQUARTERS
ROAD
STATE PARK
STATE ROUTE 727

LAKE FEATURES
STREAM CHANNEL
SHORELINE
CONTOUR (DEPTH IN FEET) 5

Location: In Clermont County, 25 miles east of Cincinnati. From Cincinnati take SR 131 east to SR 727. Go north to the lake and quiet state park.

Fishing opportunities: Largemouth, bluegill, channel catfish, crappie, rough fish and some spotted bass.

Water conditions: Fairly turbid.

Bottom composition: Stumps, mud, vegetation.

Horsepower restrictions: Electric motors only.

Camping: Stonelick State Park, (513) 625-7544.

Small seasonal boat rental.

Where prairie meets forest, the Stonelick Lake area reflects a time when warmer climates and tall grasses flowed like oceans across the Midwest. Only one-half hour from Cincinnati, the mature lake is used lightly. The fishing is good, but the scenery and peacefulness are better. The water is almost always smooth and boat traffic is slow and quiet. Once a year, however, the state park does put on a rollicking canoe race. That's about as much excitement as there is at the retreat-type lake.

In a quiet state park, this older lake has accessible shorelines. It's fairly shallow, with plenty of stumps and panfish/bass-type cover throughout.

How to catch 'em: The deepest section of the lake is at the dam, where many anglers drift and concentrate their efforts. The lake once held the record for spotted bass. The scattered weedbeds hold crappies and bass, where rubber worms and surface lures can be productive. Channel catfish are taken with crayfish and soft crawls on the bottom during the summer months. Planting of threadfin shad to increase the forage base is sometimes done. Kids can have a ball catching small bluegills from the shore using simple live bait and bobber rigs.

Hot spots: The edges and pockets around standing vegetation are best in the spring and early summer. Most anglers concentrate on the west end of the lake and the recently dredged upper end.

Underwater structure: The upper end of the lake was dredged in the mid-1990s and will hold some fish. Large sections of the lake have standing vegetation. There is no manmade structure in the lake.

Boat launching: There are two small concrete ramps. One is at the west end near Newtonsville Road and the other is just past the cemetery near the east end of the lake.

Ice fishing: Some ice fishing for panfish is done on the lake. Solid and safe ice for any length of time is rare.

Insider tips: The quiet state park has seven miles of hiking trails, a beach, day-use areas, campground and a Rent-A-Camp program where you can rent a tent and equipment. It's a great way to try camping, without the initial expense. I once locked the my keys in my car at Stonelick, and a handy park ranger and his "Long John" Jimmy bar came to the rescue. The park has a great staff!

Tappan Lake

HARRISON COUNTY ■ 2,350 acres of fishing water ■ 47 miles of shoreline

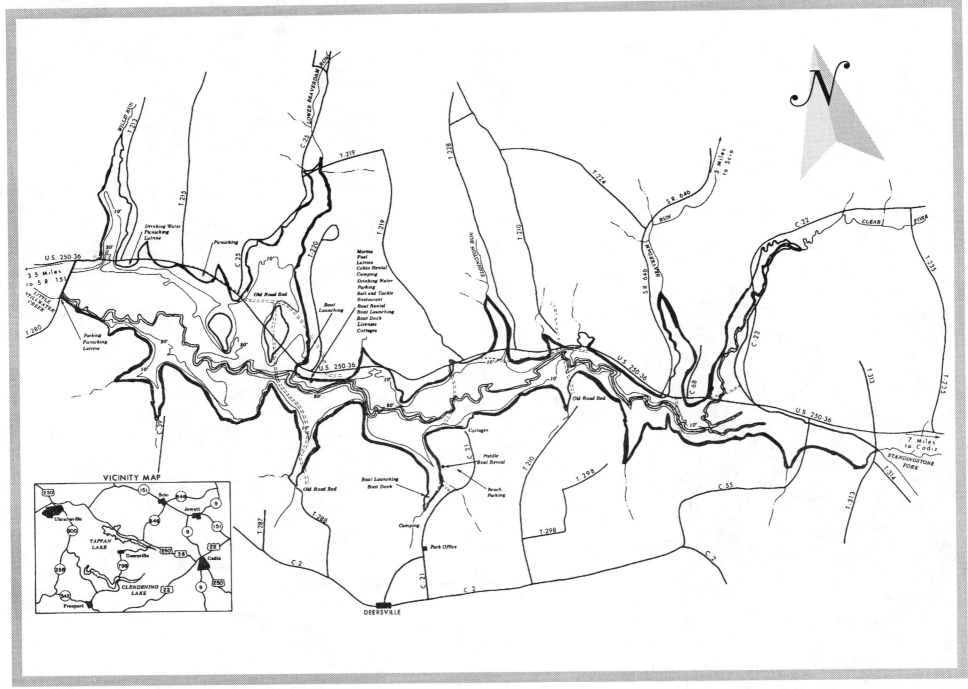

Location: In Harrison County. U.S. 250 follows the main body of the reservoir for seven miles. It's 7.5 miles west of Cadiz.

Wildlife district office: (330) 664-2293.

Fishing opportunities: Largemouth bass, crappies, white bass, bluegill, channel and flathead catfish and a few large walleye.

Water condition: Medium to clear.

Bottom composition: Mixed, mud, some gravel.

Horsepower restriction: 120 hp limit.

Maximum depth: 34 feet.

Boat rental: (614) 269-2031.

Camping: 500 sites, call (614) 922-3649.

Stocking: Saugeye.

Outlook:
Largemouth bass - good
Channel catfish - excellent
White crappies - poor
Saugeye - very good
White bass - excellent, in season

Surrounded by pines, winding

Tappan Lake has a reputation as a largemouth bass lake and draws a lot of tournament action. Tappan is also one of the few inland lakes that has a very good white bass fishery. The lake is part of the Muskingum Watershed Conservancy District, which is organized to help control floods, for conservation and to provide recreation. The group owns the lake and surrounding land, and is responsible for managing it. The dam is owned and operated by the U.S. Army Corps of Engineers and is on Stillwater Creek. It was built in 1936.

How to catch 'em: Saugeye fishing is fair to very good (15-24 inch average size), with most of the action in the deeper waters near the dam along the gravel points. Tappan is also a good crappie lake, especially in April and May. In mid-summer, particularly in August, white bass come up to the surface in schools chasing small bait fish. This is called a "jump," when the panicked bait fish literally jump out of the water (kinda like Flipper), trying to escape the swarming school of hungry silver-colored bass. To fish the jumps, try casting at the school with small Mepps-type spinners or a jig if

you need to cast a long distance. The jump (school) of white bass can be spooked easily, sending them deep. Fish the white bass jumps on hot days in the evenings.

Most largemouth are taken by casting to the shoreline in the spring or wading using artificial lures. The many bays and coves are terrific places to probe. Night fish for catfish using cutbaits or try some commercial doughballs. Bring your cane pole and a can of redworms for fast action on bluegills. Serious anglers should find the old creek channel and still or drift fish the wide spots in the lake.

Call the marina for a good fishing report at (614) 269-2031.

Hot spots: Fish for largemouth early in the season in the upper end near the headwaters. Each year biologists do an early season electro-shocking study in this area and some huge largemouth bass are rolled. In fact, 20-30 largemouth per pass in the shocking boats is considered good. In this area upwards of 100 fish are commonly rolled to the surface by biologists during the census survey. There's plenty of shoreline access points, near good reachable fishing areas.

Underwater structure: In the early 1990s, the Wildlife Division used a helicopter to move entire tree stumps into the lake. The chopper actually bombed the lake with trees stumps near U.S. 250. Today, placement of underwater structure continues. Use your sounder and check with the marina about current structure placement.

Boat launching: Two concrete ramps serve the lake. One is on U.S. 250 near the roadside rest area, and another is at Tappan Marina, (614) 269-2031. The marina rents boats and docking, and sells marine supplies, bait, limited tackle and food at a small restaurant with a great lake view. Houseboats and slow-moving pontoons are common.

Ice fishing: Not much ice fishing is done on the lake.

Insider tips: Turkey hunting along the lake is popular in the spring. Early bird anglers often hear turkeys gobbling in the distance. Watch for the white bass runs in August. The sprawling park on the lake has nature trails, camping, picnic areas, an activity center and a sandy swimming beach.

Timbre Ridge Lake

■ 100 acres of fishing water ■ 4 miles of shoreline LAWRENCE COUNTY

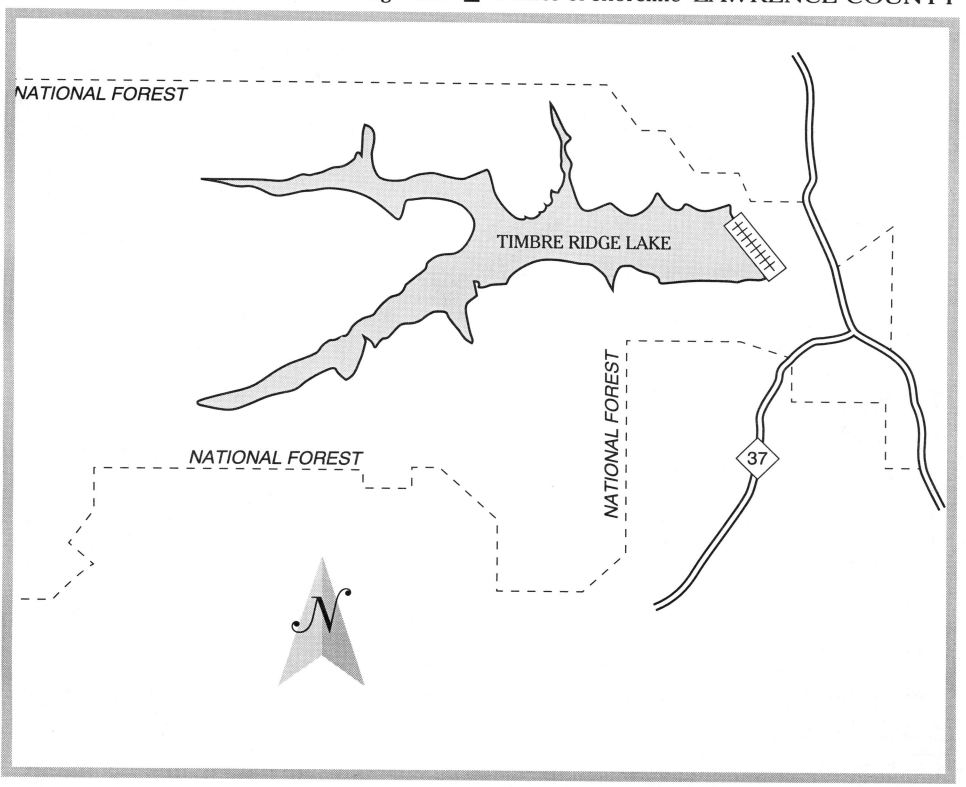

NATIONAL FOREST

TIMBRE RIDGE LAKE

NATIONAL FOREST

NATIONAL FOREST

N

37

Location: In Lawrence County. 20 miles southwest of Ironton, 20 miles northeast of Gallipolis and 15 miles north of Rio Grande. From SR 790 taken CR 37 south to the lake and dam area.

Wildlife district office: (614) 594-2211.

Fishing opportunities: Bluegill, largemouth bass and channel catfish.

Water conditions: Clear.

Bottom composition: Mud.

Horsepower restriction: Electric motors.

Stocking: Channel catfish.

Check current bass regulations.

Camping is permitted, except at launch and dam areas.

Outlook:
Bluegill - very good
Largemouth bass - good, improving

Channel catfish - good

The Division of Wildlife has a fish management agreement with the Wayne National Forest to oversee Timbre Lake's fishery. The area is open to the public and free public fishing has been in effect since 1991. Managers have imposed a slot length limit on largemouth bass in an effort to improve the bluegill fishery. At one time the lake was being developed as a resort lake. Currently some master planning is underway to determine future development, if any. The lake waters are clear and come from a protected watershed. The remote lake rarely gets turbid.

How to catch 'em: Timbre Lake has quality bluegill fishing. Many of the 'gills are 8-10 inches and when they are on the bite, dozens can be taken in an afternoon or evening. Surprisingly, many bluegills are taken in 30-foot-deep water. Try still fishing for the big bluegills that will take all types of larvae baits includ-

ing waxworms, mealworms or slip bobbers.

With regular stocking, catfishing is improving. Good-sized cats have been taken in the west half of the lake on dead minnows and chicken or beef livers. Bottom fish the clear water in the evening.

Hot spots: The remote lake has two long branches that tail off to shallow water. Deep-water bluegill fishing is best in the east half of the lake to the dam, while spring bass angling can be good in the wide branches that point west.

Underwater structure: Look for natural humps and fallen trees as the only structure in the lake. No manmade fishing devices or fish concentrating structures have been installed.

Boat launching: The small gravel ramp is at the corner of the dam. Cars and trailers must park along the road below the dam. Only small fishing boats can launch from the

narrow, gravel ramp.

Insider tips: The lake is surrounded by mature woodlands owned by the U.S. Forest Service. Swimming is allowed at your own risk. This is one of the most remote lakes covered in this book, offering anglers a chance to visit the Wayne National Forest and explore the wooded rolling hills. A couple of foot trails wander along the north shore and overland in this area. Pack out your garbage. The nearest community is Lecta at the intersection of State Routes 775 and 790.

The dam, boat ramp and parking area are closed between 10 p.m. and 6 a.m. unless lawfully used for fishing or camping. For more information about the national forest, write the District Ranger, Ironton Ranger District, 6518 State Route 93, Pedro, Ohio 45659.

Turkey Creek Lake

SCIOTO COUNTY ■ 48 acres of fishing water

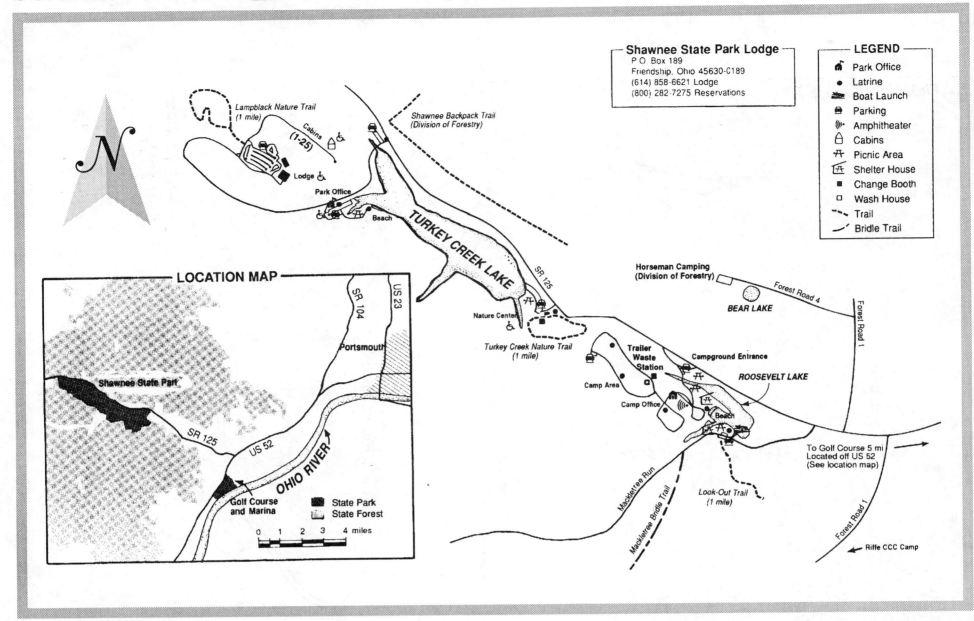

Shawnee State Park Lodge
P.O. Box 189
Friendship, Ohio 45630-0189
(614) 858-6621 Lodge
(800) 282-7275 Reservations

LEGEND
- Park Office
- Latrine
- Boat Launch
- Parking
- Amphitheater
- Cabins
- Picnic Area
- Shelter House
- Change Booth
- Wash House
- Trail
- Bridle Trail

LOCATION MAP

State Park
State Forest

0 1 2 3 4 miles

Location: In the Shawnee State Park, south central Ohio. Most anglers arrive via U.S. 23 and pick up U.S. 52 West at Portsmouth. Follow U.S. 52 west for seven miles to SR 125, and turn right for another seven miles to the state park entrance. Roosevelt Lake is also in the park, southeast of Turkey Creek Lake.

Wildlife district office: (614) 594-2211.

Fishing opportunities: Bluegill, crappies, largemouth bass, channel catfish and three species of trout.

Water conditions: Clear.

Bottom composition: Mud.

Horsepower restrictions: Electric motors.

Stocking: Trout annually and channel catfish.

Check posted bass regulations.

Maximum depth: 40 feet.

Canoe rental and bait is available.

Camping: 107 sites in the Shawnee State Park, call (614) 858-6652.

Outlook:
Bluegill - excellent
Redear - excellent
Largemouth bass - good
Channel catfish - excellent

Golden trout - excellent

Turkey Creek Lake is spring-fed and has a thermocline. Therefore, the cool lake is perfect for trout stocking—and trout catching. Many trout winter-over in the deep lake, adding to the springtime excitement. Rainbow, hybrid rainbow or browns are stocked the last weekend of April each year. All three species are present in the lake.

Nearby 20-acre Roosevelt Lake is fed by Turkey Creek Lake and was built in 1937. Roosevelt Lake has the same species of fish as Turkey Creek Lake, but it is best known for superior crappie fishing. On the north side is a big rock cliff that over the years has lost rocks into the water. These rocks have become places that concentrate crappies. Also in this 15-foot-deep area are some fallen trees and other natural features. The waters here are sometimes muddy (but it clears fast) and warm.

Roosevelt has excellent access and nearby picnic tables. It a terrific place to take kids fishing. A very small boat ramp for electric or paddled boats is on the lake. Bring your mealworms for bluegill and crappies, or a batch of colored jigs and grub bodies. Camping is near Roosevelt Lake. The bridge that crosses to the camp area is probably the best hot spot on little Roosevelt Lake. This pretty area is under a canopy of birch and hem-

lock and near a mowed open space that offers plenty of shoreline room for fly fishing. A few warmouth bass, a member of the sunfish family about the size of a rock bass, are taken from Roosevelt Lake.

How to catch 'em: After the trout stocking and as fish distribute throughout the lake, most anglers will find them in the deep water near the dam for the remainder of the season. Local anglers advise trout anglers to use garlic cheese and Velvetta cheese on a small hook. They also use corn and small light-colored spinners (Roostertails, etc.). Several year classes of largemouth bass are present in the lake as well, with good catches of 12-15 inch fish. Biologists predict that the bass fishery will continue to improve. Strict bass regulations have helped the bluegill and redear population and size. There are good harvests of 6-8 inch bluegill and some 11-inch redear sunfish have been surveyed.

Hot spots: In the spillway catch basin below the dam are some good-sized redear sunfish that will take redworms and mealworms. Stay in the deep water most of the season.

Underwater structure: The lake is also managed for channel catfish, which are heavily fished at night. On the north side of the lake, between the lake and SR 125, are some catfish spawning structures.

In the main basin of the lake, a large rock mound has been built that holds fish of all species. It is located in the dead-center of the lake. Resident beavers are also creating underwater fishing structure toward the south end. About 200 Christmas trees have been placed in the lake over the years.

Boat launching: The launch and lake are for small craft that you can row or paddle, and maybe supplement with a trolling motor.

Ice fishing: The climate of the area is very good for ice fishing and warning signs are posted.

Insider tips: If you want to escape for the day, try fishing the quiet south side of Turkey Creek Lake, called Slate Hollow Cover, accessed by a foot trail. Some shale outcrops are found at the head of the ravine in the sprawling state park. Shawnee State Park has camping, a 50-room lodge, 25 cabins, and access to the Ohio River via three two-lane boat ramps, three walking trails, auto tour, golf course and expansive day-use areas. Be careful in this rugged country. Copperheads and timber rattlers share the beautiful tract.

Tycoon Lake

■ 204 acres of fishing water GALLIA COUNTY

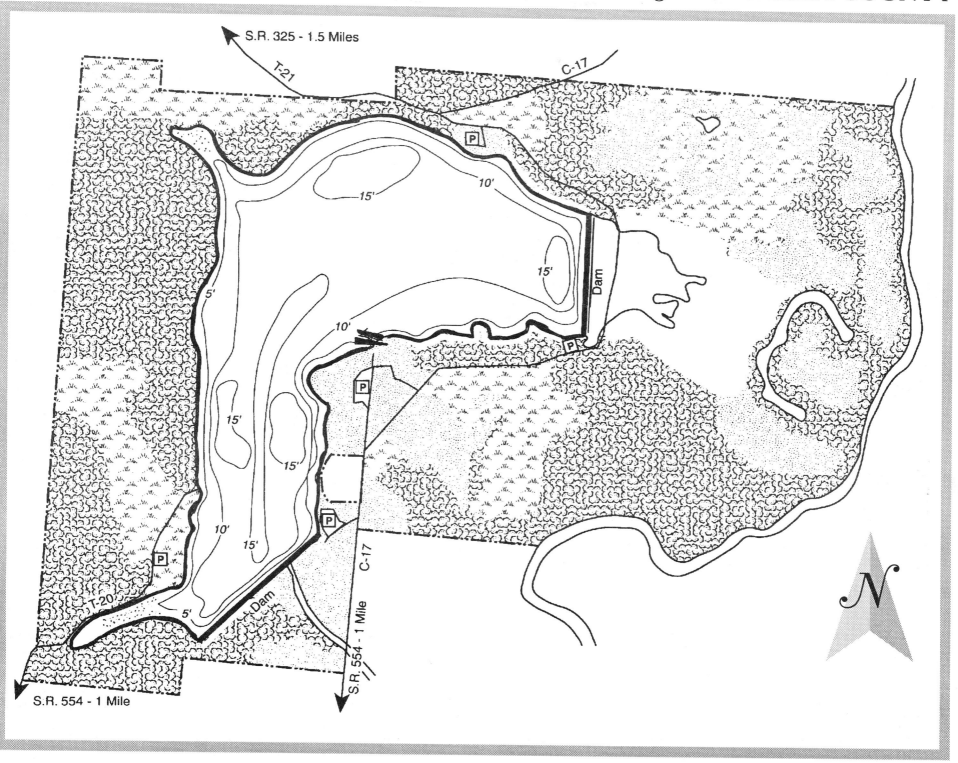

Location: In Gallia County, between SR 325 and SR 554, five miles northeast of Rio Grande. From SR 325 access to the area is gained by TR 21 (Eagle Road). From SR 554 access is provided off TR 20 and CR 17 (Tycoon Road). The lake is 52 miles from Chillicothe, 22 miles from Jackson.

Wildlife district office: (614) 594-2211.

Fishing opportunities: Largemouth bass, bluegill, redear, channel catfish and crappies.

Water conditions: Fairly clear.

Bottom composition: Mud.

Horsepower restriction: Electric motors only.

Stocking: Channel catfish as needed.

Average depth: 12-14 feet.

Special regulations: Check the slot limit on bass.

Outlook:
Largemouth bass - excellent
Bluegill, redear - fair
Channel catfish - excellent
Crappie - good

The small lake has a high density of hybrid bluegills and redear sunfish. During the spring, large numbers of crappies can be taken at the lake, where the fishing pressure is heavy, especially on spring and summer weekends. The topography of the 204-acre lake is gently rolling to hilly. About 54 percent of the uplands are wooded, mainly with oak-hickory types. The lake is shallow and the shorelines sloping and composed of silt loam soils. The lake has two dams.

How to catch 'em: Local experts say waxworms and redworms catch everything—but bass anglers typically use a variety of spinners to probe the bean-shaped lake. In front of both dams the water reach-es a depth of about 14 feet and can hold fish after spawning and through the summer. The best largemouth fishing is early in the season when many 10-15 inches fish are seen.

Bluegill are abundant, but small, with an average of only five inches. Sunfish typically average six inches, fitting nicely into a frying pan. Channel catfish are stocked in the lake with some regularity. The cats do well in the warm water. A few 28-pound whiskers have been recorded at Tycoon. The west shoreline is said to hold many 15-20 pound fish.

Hot spots: The lake has two old roadbeds. One, at the south end of the lake, it is the extension of T-20, which runs across the lake to the small parking lot on the east side of the southern dam. The other roadbed worth fishing is at the north end of the lake, and bisects the lake from the parking lot across to the shoreline. These are excellent linear areas for panfishing. The north underwater roadbed is excel-lent for large bullheads. The sub-merged roadbed to the west is best known for good bass and panfish-ing.

Underwater structure: No man-made structure has been placed, and the bottom is mostly feature-less. The lake has some scattered weedbeds.

Boat launching: A newer launching ramp is accessible to anglers and boaters with disabilities. There are also an accessible rest room and small picnic area with fire rings.

Ice fishing: Few anglers ice fish the lake, but biologists suggest that win-ter panfishing might be very good.

Insider tips: Near the boat ramp, campers may stay a night or two. There is no official campground, but the small launch area has parking, latrine and picnic tables. The 684-acre wildlife area that includes the lake is an excellent waterfowl and wildlife watching area.

Van Buren Lake

HANCOCK COUNTY ■ 53 acres of fishing water ■ Two miles of shoreline

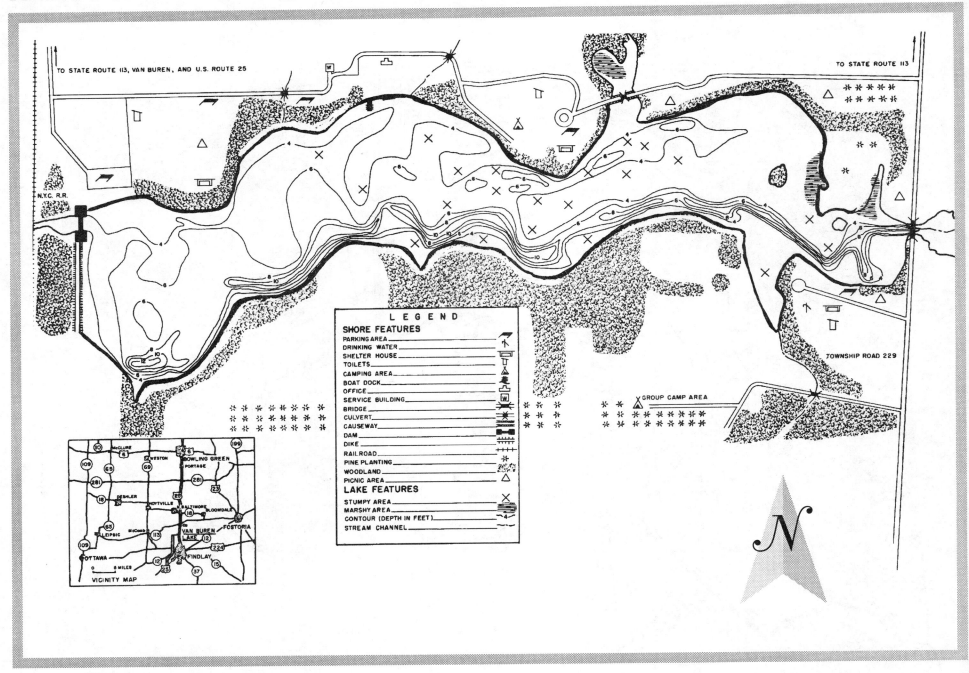

Location: In Hancock County, eight miles north of Findlay, one mile east of I-75 on SR 613.

Wildlife district office: (419) 424-5000.

Fishing opportunities: Largemouth bass, bluegill, crappie and bullhead.

Water conditions: Turbid.

Bottom composition: Mud.

Horsepower restriction: Electric motors only.

Stocking: Not since 1987.

The lake is built on a stream and is turbid. Often dredged, the small lake is an average fishery in a small state park that features a playground, 40 campsites (15 at waterside and the group campground can accommodate 200), 2.5 miles of trails and all the peace and quiet you can tolerate. The rolling wooded shoreline is shallow and often a place where if you don't catch any fish, you will at least see some interesting wading birds.

How to catch'em: Bring your rowboat or canoe, cane pole or graphite rod and quietly paddle around the narrow lake casting at the shoreline for largemouth and bluegills. There are no secrets in the lake. It's shallow and meant only to be a relaxing place away from lots of people and boat traffic. A small bay by the dam and on the south shore are considered the two best spots in the lake.

Shoreline access: The shoreline is the lake's biggest advantage. The gentle waters and complete access provide a wonderful place to bring children, a cooler filled with lunch, and a place to spend an afternoon fishing.

Boat launching: A single-lane ramp serves the lake.

Ice fishing: Limited, the shallow lake is a poor ice fishing destination.

Insider tips: The lake has complete shoreline access. A large commercial campground is located next to the park and lake.

Van Wert Reservoir I and II

■ No. 1 - 65 acres, No. 2 - 62 acres of fishing water VAN WERT COUNTY

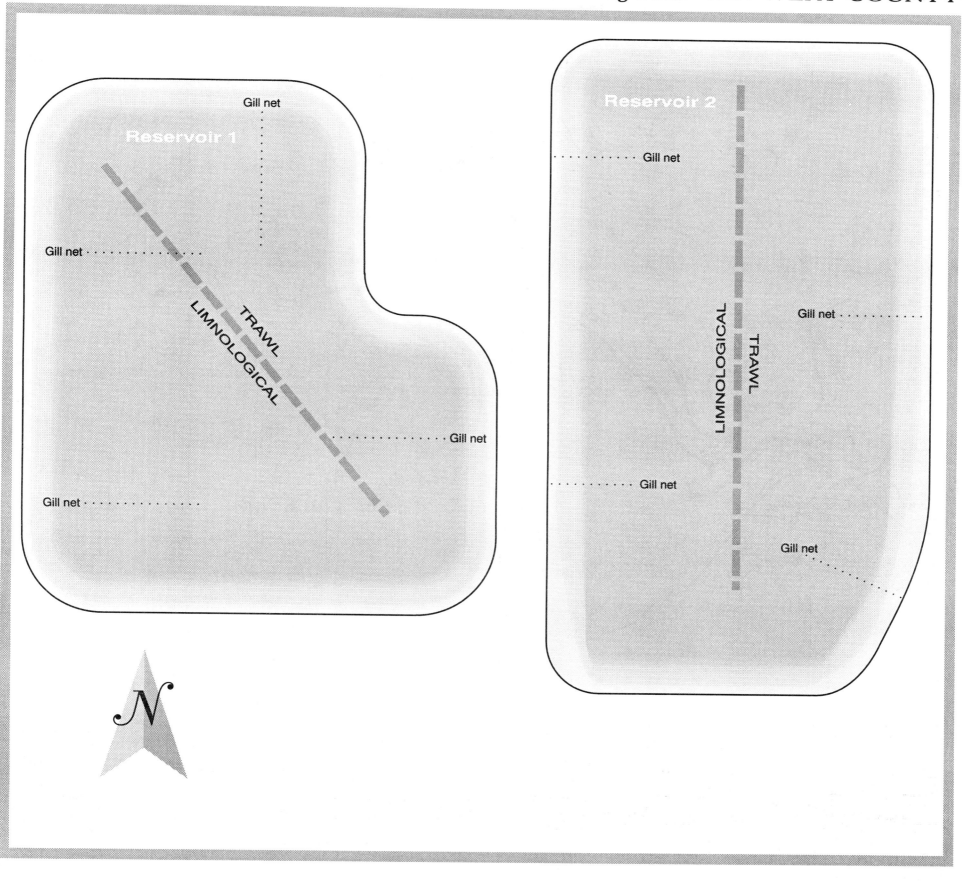

Location: In southwestern Ohio, off Rt. 127, one mile south of Van Wert. 20 miles north of Grand Lake St. Marys.

Wildlife district office: (419) 424-5000.

Fishing opportunities: Walleye, largemouth bass, channel catfish, bluegill and yellow perch.

Water conditions: Clear.

Bottom composition: Flat and muddy.

Horsepower restrictions: Electric motors.

Stocking: Maintenance stocking of walleye and catfish.

Outlook:
Walleye - good
Smallmouth - excellent
Channel catfish - good
Bluegill - good

Both of the reservoirs are upground with cool, clear water offering good walleye and smallmouth bass action. The reservoirs may be used one hour before sunrise and up to one hour after sunset.

How to catch 'em: Walleye and saugeye populations are good and run in the 13-18 inch size. The lakes also have an excellent population of smallmouth averaging 10-15 inches in size. Catfish populations are also strong with 14-20 inch fish common.

Hot spots: Shoreline anglers have access around the entire perimeter of both reservoirs.

Underwater structure: Both reservoirs have Christmas tree spawning structures. Look for the fish attractors for the best fishing opportunities. In 1990, 26 fish structures were placed in Van Wert Res. no. 2. The are along the east and west shoreline and reachable for shoreline fishermen. Reservoir no. 1 is L-shaped and has little underwater structure.

Boat launching: The maximum length on boats is 17 feet.

Ice fishing: Ice fishing is allowed, but the lakes are lightly used in the winter.

Insider tips: Try weight-forward spinners and look for excellent bass fishing in the early spring.

Lake Vesuvius

LAWRENCE COUNTY ■ 143 acres of fishing water ■ 8 miles of shoreline

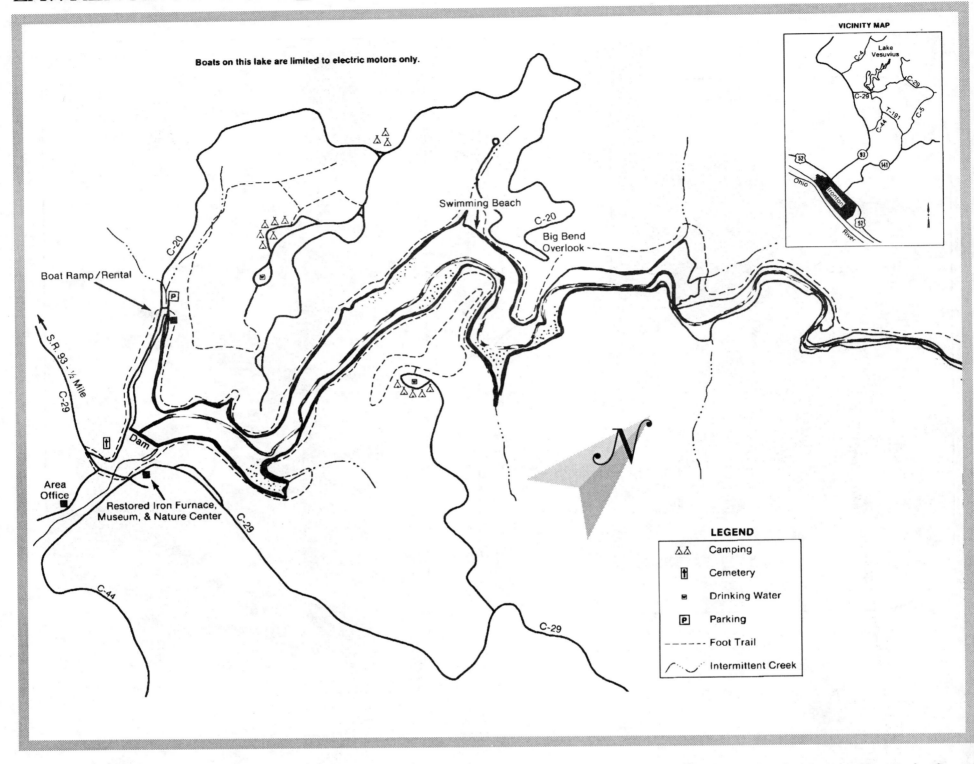

Boats on this lake are limited to electric motors only.

VICINITY MAP

LEGEND
- △△ Camping
- Cemetery
- Drinking Water
- P Parking
- ----- Foot Trail
- Intermittent Creek

Location: In Lawrence County, 11 miles north of Ironton and 32 miles south of Jackson, with access from SR 93. 131 miles from Cincinnati, 105 miles from Columbus and 29 miles from Huntington, WV.

Wildlife district office: (614) 594-2211; U.S. Forest Service Ranger, Wayne National Forest, Ironton District, (614) 532-3223.

Fishing opportunities: Largemouth bass, crappies, channel catfish and bluegill.

Water conditions: Muddy, turbid.

Bottom composition: Mud, some stumps.

Stocking: Saugeye and channel catfish.

Horsepower restriction: Electric motors only.

Maximum depth: 27 feet.

Boat rental.

Camping: Two campground operat-ed by the Wayne National Forest.

Outlook:
Bluegill - fair
Largemouth, spotted bass - fair to good
Channel catfish - excellent
Saugeye - good

Under a fishing agreement with the U.S. Forest Service, the Wildlife Division manages Lake Vesuvius for channel catfish. Every other year, yearling catfish are stocked. Due to the muddy water and other condi-tions, the lake is not a good bass fishery. Both saugeye and channel catfish, however, do well. The lake was built by the Civilian Conservation Corps in 1939 and it drains a 7,104-acre watershed. The hilly area has rapid runoff, making the lake turbid.

In places the lake has good stands of aquatic vegetation and rock shorelines.

How to catch 'em: Largemouth and spotted bass turn on as the water warms in March. Bass anglers often flip plastic worms in the lily pads in the upper end of the lake until early summer. Along the shore and rocky area, try crankbaits and jigs with tails. Try fishing along the face of the dam when the water is warm and bass can't be found around other structure.

Saugeye up to 18 inches are caught as the fishery improves. Saugeye are suited for the turbid water and can be taken by drifting a fat night-crawler, using a weight-forward spin-ner, casting light-colored crankbaits or jigging with a bright or sparkling twister tail. The lake is best for channel cat fishing. They are often found in large numbers where the lake narrows to the channel of Storm Creek and near the dam in July and August. Bring your chicken livers and fish on the bottom for some excellent action.

Bluegill size is small, but they are abundant. Biologists say the lake does cycle, relative to bluegill fish-ing. The best time of the year is late April to late May when the bluegill are on the spawning bed along shoreline points. Use tiny hooks. Simply cast waxworms at the beds or cast popper and rubber bugs with a fly rod.

Hot spots: On good is in front of the dam and the mouth of the first bay east of the dam. For largemouth, try the feeder stream at the upper end of the lake in the spring.

Underwater structure: Bundles of Christmas trees have been sunk in the lake, mostly between the beach and the dam along the shorelines. The trees have helped to attract crappies and other species seeking cover.

Boat launching: A single ramp (small fee) serves the lake north of the dam.

Insider tips: Shoreline fishing is somewhat limited. The Wayne National Forest operates two camp-grounds, swimming beach, boat rentals, trails, concession and other amenities.

Veto Lake

■ 160 acres of fishing water ■ 6 miles of shoreline WASHINGTON COUNTY

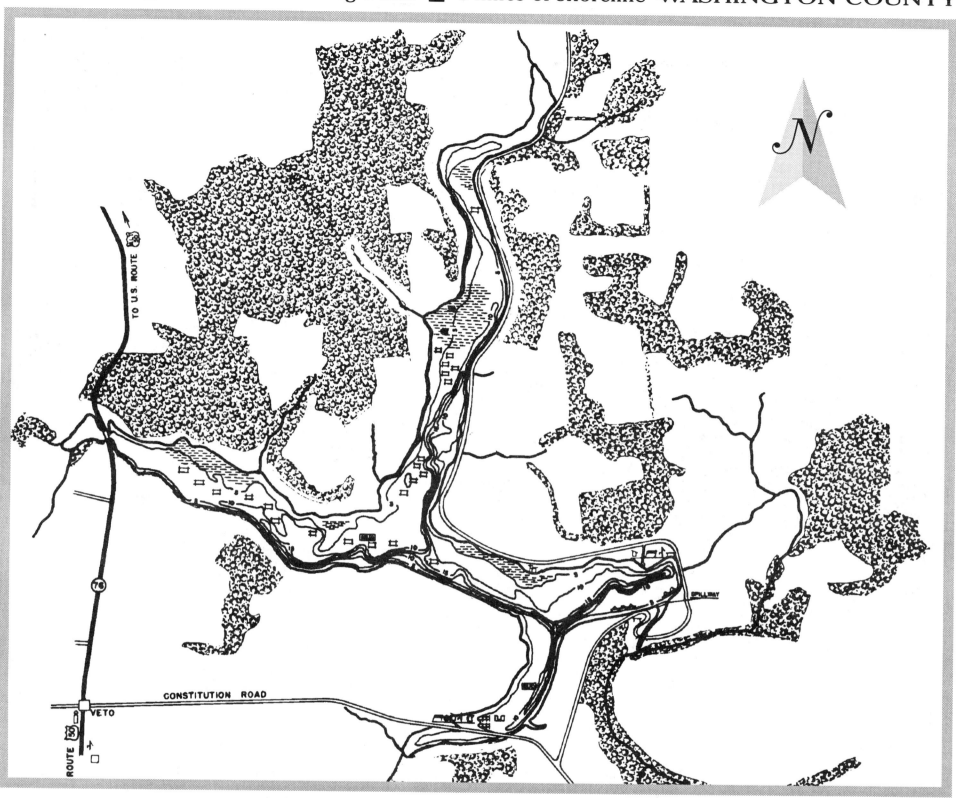

Location: In Washington County. From U.S. Route 50, take SR 339 south to the lake.

Wildlife district office: (614) 594-2211.

Fishing opportunities: Bluegill, redear sunfish, largemouth and spotted bass, channel and flathead catfish and saugeye.

Water conditions: Very muddy and dark early season.

Bottom composition: Mud, sticky.

Horsepower restriction: 10 hp.

Stocking: Saugeye and channel catfish.

Outlook:
Bluegill, redear - fair
Largemouth, spotted bass - good
Channel catfish - excellent
Saugeye - fair

Narrow and curving, Veto Lake is a difficult lake to manage from a fish biology point of view. It is very shallow and part of a large watershed. There is a lot of flushing action through the lake. Nevertheless, this is one of the best channel catfish lakes in the region. Bass fishing is good to very good much of the year. In 1988, the lake was drawn down and the Division of Wildlife seeded and fertilized the shoreline during construction of the launching ramp. After construction was done, it was filled with water, flooding this new vegetation that has helped clear the water and provided a new charge of nutrients in the lake since. In this whole process, bass surveys were conducted, showing the technique helped. This special year class is still in the lake, and they are getting pretty darn big.

How to catch 'em: Big channel cats, many in the 8-12 pound class, are taken near the emergency spillway and the dam. Most anglers use simple chicken livers and nightcrawlers. Crappie fishing can be excellent at times. Saugeye prospects are improving at the X-shaped lake. The first saugeye stocking was done in 1990 and the favorable forage base and survival rate offer fair to good fishing. Many saugeye are in the 18- inch range.

If you know how to catch bass in muddy water, you can catch some trophy largemouth from Veto Lake. Buzz baits work later in the summer, as does the Kentucky method, which is a long cane pole and a large minnow or sucker on the end. The technique is to simply repeatedly dip the live bait into the water while moving into, and away from, the shoreline as you drift. Sometimes when the intrepid low-tech angler lifts the cane pole, a big bass can be swinging from the end of the line.

Flathead catfish are also found in the winding lake, with some 40-pound fish reported. On occasion, a hybrid striper, which were brought in from the river by people, are caught along with largemouth and spotted bass. In fact, a 16-pound striper, which is a near state record, was taken out of the lake several years ago.

Hot spots: Shoreline access is extensive.

Underwater structure: In the 1980s more than 1,000 Christmas trees were submerged in the lake. In more recent times, 400 trees have been bundled, weighted and dropped into the colored water.

Boat launching: The single-lane launch, built in 1988, has been improved to include a hard-surfaced parking lot and a floating loading platform that is accessible by anglers with any disabilities.

93

Wauseon Reservoir 1 & 2

FULTON COUNTY ■ No. 1 - 40 acres, No. 2 - 45 acres of fishing water

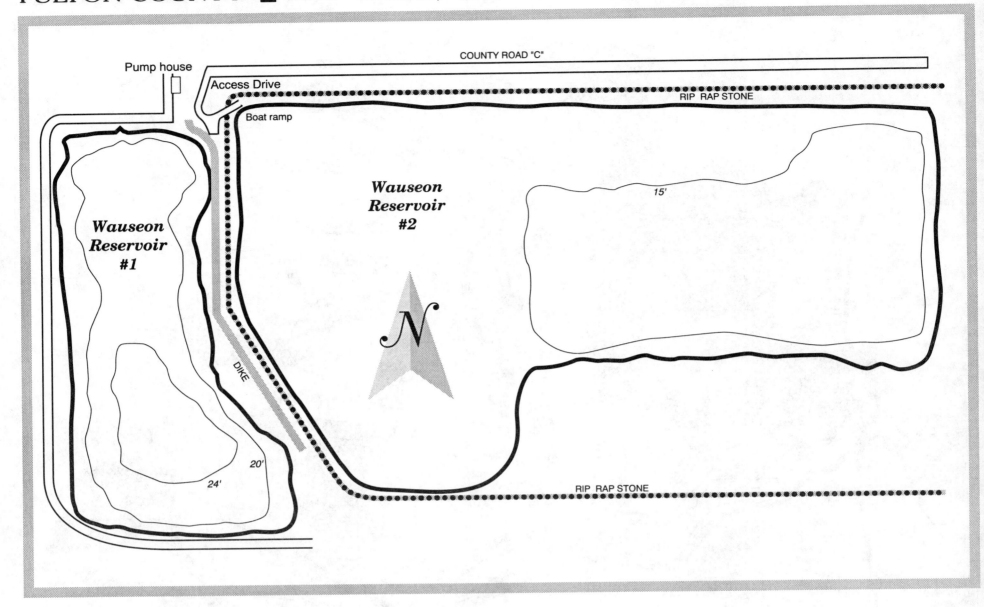

Location: In northwestern Ohio, south of the village of Wauseon off County Road C.

Wildlife division office: (419) 424-5000.

Fishing opportunities: Yellow perch, channel catfish, walleye and largemouth.

Water conditions: Medium clear.

Bottom composition: Mud.

Horsepower restriction: Electric only.

Stocking: Walleye and cats, alternate years.

Outlook:
Saugeye - good to very good
Crappies - good
Channel catfish - good
White bass - excellent
Yellow perch - fair
Largemouth bass - good

There are two bodies of water at Wauseon Reservoir. Reservoir No. 1 is the smaller of the two. No. 2, with its riprap shoreline, is known for its terrific white bass population. The reservoirs are south of the village of Wauseon. Reservoir No. 1 is up to 24 feet deep and adjacent to the larger No. 2.

How to catch 'em: Bring your jigs and minnows for white bass in reservoir No. 2. Natural color jigs and grub bodies also work in the clear water on the reservoir. Saugeye and walleye can be taken off the windswept shoreline using small crankbaits, minnow imitators and jigs with minnows. Drift in the deeper water during the summer. Walleye average 12-22 inches.

There are good populations of both white and black crappies in the reservoirs. The popular panfish average 9-13 inches and are evenly distributed around the small reservoirs. Many can be taken from the shoreline by youngsters. Bring live bait and bobbers for some good early season family panfishing. Channel cats can range to 25 inches long and give small anglers a real fight.

Hot spots: Shoreline access is excellent. Work the shoreline in the spring, deeper water in the summer. Fish from the dike of riprap and near the outlet stand pipe. Some bank anglers also concentrate near the small gravel launching ramp.

Underwater structure: Both reservoirs are nearly featureless. Anglers will need to drift and cast, checking depth and temperature ranges where fish might be holding.

Boat launching: Although there is a hand-made gravel launching ramp, it is rough. It's best to hand-launch car-top boats in both small reservoirs.

Ice fishing: Ice fishing is not popular on the reservoirs, yet district biologists believe there is opportunity.

Insider tips: These are good day trip lakes, where a family can spend an afternoon around small bodies of water allowing all ages of kids a chance to fish. Bring bait with you.

West Branch Reservoir (Kirwin Lake)

■ 2,350 acres of fishing water   ■ 40 miles of shoreline   PORTAGE COUNTY

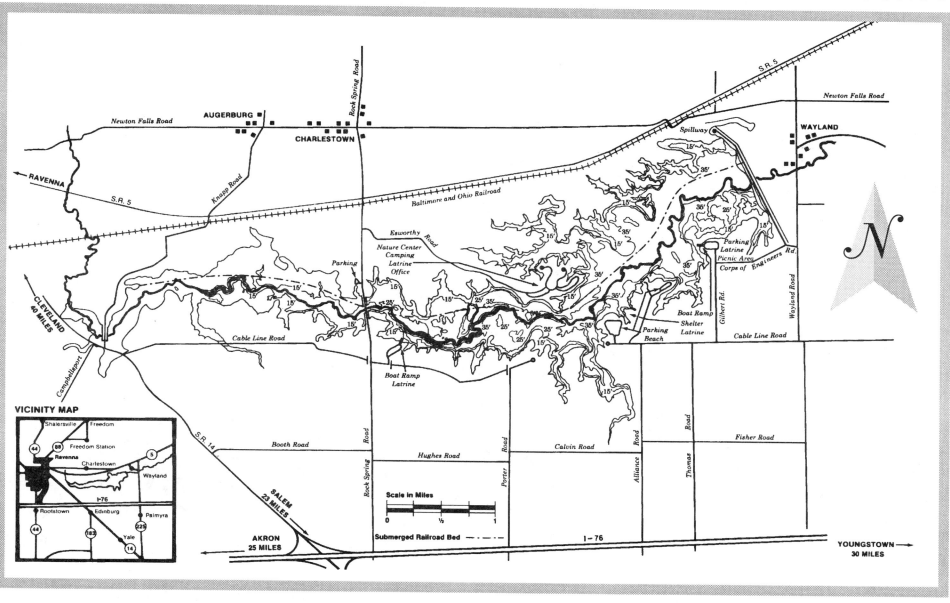

Location: In Portage County. From I-76, depart at Exit 38 and head north to SR 44/5 for three miles to Ravenna. Continue west on SR 5 for about six miles. It's 40 miles from Cleveland.

Wildlife district office: (330) 644-2293.

Fishing opportunities: Muskie, saugeye, white and black crappies, largemouth bass, hybrid striped bass and bluegill.

Water conditions: Medium clear to dark.

Bottom composition: Mostly mud, some firm areas.

Horsepower restrictions: None; no wake 300 feet to shore.

Stocking: Muskie, saugeye.

Maximum water depth: 55 feet.

Camping: 103 sites at West Branch State Park; (216) 296-3239.

Check bass regulations.

Outlook:
Muskie - fair
Saugeye - fair to good
Crappies - fair
Hybrid striped bass - poor

West Branch is a big, wide open lake with plenty of powerboats zooming from end to end. The upper end of the lake does have a speed limit. Unfortunately, the best fishing, near the dam, is also where most of the

powerboaters play.

To ease flood problems and supply water, the U.S. Army Corps of Engineers constructed a dam in 1965 that turned the West Branch of the Mahoning River into Michael J. Kirwan Lake. In the process they created a recreational haven for anglers, boaters, swimmers and campers in the neighboring state park. The north half of the state park is a glaciated plateau, a lobe of the Kent terminal moraine, while the middle is the lake that stretches seven miles and has dozens of productive shoreline coves, inlets and numerous forks.

How to catch 'em: The lake has trophy muskie potential. Muskie anglers will be among the powerboaters as they concentrate on waters east of the causeway. As with Leesville and Piedmont, night fishing for muskie has become popular and productive, all while avoiding the heavy daytime recreational boat traffic. The largest muskie taken during a netting survey was 46 inches in 1996. Some nighttime muskie anglers suggest adjusting the trolled lure to sometimes be near the boat, in the edge of the wave, shallow and deep. Anglers are learning muskie occupy virtually all depths and regions of the lake at night during the hot summer.

Saugeyes can range up to 22 inches and are typically taken off the humps, along with walleye. Bass,

saugeye and walleye can also be found along the shoreline, especially at night or early in the season. When trolling, try to stay over the sunken roadbeds and in the deep water near the dam for stripers and other species. Crappies average about eight inches and are evenly distributed, but best found in the tops of felled trees, vegetation or brush. Catfishing is excellent at West Branch, especially at night when the water warms in mid-summer. Many catfish are taken on live bait fished on the bottom.

Hot spots: At one time the state record tiger muskie came from these waters. It was a 26-pound, 45-inch-long fish taken at mid-lake by a trolling angler in mid-August 1984. Shoreline anglers will enjoy the Fisherman's Parking Lot on the north side of the causeway, where there are parking, toilets, picnic tables and a place where you could hand-launch small boats. Shoreline fishermen should also try areas near the dam. Local anglers usually stay in the eastern section of the lake from the causeway when after walleye or saugeye. Bass in the spring can be found in the western section from the causeway.

Underwater structure: West of the causeway is shallow and there's plenty of vegetation where bass congregate. There are few, if any, manmade structures in the lake other than submerged roadways and a few humps. Depth breaks and

points, especially at the mouths of small bays, are typically good places to begin your day.

Boat launching: Two major launches serve the lake, one on the east end and one on the south side. These launches can be filled with powerboaters early each weekend through the summer. The east ramp at the end of Gilbert Road at the southeast corner of the lake has four cement lanes and two loading docks. The ramp is across a small cove from the park marina which features slip rentals, gasoline, marina supplies, bait, boat rentals and food. The West Marina (216-296-9209) is at the end of Alliance Road on the south side of the lake.

Ice fishing: In part because of poor panfishing, the lake isn't ice fished much.

Insiders tips: The hybrid striped bass are no longer stocked and are slowly dying—fished out. Nevertheless, an occasional 30-pounder is taken. Look for saugeye and walleye fishing to improve. Muskie are stocked at half the rate of Leesville Lake, giving these fish an opportunity to grow larger on the forage base of gizzard shad. Adjoining West Branch State Park has 12 miles of hiking trails, park marina with gasoline, marina supplies and bait, campground and sprawling day-use areas.

Lake White

PIKE COUNTY ■ 323 acres of fishing water ■ 8 miles of shoreline

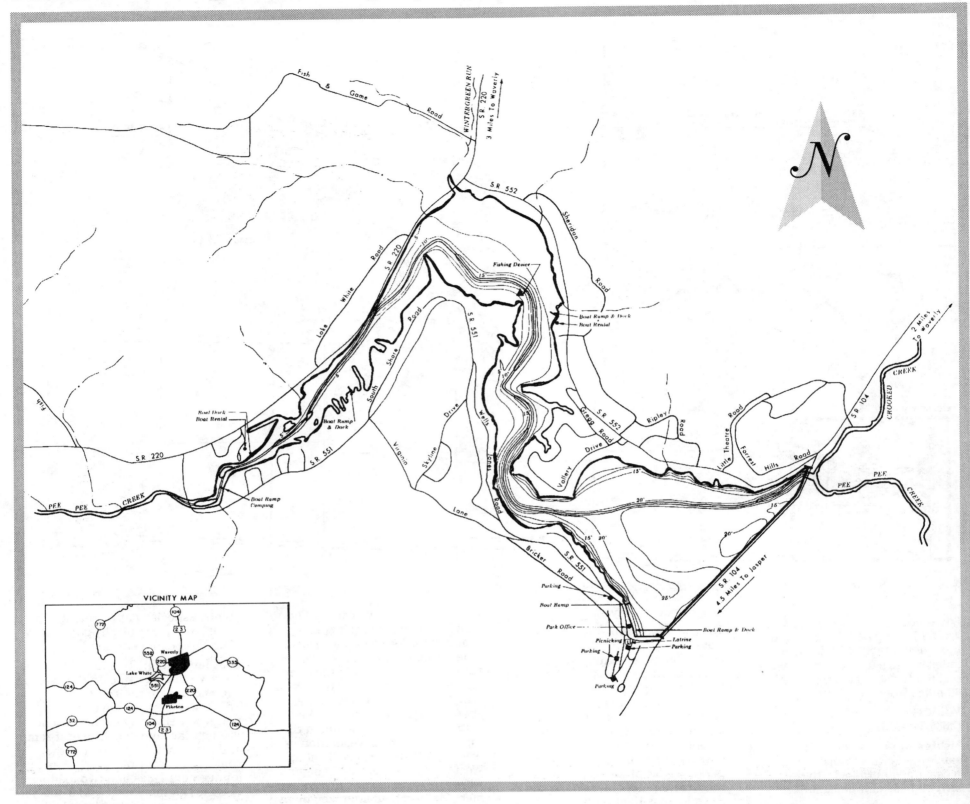

VICINITY MAP

Location: In Pike County, four miles southwest of Waverly, at Routes 104 and 220.

Wildlife District office: (614) 594-2211.

Fishing opportunities: Largemouth bass, saugeye, crappies, bluegill, bullhead and channel catfish.

Water conditions: Medium clear.

Bottom composition: Firm, mud.

Horsepower restrictions: None.

Stocking: Saugeye and channel catfish.

Boat rental.

Camping: Private and state parks, call the state park at (614) 947-4059.

Outlook:
Bluegill - fair
Largemouth bass - good
Channel catfish - excellent

Saugeye - good

Shoreline access is limited to the area near the state park headquarters, and sometimes the unlimited horsepower boats and water-skiers can keep fishing relegated to weekdays or early and late in the day. Try visiting during the colder seasons—early spring and fall. Many private docks surround the lake. With water temperatures good for skiing, the lake can be busy. Saugeye have been planted in White Lake, the second longest of any lake in the state. The lake has also received more consistent annual stocking than any other lake in the state. Ten-pound saugeye are ever-present in the small lake.

How to catch 'em: The state record spotted bass came out of Lake White 30 years ago. There is also a good population of largemouth as well. But the real stars of the lake are saugeye and channel catfish. In spite of heavy boat traffic, bass angling can be good. There are a lot of 10-19 inch bass, many of which can be taken on jigs and spinners in the early season. Shorelines and points near deep water are good places to find mid-day bass in March through early May. When the water temperatures rise to 65-70 degrees, bass will begin to roam the shallow gravel shorelines looking for spawning beds. At this time, rubber worms and spinners will bring up fish. During the summer, fish the deep channel and dropoffs to 15 feet of water. Once fall temperatures drop, head back to the shorelines where bass are feeding.

Saugeye growth rates are slow, but the state classifies the fishing as good. Keep plenty of jig styles and colors working, and tip them with lively minnows. Crappies are evenly distributed and can be taken in good numbers on jigs near brush or fallen trees in April and May. These areas will also produce average-sized bluegill. Lake White is a great catfish lake. Night fish the gravel bars with nightcrawlers or cutbaits.

Hot spots: Fish at the dam or the upper half of the lake, from the dam back.

Underwater structure: Anglers should focus on the creek channel that meanders through the lake. Concentrate on points and the mouth of narrow bays.

Boat launching: The busy launch is near the state park headquarters.

Insider tips: The unlimited horsepower rating makes fishing tough on the lake during the summer vacation season. Plan some night fishing on the small lake. The lake was formed by damming Pee Pee Creek.

Willard Reservoir

■ 215 acres of fishing water ■ 2.3 miles of shoreline HURON COUNTY

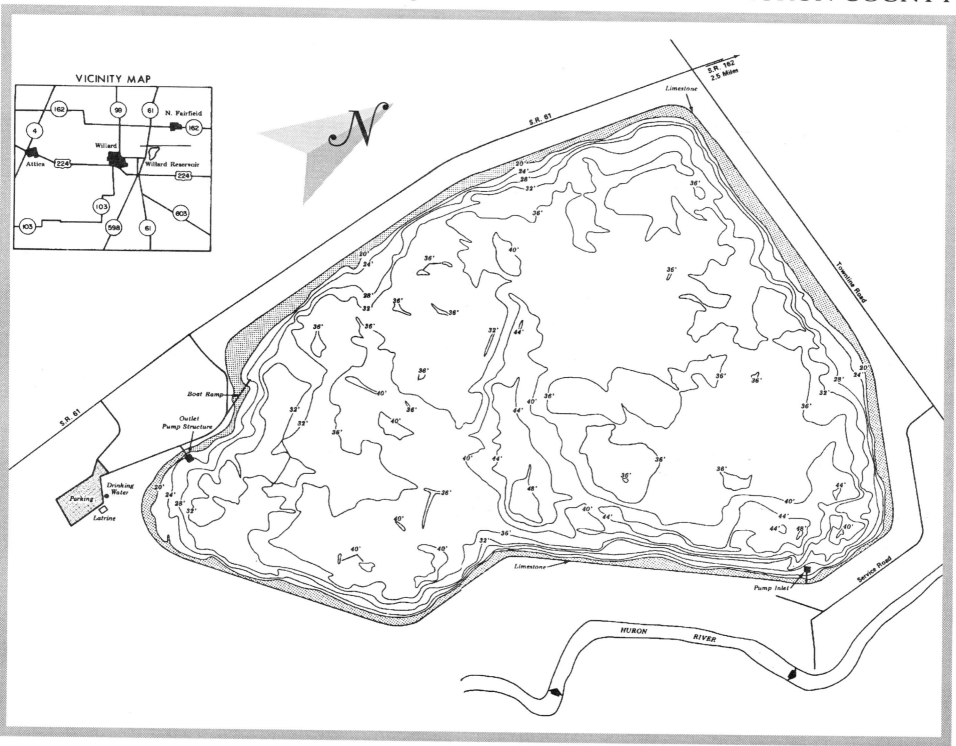

Location: In Huron County on SR 61, two miles north of New Haven.

Wildlife district office: (419) 424-5000.

Fishing opportunities: Small- and largemouth bass, bluegill, walleye, yellow perch, crappies, bullheads and channel catfish.

Water conditions: Clear.

Bottom composition: Clay and silt.

Horsepower restriction: Electric motors only.

Stocking: Alternate years, channel catfish and walleyes.

Depth: Up to 35 feet.

Outlook:
Walleye - fair to good
Yellow perch - fair and big
Smallmouth bass - good
Largemouth bass - fair
Bullhead - good
Channel catfish - good to very good

Willard is an upground reservoir

that was built in 1971 adjacent to the Huron River. It supplies water to the city of Willard and offers good fishing to the rest of us. The reservoir has a lot of deep water and the bottom is mildly bumpy, with a few significant depth changes.

How to catch 'em: Drift fish for walleyes (average size 13-24 inches) and channel catfish. A few depth breaks in mid-lake are considered good locations to try, as are wave-washed shorelines in the spring. Use weight-forward spinners, weighed spinners, worm combinations or Lindy rig-type lures. Some local experts claim slow trolling for walleye in the summer can be productive. Smallmouth (average size 10-18 inches) tend to hold near the stone shoreline and take live baits of nightcrawlers, minnows and crayfish, as well as spinners and crayfish-colored crankbaits.

Largemouth also like the shoreline and shallower waters. Visit in the spring and try live bait or rubber worms. Many bank fishermen can

do well on largemouths during the spring and early summer.

Bluegills love the water inlets/outlets near the pumping stations. Dip redworms or larval baits using ultra light equipment for a lot of fun. Bring your balloons for big catfish and a can of worms for lots of bullhead bites in any part of the lake. Fish the bottom for both of these whiskered fish. Perch anglers will find some big fish off the shoreline structures in the early morning or at dusk. If you are a good angler, you can catch a good-sized bunch. Most of the perch are 6-8 inch, taken on minnow and worms.

Hot spots: The best shoreline fishing is along the south side of the reservoir. Here, the gentle banks allow for easy access, and the depth changes nearby offer good fishing. Built like a bathtub, the relatively featureless lake does offers some good possibilities near the pump houses. Anglers often concentrate at the inlet, near the service road at the east side of the lake. This is a good panfish area. Try near the

inlet for all species, especially smallmouth bass—bring your small Mepp's spinners.

Underwater structure: Some Christmas trees have been clumped together along the edges of the reservoir in eight to 10 feet of water. The Christmas trees are accessible to shore fishermen. A few rock piles are also in the reservoir.

Boat launching: A two-lane concrete launching ramp is at the south end of the reservoir off SR 61. Near the launching ramp are a latrine, drinking water and a large hard-surfaced parking lot. This area is like a small city park.

Ice fishing: It's not allowed

Insider tips: The reservoir's bottom is pretty uniform. The shallow waters along the limestone rip rap shoreline provide more food than the deeper waters, serving to concentrate the fish. Spring is the best time to fish Willard. Upground reservoirs are unique to Ohio.

Wills Creek Lake

COSHOCTON & MUSKINGUM COUNTIES ■ 900 acres of fishing water

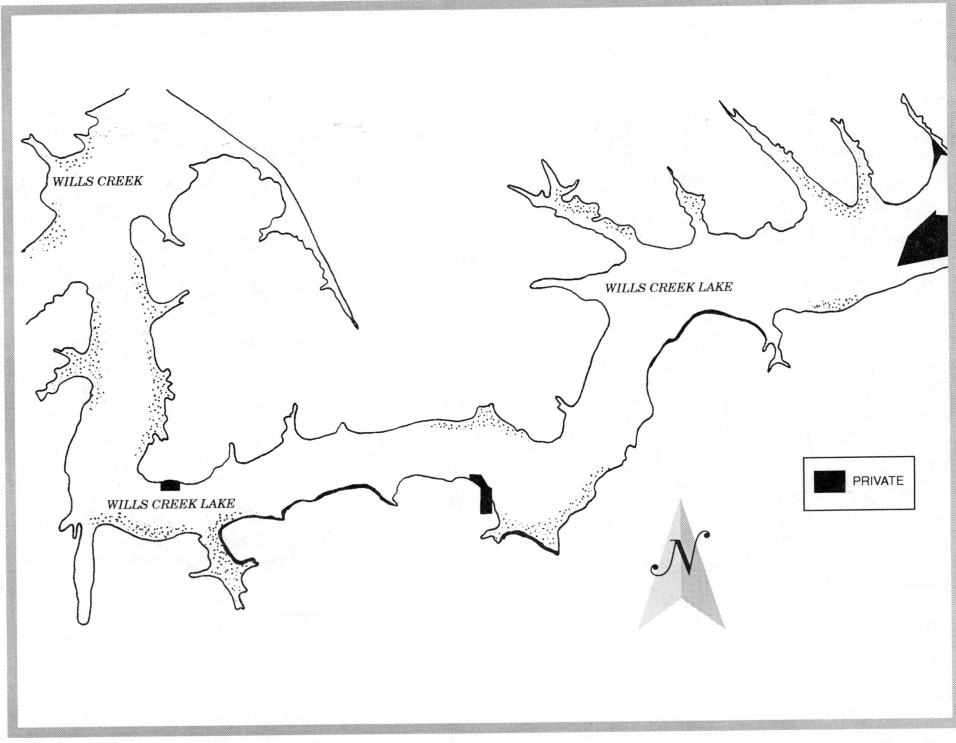

PRIVATE

N

Location: In Coshocton and Muskingum counties. SR 83 bisects the lake. SR 93 skirts the east end of the lake, south of West Lafayette and Coshocton.

Wildlife division office: (614) 594-2211; Wills Creek, (614) 829-2425.

Fishing opportunities: Saugeye, bluegill, crappie, largemouth bass, white bass, flathead and channel catfish.

Water conditions: Brown, stained, colored.

Bottom composition: Mud, some gravel.

Horsepower restriction: 10 hp.

Stocking: Saugeye.

Outlook:
Bluegill - fair
Largemouth bass - good
Channel catfish - excellent
Saugeye - excellent
Muskie - poor

Many local dyed-in-the-wool bass anglers give up chances to fish other lakes to ply their skill on Wills Creek. According to fisheries biologists, these bass anglers kept the lake a secret for many years. Saugeye anglers love it too. In fact, a state record saugeye was once taken from Wills Creek. It weighed 10 pounds, four ounces and was taken on a jig and twister tail near the dam, in the tailwaters. Wills Creek, with its clean (non-farm or industrial) runoff and partial gravel bottom, is considered one of the best saugeye natural reproduction lakes in the state.

Anglers should take heart. Wills Creek, with all its shallows and mud flats, is tough to figure out. The best advice is to put in at the small boat ramp and head for the dam. Up river/lake is stream-like and shallow. Currently the lake is not heavily fished or managed; however, the state is considering improvements and increased managment. Use your slow moving river techniques at Wills Creek. Try drifting against a

tight line and vertical jig, and bounce off the bottom.

How to catch 'em: The body of water is more like an oversized creek than a lake. Undeveloped, the lake is scenic and the fishing can be very good. There is a green buffer zone between the lake and any development. Station staff report that walleye, saugeye and largemouth bass love chasing a Mepp's-type twister tail with a two-ounce weight jigged along the bottom. Keep the jig moving, or you will get hungup. Jig gently; maybe you can hook up with a new state record, possibly native born, saugeye.

Bluegill are heavily populated, with individuals averaging about six inches. Natural reproduction of channel catfish make the lake popular for diehards. Some 20- and 30-pound catfish are reported each year.

Hot spots: Below the settling basin, and from the shoreline at the dam are the best spots. The trailwaters below Wills Creek Dam on to Muskingum River is also a very good smallmouth fishery. Brushy

areas are terrific for spring and early summer crappie.

Underwater structure: Water levels can vary dramatically. No manmade structure have been placed. A decent amount of natural snags and contours hold fish.

Boat launching: Limited boat access has made fishing good, and the bass population underused. The primitive launch ramp is designed for small fishing boats and anglers should take care to feel their way around a bit before increasing speeds. Go slow, due to the silting nature of the lake and wide swings in water depth. The shallows and channels change and can be difficult to find. The shifting of channels makes the lake hard to mark with buoys. A small picnic area is at the ramp.

Insider tips: The lake is in a 4,846-acre area operated by the watershed district. An occasional muskie is taken at Wills Creek.

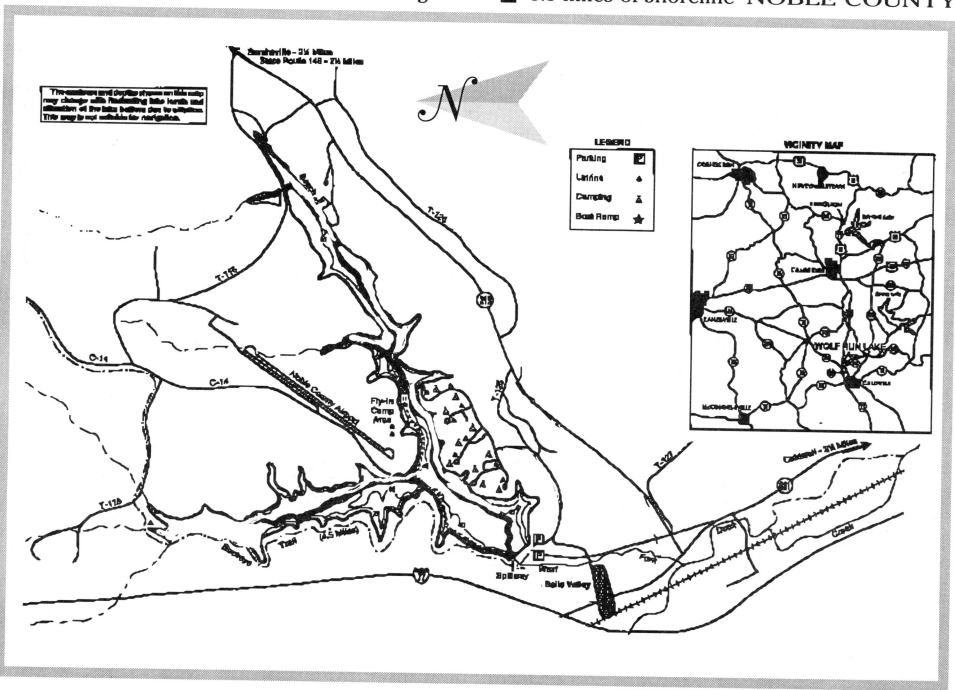

Location: In Noble County, three miles north of Caldwell. Access from I-77 is at the Belle Valley Interchange with SR 821. The lake is 146 miles from Columbus, 103 miles from Akron and 19 miles from Cambridge.

Wildlife district office: (614) 594-2211.

Fishing opportunities: Golden trout, bluegill, largemouth bass, crappie and channel catfish.

Water conditions: Clear.

Bottom composition: Firm, mud.

Horsepower restriction: 10 hp.

Stocking: Rainbow trout, channel catfish.

Special regulation: Check slot length limit.

Depth: Dropoffs to 30 feet of water.

Camping: 140 sites at the state park;, call (614) 732-5035.

Outlook:
Bluegill, redear - fair
Largemouth bass - good
Channel catfish - excellent
Golden trout - good

Rainbow trout, largemouth bass and channel catfish are the key managed species at Wolf Run Lake. The nearby state park features camping, a beach, day-use areas, camp amphitheater and hunting. The rock outcroppings and deep dropoffs make Wolf Lake an interesting lake to figure out.

How to catch 'em: "Golden" (rainbow) trout are stocked annually and provide good fishing from March through fall. The very best time to go after trout is after a few warm days in March. When the water begins to warm, the fish can turn on to lightly presented thin-blade spinners, cheeseballs, worms or tiny spoons. Some anglers like Powerbait and salmon eggs also. Plan to carefully work the shelves and sharp dropoffs with these lures. As summer warms up, the trout move to progressively deeper water, where some are taken in 15-20 feet on the same basic lures, but slower presentation.

The many interesting coves offer excellent spring largemouth fishing. These are shallow places where thick wiggling nightcrawlers can take lots of fish in the early season. As the water warms to 50 degrees or more, the shallow bays can still hold fish, but plastic worms and various colored and skirted spinners will do a better job of teasing the bucketmouths. Post spawn, the long sloping points will focus the bass population. Use deep-divers and work the lure slowly and methodically. Evening anglers should try some noisy topwater baits for thundering surface hits. The largemouth population is diverse and multi-year classed. Fish range from 5-23 inches.

Most catfish anglers work the shallower parts of the lake at night using standard cutbaits, prepared baits or gobs of crawlers. Panfishing is best in the early season, May to mid-June. Bluegills average 6.5 inches. Use light line and small baits and hooks in this clear lake. Huge catfish have been taken from the placid lake. Try crayfish, redworms or beef livers on the bottom at night.

Hot spots: Most of the trout are taken at the dam (especially after stocking). This is also where many of the trout stay as summer progresses, due to water temperature and oxygen level. Public access and shoreline fishing are good around the lake. Local anglers say the shoreline across and west of the beach have structure that holds fish. Other hot spots include three small bays on the east side of the western spur. Some steep dropoffs plunge to 30 feet of water and can be productive zones to bounce baits down and across.

Underwater structure: 38 units of brush and downed trees were placed in the lake in the early 1980s. Drift over the creek channel. About 420 Christmas trees were placed in the lake in the early 1990s. Some felled shoreline trees are in place and help hold panfish.

Boat launching: The modern launching ramp, with tie-ups, is on the southeast side of the lake.

Insider tips: A 65-pound shovelhead catfish was taken in an early 1990s Division of Wildlife net survey (and 45-pounders have been caught). Ten-pound largemouth bass have also been caught at Wolf Run. There is fly-in camping near the Noble Airport. Come to this lake equipped with your own bait. This is an easy lake for boat handling.

Zepernick Lake

COLUMBIANA COUNTY ■ 39 acres of fishing water

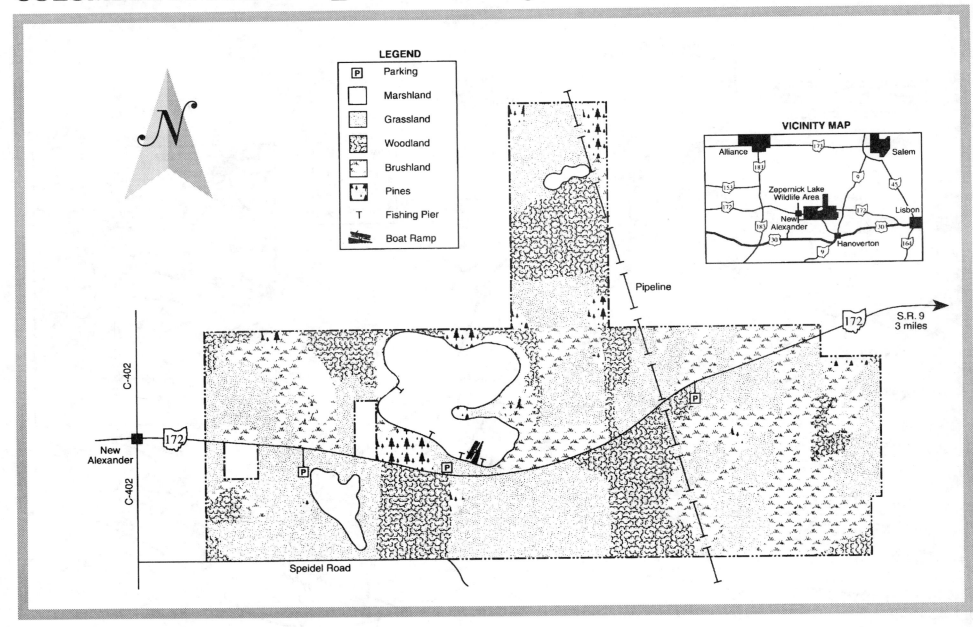

LEGEND

- P Parking
- ▢ Marshland
- Grassland
- Woodland
- Brushland
- Pines
- T Fishing Pier
- Boat Ramp

VICINITY MAP

Location: In Columbiana County, five miles from Guilford Lake and four miles northwest of Hanoverton in western Columbiana County. The lake is in the state-owned Zepernick Wildlife Area. Route 172 bisects the forested tract. The lake is 50 miles from Steubenville, 36 miles from Akron and 29 miles from Youngstown.

Wildlife district office: (330) 644-2293.

Fishing opportunities: Largemouth bass, crappies, redear sunfish, yellow perch, bluegills, catfish and some chain pickerel.

Water conditions: Medium clear, can be muddy after rains and in the spring.

Bottom composition: Mud, silt.

Stocking: Irregular stocking of largemouth bass.

Bait and tackle: Hilltop Bait, (330) 424-5760.

Outlook:
Largemouth bass - Very good
Channel catfish - Good
Perch - good
Crappies - fair to very good
Chain pickerel - poor
Redear sunfish - good

The scenic lake is in the middle of the 518-acre Zepernick Wildlife Area on the glacial plateau of northeastern Ohio. The area is forested and gently rolling to steep with a few poorly drained pothole areas. South of Rt. 172 and Zepernick Lake is a seven acre lake locals call, Rough Pond. There is poor access to the pond, but anglers that walk in report good springtime success. There is also a five-acre pond that is man-made and very marshy.

Zepernick Lake is the perfect retreat, especially during the week when few anglers are on the water. The quiet wildlife area is about 35 percent cultivated and the rest is second-growth hard- and softwoods. There area offers some squirrel hunting, but is best for rabbit and ring-necked pheasant along corn-field strips, brushy field edges and woodland borders. Raccoon and woodchuck hunting can also be good. Waterfowl hunting is limited.

The state purchased the tract in 1954 and the original lake was only 25 acres. It was enlarged and improved and is stocked occasionally. Other improvements to the area is management for small game hunting. Sections of the tract are cultivated and areas have been planted with conifers.

The wildlife division has stocked grass carp in an effort to keep the intimate lake clear and productive. Remember to release any grass carp you catch.

How to catch 'em: Zepernick Lake is a fun lake to buzz spinners in a shallow stump field for largemouth bass. Local angler swear by live shiner minnow as live bait, Mr. Twisters, chartreuse and white or yellow spinnerbaits, rooster tails, bangtails and Plowjockey plastic worms with a natural-colored clear tail. Some bass anglers also like peach-colored worms that they use to flip in the stumps.

For panfish, stay in the southern one-third of the lake and near the bay by the boat ramp. Panfish anglers typically use small Mr. Twisters and waxworms or maggots tipped on a small hook. Again white chartreuse are the most productive colors. Staff at the Hilltop Bait shop says some years pink is a hot color, especially in the spring when the water is colored.

Perch tend to hold in the middle of the lake. Mealworms and maggots work well on the redear sunfish. Some sunfish anglers also use a small brightly-colored twister tail. Crappies are taken all over the lake, especially near brush tops and any floating vegetation.

Catfishing is good in the small lake. Many local angler rely on Magic Bait, preserved chicken livers and Mr. Stinker, a volatile prepared stinkbait. Wear rubber gloves when using Mr. Stinker, it has a foul Limburger cheese smell.

Underwater structure: The stump field on the north shore is an excellent spot. Otherwise the lake is mostly featureless with only vegetation and small humps. The lake turns over once a year. Some anglers like to work near the peninsula, especially on the north side.

Hot spots: The north edge of the lake for largemouth bass and the south half of the lake is best for panfish. Some angler like to work the point off the peninsula and deep water for perch. Kids will have fun shoreline fishing along the south shore and near the small launching ramp.

Boat launching: There's plenty of parking on the hard-surface lot that serves the ramp.

Insider tips: Nearby Guilford Lake is a terrific panfish lake. A few large chain pickerel are occasionally taken from Zepernick. Nearby Glenn's Archery and Tackle also knows the lake well. The lake has an average growth of aquatic vegetation. Try tiny Rough Pond for chain pickerel. The lake is busy in the springtime with pan fishermen. A portable toilet is in the parking lot.